Economic Restructuring
and Social Exclusion

DATE DUE

A new Europe?

Economic restructuring and social exclusion
Editors: Phillip Brown and Rosemary Crompton

Social change and political transformation
Editors: Chris Rootes and Howard Davis

Economic Restructuring and Social Exclusion

Edited by
Phillip Brown & Rosemary Crompton
University of Kent at Canterbury

UCL
PRESS

First published in 1994 by UCL Press

UCL Press Limited
University College London
Gower Street
London WC1E 6BT

The name of University College London (UCL) is a registered trade mark
used by UCL Press with the consent of the owner.

ISBN:
1-85728-149-7 HB
1-85728-150-0 PB

British Library Cataloguing in Publication Data.
A catalogue record for this book is available from the British Library.

Typeset in Baskerville.
Printed and bound by
Biddles Ltd., Guildford and King's Lynn, England.

Contents

CONTENTS

Contributors

Sheila Allen   University of Bradford

Sara Arber   University of Surrey

Phillip Brown   University of Kent

Irene Bruegel   South Bank University

Terry Cox   University of Strathclyde

Rosemary Crompton   University of Kent

Jay Ginn   University of Surrey

Ariane Hegewisch   Cranfield Institute of Technology

Patricia Kennett   University of Bristol

Scott Lash   Lancaster University

Arnlaug Leira   Institute for Social Research, Oslo

John Lovering   University of Bristol

Marie Macey   University of Bradford

Mark Mitchell   University of Portsmouth

Larry Ray   Lancaster University

Dave Russell   University of Portsmouth

Acknowledgements

We would like to thank Nicola Kerry and Christel Lane for their invaluable contribution to the organization of the British Sociological Association (BSA) Conference at the University of Kent, and to the production of this volume. We are also indebted to Nick Dalziel, until recently Publications Officer of the BSA, for his help in securing the publication of this and its companion volume.

Introduction

Rosemary Crompton & Phillip Brown

I

As the 20th century draws to a close, the economic and political changes in contemporary Europe seem to be as profound as those that dominated the concerns of Sociology's founders in the 19th and early 20th centuries – economic crisis, nationalist wars, and social instability. Nevertheless, in western Europe the compulsion of economic necessity, as well as a determination to try to control the propensity to military adventure that has dominated European history, has resulted in the creation of the European single economic market. The Single Market among the 12 member states has formed an alliance with nations who are part of the European Free Trade Association (EFTA) to provide a barrier-free market of approximately 400 million people in 19 countries.[1]

However, the parallel shifts to political integration, together with attempts to create a single currency, have proved to be far more difficult ambitions to realize. They have raised the thorny and emotive issues of sovereignty, national identity, and democratic accountability. These facts are hardly surprising. Among the nation-states that now make up the European Community (EC), there has always been a wide variation in economic structures and national political complexions. In respect of economic issues, some sociologists have emphasised the significance of "societal effects" – that is, identifiable and relatively enduring national differences – which are manifest in key areas of economic activity such as organizational structure and functioning. These "societal" differences persist even when crucial variables such as technology, size, and industrial sector are held constant in cross-national organizational comparisons (Maurice et al. 1986). There are many other significant differences between the nation-states of Europe. In

1

important areas such as industrial relations, for example, countries such as Germany are characterized by a broadly corporatist strategy, with the mutual involvement of unions, employers, and the state. In Britain, in contrast, corporatist attempts have been largely overshadowed by the voluntarism and conflict that have dominated employer–worker relations. There are also crucial, and long-standing, national differences in fundamental political matters such as the definition of "citizenship". France, for example, holds to a universalistic definition of the term that, while emphasising equality, is not particularly tolerant of cultural difference – particularly when religious affiliation might seem to assume priority over allegiance to the state. Germany, in contrast, defines citizenship in a particularistic manner, in relation to "volk" or ethnic origin.

These kinds of differences are reflected in national responses to EC initiatives. Although, therefore, the Maastricht treaty is likely to be ratified by all EC member states, Britain and Denmark have negotiated special clauses claiming national exemptions from politically unacceptable parts of the treaty. The Conservative representatives of the British government have negotiated an "opt-out" clause on the single currency and exemption from the Social Charter, which relates to minimum wages, part-time work, working conditions, and so on. Douglas Hurd, the then Foreign Secretary, warned that such protective legislation would lead to the "bad old days" of the 1960s. This stance may be seen as an expression of the vanguard neo-liberalism of the present British government. Nevertheless, the issue continues deeply to divide the British Conservative party, both inside and outside the House of Commons. The Danes have voted in a referendum to claim exemption from the single currency, and Mitterand suffered the embarrassment of the extremely narrow "yes" vote in France.

In eastern Europe it is the disintegration of the erstwhile Soviet Union, together with its satellites, that has dramatically defined the agenda. Economically, all east European nations have lurched, with greater or lesser speed and success, towards the creation of capitalist markets. This has involved programmes of privatization, intended to free the economy from excessive state controls and to foster a culture of enterprise among the population. The process of political liberalization that has accompanied the break-up of the Eastern Bloc has highlighted the problem of finding democratic and economic solutions to deep-rooted antagonisms between ethnic and religious groups within as well as between nations. In the Balkans, ethnic conflicts have torn Yugoslavia apart. The scale of the challenge that confronts these nations is exemplified in the case of Eastern

Germany. In 1989 Chancellor Helmut Kohl promised that re-unification could be achieved without the raising of taxes in West Germany. Despite substantial investment, East German businesses remain uncompetitive, unemployment is rising, and the neofascists have taken to the street, fire-bombing hostels for Turkish "guest workers". Tax increases have become inevitable, and a trillion Marks will be required to alleviate existing problems (Stern 1992).

New competitive pressures

The establishment of powerful trading blocks in western Europe, North America, and Southeast Asia has created a global "golden triangle". In conditions where nation-states are unable to manipulate trading relationships in order to win a competitive advantage – for example, through the imposition of trade barriers – they will seek to exhibit governing competence through "supply side" policies that contribute to the conditions in which competitive advantage can be sought through attracting inward investment, encouraging entrepreneurial activity among the nation's workforce, and developing new skills and forms of work organization. Thus in all European countries the question of how to enhance the cognitive and technical skills of the labour force has become a major political issue, despite differences in the way national governments seek to exploit the power of the state to manipulate internal trading conditions. This is because all new forms of work organization involve attendant changes in forms of social regulation and involvement, as well as in the nature of work, power, and authority.

As a consequence of these new forms of competitive pressure, processes of regional economic integration are being accompanied by what some argue are fundamental changes in the pattern of production, distribution, and consumption. The process of globalization, especially of economic markets, has been accompanied by rapid technological change and a revolution in communications. This has facilitated an increased demand for "flexibility" in relation to where production is to be sited, the way organizations are structured, and the way labour power is utilized. In highly competitive markets, especially for mass produced goods and services that can be provided more cheaply in the newly industrialized countries (NICs), there is a growing assumption throughout western Europe that economic advantage may be best achieved through the creation of markets for "high value added" products and services that depend on the skills, insights, and talents of the indigenous labour force, rather than through competition based on cost. However, like all forms of competition, such a strategy will involve losers, as well as winners.

Thus one possible outcome of the development of new competitive strategies within the Single Market is the creation of a "two tier" Europe. It is argued that this is at least in part a consequence of the different ways in which European nation-states have already responded to the economic crises of the 1970s and 1980s, despite homogenizing features such as the moves towards the creation of a Single Market in western Europe. In broad terms it can be suggested that European societies confronted choices. These were between on the one hand, trying to adapt the rigid, hierarchical divisions of labour, and the low skill and low trust relationships that characterize the "Fordist" production regimes that dominated the 1950s and the 1960s societies to these new conditions, or on the other, to shift to systems of flexible production and organization based on flatter hierarchies, adaptable and highly skilled workers, and a breakdown of the divisions that currently exist between mental and manual labour and learning.

Thus Leborgne and Lipietz (1990) have argued that unless significant policy reforms are introduced, the pressure towards the creation of a two-tier Europe within a "Single Market" will increase, to the distinct disadvantage of countries such as the United Kingdom and France. They suggest that an important reason for an increasing polarization in economic fortune is the direct result of the United Kingdom and France adopting Fordist strategies to deal with the "supply side" crisis (i.e. unemployment) in the 1980s. They note (1980: 180):

> Among businessmen, some (mainly in the United States, the United Kingdom and France) staked everything on reducing the cost of labour: temporary employment, subcontracting, relocation towards the Third World and automation. Others, however, mainly in Japan, the Scandinavian countries, the Federal Republic of Germany and some regions of Italy, preferred to rely on a new social pact, negotiated at enterprise, sectoral or national level, dealing with the actual organization of work. The employees were invited to join in the fight for quality and productivity.

Although the advantages of the "Single Market" appear to favour those member states who have adopted these kinds of neo-corporatist strategies to deal with new economic pressures, this has not prevented criticisms of "social dumping" (job-poaching) being levelled at Britain. Social dumping involves the movement of investment to countries with the lowest standards (i.e. minimum wages). Britain's decision to opt out of the Social Chapter is increasingly being seen to create an unfair competitive advantage, even if this means low wages and poor working conditions for British workers. Thus the President of the European Commission, Jacques Delors, recently attacked the decision by Hoover, the US multinational, to relocate from Dijon in France to Cambuslang in Scotland.[2]

Forms of social exclusion

A major consequence, therefore, of economic restructuring throughout Europe has been an intensification of competitive pressures, and this is likely to reinforce divisions between rich and poor nations and people. Max Weber argued that, as competitive conditions intensify, so social groups will seek to curb competition:

> Usually one group of competitors takes some externally identifiable characteristic of another group of (actual or potential) competitors – race, language, religion, local or social origin, descent, resident, etc. – as a pretext for attempting their exclusion. It does not matter which characteristic is chosen in the individual case: whatever suggests itself most easily is seized upon. Such group action may provoke a corresponding reaction on the part of those against whom it is directed. (Weber 1968: 242)

As a consequence, competitors form an "interest group" towards outsiders. One example of this is the way the promotion of the economic and social progress of European citizens has led to attempts to exclude non-EC nationals. Here the rules of exclusion are not based not on the specific attributes of individuals, but on the generalized attributes of social collectivities (for example, foreigners – Parkin 1974: 6). Thus the creation of a "fortress Europe" that imposes barriers on east Europeans and Africans seeking entry to EC member states may be seen as an example of what Parkin (1974) describes as "collectivist" exclusionary rules.

These can be contrasted with those forms of exclusion that typically affect the life chances and material circumstances of those who have EC citizenship rights. The dominant forms of social exclusion within most European countries are based not on political or legal restrictions, limiting access to civil rights, education, or professional occupations, but on the outcome of ostensibly universal criteria of achievement, reflecting personal qualities, efforts, and attributes. As Parkin has argued, during the 20th century there has been a gradual shift from "collective" to such "individualist" exclusion rules, associated with the development of the universalist rights of "citizenship" (Marshall 1963), within nation-states.

However, the powerful and the privileged have also attempted an "appropriation of market opportunities". Competition takes place not only at the level of the firm, but also in the labour market, within which both individuals and groups seek both protection and advantage. Trade unionism (which was described by Marshall as "a secondary form of industrial citizenship parallel with and supplementary to the system of political citizenship"), as well as other forms of collective occupational activity, have been one of the ways in which groups have sought to provide themselves with market shelters. These collective strategies of protection, however, are in decline, as a consequence of direct political attack as well as economic and technological restructuring. Thus we might expect to see an intensification of more individualistic efforts in this regard as a consequence of both rising unemployment and increasing uncertainty about job tenure. The expectation of permanent employment has declined, and career progression through internal labour markets has hit against the logic of flatter organizational hierarchies and the threat of take-over, merger, down-sizing, and closure.

Thus, increasingly, much everyday behaviour is not geared directly towards the exclusion of others, but rather to ensuring the inclusion of individuals or their family members, in terms of access to educational credentials, superior jobs, promotion opportunities, etc. As Parkin has noted:

> Individualist criteria of exclusion through the application of universal rules cannot guarantee the liberal conditions of justice as long as the state tolerates the intrusion of socially inherited handicaps and easements that directly affect the individual's capacity to perform. (Parkin 1974: 7–8)

In other words, some individuals are more equal than others. For example, middle class parents frequently hold contradictory values: "We believe in equality of opportunity. All children should have an equal chance of educational success." Yet in the next breath, "Of course, we want the best for our child", which leads them to invest in private education. This effectively ensures the absence of equity in "the competition for a livelihood" (Weber 1968: 341). It is, therefore, not only the question of social groups being able to control (or monopolize) market opportunities that is important, but equally their ability to appropriate market opportunities that they do not necessarily control directly. It is the access to such market opportunities or "life chances" that Weber described as contributing to the "class situation" of social groups.

Inequality, poverty and exclusion

As has been noted above, after the Second World War there was a rapid expansion of what Marshall described as "social citizenship" in western industrial societies, that is, "the right to a modicum of economic welfare and security [and] the right to . . . live the life of a civilized being according to the standards prevailing in the society" (1963: 74) – the rights, in short, associated with the development of the modern "welfare state". As many commentators have noted, the extension of welfare rights was associated with macro economic policies that were broadly Keynesian in their inspiration. Thus this period was also one of the rapid expansion of productive activities, together with mass consumption. This particular combination of production, consumption, and state regulation has been described as "Fordist" (Harvey 1990). In broad outline, it also has many similarities to what have been described as "left corporatist" modes of political and economic regulation (Lembruch & Schmitter 1982).

However, the social democratic dream of universal rights of citizenship and social justice has never been fully realized. Even in the most successful economies, moves towards universalism proved to be zero-sum in that the gains of the majority were at the expense of significant minorities, particularly immigrants, guest workers, and working class women, who were drawn into paid employment in ever greater numbers. In many cases, immigrant groups were excluded because, as has been noted above, the category of "citizen" may be a basis for exclusion as well as inclusion. We will need, therefore, to build upon our knowledge of existing social divisions within and between European nation-states and, in the New Europe, there is evidence that social and economic polarization and inequalities are increasing (Davis 1992).

As a consequence of these widening inequalities, it has been argued that a permanent "underclass" has developed, or is in the process of development, in Western industrial societies. The underclass concept has most recently been used in the United States to describe the ghetto poor. With the intensification of long-term unemployment, poverty, and urban unrest, it has been suggested that a similar "underclass" is emerging in Britain (Murray 1990). A feature of neo-liberal arguments such as those of Murray is that the supposed "underclass" is held to be morally responsible for its own deficiencies – that is, that the "underclass" has lost the will to work, is welfare dependent, and so on.

The focus of Murray's discussion of the "underclass", therefore, is not the structure of inequality but the personal character and demoralization that, he argues, have resulted directly from misguided social attitudes and welfare policy reforms in the 1960s and 1970s. The logic of this account of the underclass not only leads to programmes such as "Workfare" in the USA, but ultimately to the questioning of entitlements to citizenship itself:

> The question is no longer what the worst-off members of the community should receive. Now the question is who should be considered a bona fide member of the community in the first place.
>
> (Mead 1991: 11)

One should always be aware, however, that the practice of blaming the poor for their own circumstances has a very long history indeed (Bendix 1964). Considerable care, therefore, should be exercised in the use of the "underclass" concept.

Nevertheless, among the very poorest, two broad categories of disadvantage may be identified. These are first, those groupings that are defined by collectivist exclusion rules. In the "New Europe" this category might include immigrant groups, such as "guest workers" in Germany, who are granted residence but not citizenship rights. In general terms, such groups may be described as a potential source of a "non-citizen" underclass. Secondly, there are those who are excluded, for one reason or another, on individual grounds, rather than because of their collective exclusion from citizenship. Thus, for example, the very poor in Britain may be broadly described as a potential "citizen" underclass who, although formally holding full rights of national citizenship, are effectively barred from full participation in the society in which they live due to social, economic, and cultural deprivation.

Economic change and social institutions

Variations in national responses to changing global markets are inextricably connected to differences in "welfare regimes". Among European nations, "three worlds" of welfare capitalism have been identified (Esping-Andersen 1990), which relate to the national differences that have already been discussed. These are a) social democratic or universalist (for example, the Nordic countries); b) corporatist (for example, Germany and, to a lesser degree, France); and c) liberal (the UK). In the UK, the Conservative government has increasingly sought, over the last decade, to extend the principles of classic liberalism to the welfare state. Thus, as we have seen, the problem of economic exclusion has focused on the morals and conduct of the poor.

The fate of individuals, families, and nations therefore needs to be understood in terms of the global transformation taking place within the advanced capitalist societies as well as in terms of the specific historical, social, economic, and political conditions that pertain in any given country. As we have seen, national differences have persisted alongside what are held to be global shifts towards new forms of competition, the adoption of new working practices, retraining, flexibility, and so on. The outcome of these new competitive pressures has led to suggestions that increasing differences in national levels of material prosperity are developing in Europe. These arguments have been paralleled by debates relating to the emergence of a supposed "underclass", reflecting increasing divisions and inequalities *within* nation-states. Were a pan-European "underclass" to develop, comprised mainly of non-citizens, in tandem with the Single Market, the consequences could be very serious indeed. Nevertheless, even short of this gloomy prospect, it seems that despite the rhetoric of easier travel, business boom, improved quality of life, job flexibility, and so on, following from the "free movement of goods, services, capital and people" (Owen & Dynes 1992), individuals and groups will also seek, as they always have done, to protect themselves from the anarchy of the market. Thus we may also expect to see the perpetuation of established exclusionary practices, and the possible emergence of new ones.

II

The chapters in this volume reflect all of the themes discussed above. Kennett (Chapter 1) argues that, despite its cosmopolitan veneer, competitive pressures are intensifying in the "New Europe", and material inequalities are increasing sharply. Her analysis draws upon "regulation theory" – that is, a set of arguments that suggest that capitalist development describes not just a set of economic institutions, but also the parallel development of political and ideological forms. She argues that the decline of "Fordism" (which we have described as mass production and mass consumption, in combination with broadly Keynesian economic and welfare policies), and with it the corporatist accommodation between capital and labour, has already taken place. It is not, as yet, possible to be confident as to the nature of the "post-Fordist" regime of accumulation that will eventually emerge, but all the signs are that it will involve a new "toughness" in welfare, increasing poverty, and an increasing hostility to outsiders. Kennett suggests that relatively weak corporatist remnants, such as the EC Social Chapter, will in fact be too insubstantial to prevent the intensification of inequalities, and the development of new forms of inequality.

Increases in inequality, therefore, involve building on the old as well as creating the new. One of the most entrenched set of institutionalized inequalities is that associated with gender. Over the last two decades, feminist work within the social sciences has both documented gender-related inequalities and demonstrated their systematic linkages with other social institutions. In particular, the development of "new" forms of flexible working associated with the move to "post-Fordism" has been closely associated with the expansion of women's paid employment, particularly in respect of part-time work. However, Bruegel and Hegewisch's (Chapter 2) comparative analysis of national differences in part-time employment suggests that the situation is complex. There are significant national differences in levels of part-time working. These differences indicate the continuing importance of institutionalized national peculiarities, as would be emphasized by those sociologists who have stressed the relevance of "societal" effects, and the precise explanations for women's part-time working will vary from country to country. Nevertheless, Bruegel and Hegewisch conclude that, on balance, labour shortages have probably been more significant causal forces in the expansion of part-time employment than a conscious strategy of flexibility on the part of employers – although both factors will contribute.

In part because of features such as part-time working, women remain concentrated in low-level jobs. Thus the increase in women's employment has not been accompanied by any very significant improvement in the material circumstances of women. Indeed, as Ginn and Arber's (Chapter 3) comparative analysis of women's pension entitlements in Denmark, Germany, and Britain demonstrates, work-related inequalities among women are carried over into female poverty in later life. However, national differences, linked to variations in the manner of welfare state provision, are very significant in determining the extent to which women receive some sort of pension compensation in spite of these work-related inequalities. Using the framework developed by Esping-Andersen, Ginn and Arber demonstrate that the British liberal welfare state renders British women, in comparison to Danish and German women, most vulnerable to poverty in old age. British women might possibly gain some enhanced protection from universalist, EC-wide provision such as that envisioned in the Social Chapter – but, as we have seen, the present government's policy has been actively to resist such developments. Esping-Andersen's framework is also deployed by Leira (Chapter 4) in her analysis of the work and family experiences of women in Scandinavia and Europe. In addition, Leira draws upon Pateman's (1989) influential feminist critique of classical contractarianism and the development of "citizenship". As Pateman has argued, the template for the "citizen" has been masculine and, in particular, the benefits of social citizenship have accrued to men as workers, rather than directly to women as carers. Thus, even as "citizens", women have not necessarily gained from supposedly universalist citizen rights. Leira argues, therefore, that welfare state institutions must recognize the need for support for women and men as carers and earners.

It has been argued, therefore, that women have suffered a serious disadvantage in that "citizenship" has been articulated in relation to the "worker" rather than the "carer". Nevertheless, women have been able to gain from the fact that the universalistic ideology of citizenship has provided an important framework within which the claims of (relatively) excluded groups who are nevertheless "citizens" – such as women – may be articulated. However, these claims cannot even be articulated unless minimal citizenship rights, such as membership of the national community, are granted. Thus "citizenship" has provided a significant element in frameworks developed for the analysis of race and ethnicity (Parsons & Clark 1967; Rex 1986). In their theoretical paper, Allen and Macey (Chapter 5) examine recent developments in relation to our understandings of race, ethnicity, religion, and gender. They argue that, despite what might appear to be a degree of conceptual confusion, existing sociological paradigms still have a lot to offer in the analysis of these important areas. In particular, they stress the persisting material base of structured perceptions and inequalities in respect of race and ethnicity, and warn against a too-enthusiastic embracing of alternative, "postmodernist" understandings, despite the increasing diversity that characterizes the modern world. A similar note of caution is sounded by Mitchell and Russell (Chapter 6) in their discussion of race, citizenship, and "fortress Europe". They suggest that "the right to be different can never be unconditional". Thus the multi-culturalism that has been influential in shaping British attitudes to "race relations" has been relatively unwilling to face up to the "difficult but necessary question of the boundaries and limitations that any modern society must impose upon culturally distinct groups". A positive aspect of the British case is that, in fact, the acquisition of citizenship rights is not hedged around by the same restrictions as it is in, say, Germany.

As we have noted, the acquisition of these rights can form at least the basis of a claim to social equality on the part of disadvantaged ethnic groups.

This point is emphasized by Lash (Chapter 7) in his discussion of the variations in the composition of the supposed "underclass". Lash contrasts the "citizen" underclass of the United States and Britain with the lot of the very poorest – immigrant workers – in Germany. Germany, he argues, possesses a number of institutional features that will inhibit the development of a citizen underclass. In particular, the corporatist welfare state, which, among other things, discourages women in respect of employment (although, as Ginn and Arber demonstrate, married women in Germany have substantial derived benefits as wives), and delivers substantial benefits to "citizens". Thus in Germany, despite a liberal policy on immigration, the most disadvantaged are non-citizens. Lash suggests that these non-citizens may form the basis of a specific German "underclass".

As well as the likelihood of the development of increasing inequalities within and between nation-states, therefore, there is also the possibility that a pan-European "underclass", composed of different nationalities but sharing a common "non-citizen" status in the countries in which they actually live and work, might develop. It is paradoxical that important recent developments that might have been considered in a highly positive light might actually be fuelling these negative developments. These are associated with the collapse of the repressive, "state-socialist" regimes in the Eastern Bloc, which has led to the winding down of the permanent arms economy together with hopes of a peace dividend.

However, as Lovering's discussion (Chapter 8) suggests, it is likely that one of the most immediate outcomes of the peace dividend will be an increase in unemployment. More sinister, however, is the possibility that unregulated arms competition will simply serve to provision the increasing number of (relatively) small-scale conflicts that have been fuelled by the collapse of central controls and increasing nationalist pretensions. Yet again, the regulatory controls – such as they are – of the "New Europe" appear unable to achieve effective intervention to remedy the situation. The situation is especially acute in eastern Europe. Two papers, by Ray and Cox (Chapters 9 and 10), focus upon the rapidly changing situation in these countries. Both are frankly pessimistic concerning short – and medium – term developments. Ray argues that in Soviet-type societies, the old elite stratum, the nomenklatura, have sought to transform their bureaucratic power into economic capital. The mass of the population remain excluded from access to the sources of power and prosperity, and a viable private enterprise economy seems a very remote possibility. Similarly, Cox argues that long-established inequalities grounded in state-socialist arrangements are being carried forwards into the New Europe in the East. Empirical evidence suggests that the small-scale private sector is growing, but that it retains a subordinate and subsistence character. State enterprises are being privatised only slowly, and it is not yet clear whether this will provide a viable commercial base.

Finally, it should be stressed that the final drafts of the chapters that follow were delivered during the first few months of 1993. In the light of the rapid changes that are still taking place, they should be read with this date in mind.

Notes

1. Financial Times Survey, "European Business Location", 21 October 1992.
2. See Financial Times, "Delors seeks social policy on jobs crisis", 2 February 1993.

References

Bendix, R. 1964. *Nation-building and citizenship*. New York: John Wiley.

Esping-Andersen, G. 1990. *The three worlds of welfare capitalism*. Cambridge: Polity.

Davis, H. 1992. Social stratification in Europe. In *Social Europe*, J. Bailey (ed.). Harlow, England: Longman.

Harvey, D. 1990. *The condition of postmodernity*. Oxford: Basil Blackwell.

Leborgne, D. & A. Lipietz 1990. How to avoid a two-tier Europe. *Labour and Society* **5**, 177–99.

Lembruch, G. & P. C. Schmitter (eds) 1982. *Patterns of corporatist policy-making*. London: Sage.

Marshall, T. H. 1963. Citizenship and social class. In *Sociology at the crossroads*. London: Heinemann.

Maurice, M., F. Sellier, J.-J. Silvestre 1986. *The social foundations of industrial power*. Cambridge, Mass.: MIT Press.

Mead, L. 1991. The new politics of the new poverty. *The Public Interest* **103**, 11.

Murray, C. A. 1990. *The emerging British underclass*. London: IEA Health and Welfare Unit.

Owen, R. & M. Dynes 1992. *The Times guide to the Single European Market*. London: Times Books.

Parkin, F. (ed.) 1974. *The social analysis of class structure*. London: Tavistock.

Parsons, T. & K. B. Clark 1967. *The negro American*. Boston: Beacon Press.

Pateman, C. 1989. *The disorder of women*. Cambridge: Polity.

Rex, J. 1986. *Race and ethnicity*. Milton Keynes, England: Open University Press.

Stern, F. 1992. A nation divisible and indivisible: a German example. *RSA Journal* (Aug/Sept), 587–94.

Weber, M. 1968. *Economy and society* (ed. G. Roth and C. Wittich). New York: Bedminster Press.

Chapter 1

Exclusion, post-Fordism and the "New Europe"

Patricia Kennett

Introduction

European integration has gained added momentum as the Single European Act has provided the dynamic for economic and monetary union. The globalization of capital and the restructuring of labour markets have been accompanied by new types of social and economic regulation and new strategies with supra-national dimensions. This chapter attempts to make sense of these developments with regulation theory (Aglietta 1979; Lipietz 1982, 1985; De Vroey 1984; Jessop 1990) providing a framework within which to analyze the dynamics of events. The overall aim is to look at processes of marginalization, and the transformations in the political and social spheres as the "mode of regulation" evolves within a specific regime of accumulation.

The chapter will begin by outlining regulation theory and explaining the perceived nature of the transition from Fordism to post-Fordism. The task of identifying a transition is difficult in that the nature of Fordism and modernism is still itself disputed. By drawing on empirical evidence, however, it is possible to develop an insight into the nature of post-Fordist society and to investigate the fate of particular groups within the "New Europe". This chapter seeks to penetrate the facade of a "cosmopolitan" Europe and will concentrate on issues of joblessness, poverty, and homelessness in societies where a growing number of people are experiencing social and economic dislocation and exclusion.

Regulation theory

That capital must reorganize has been recognized by a number of diverse sources. Schumpeter (1934) sees capitalism as a system of change, a gale of

14

creative destruction, characterized over time by the emergence of new commodities, techniques of production, markets, and industrial organizations. For Marx, the organizing logic of the capitalist mode of production requires that surplus is appropriated from labour by paying it less than the value it adds to the labour process. Thus, capital may develop strategies to ensure the realization of productive effort, e.g. particular types of production and management technology comprising a specific pattern of production and consumption.

A central theme of regulation theory is that capitalist development or capitalist accumulation is not just an economic process but is associated with a wide range of institutions, including not only economic institutions, but also political and ideological ones (Kotz 1990). Each capitalist development of society can be associated with different *regimes of accumulation*. Each is associated with a particular *mode of social and political regulation* that forms the:

> totality of institutional forms, networks and norms (explicit or implicit) which together secure the compatibility of typical modes of conduct in the context of an accumulation regime, corresponding as much to the changing balance of social relations and to their more conflictual properties.
>
> (Lipietz 1985: 121, cited in Jessop 1989: 262)

Thus, capitalist development is conceived as a series of specific stages of the accumulation process in which the modes of regulation are "codifications of social regulations", defining the "rules of the game" (Dunford 1990).

Extensive to intensive accumulation strategies

Within a regime of predominantly extensive accumulation in the 19th century (Aglietta 1979: 71), workers were involved as producers, meeting their consumption needs mainly through petty commodity and subsistence channels (Harvey 1989). This was followed by a regime involving a combination of extensive and intensive accumulation, complemented by a mode of competitive regulation that "at the level of the nation-state was economically liberal and non-interventionist" (Peck & Tickell 1991: 9). Capitalist relations reached into new industrial sectors such as iron and steel, railway construction, and shipbuilding (Dunford 1990) and established new trading areas in the USA, Europe, and the rest of the world. From the 1930s, the introduction of mass production and mass consumption heralded the historical transition to a regime of intensive accumulation (Aglietta 1979) as the emerging mode of monopoly regulation facilitated parallel development in advanced capitalist countries.

Transformation of the regime of accumulation and mode of regulation is necessary with a long-term or structural crisis, which becomes evident with a significant reduction in the rate of accumulation over a prolonged period of time. Crisis indicates that the mode of regulation is no longer adequate to the regime of accumulation. The Great Depression of the 1930s, for example, can be recognized as the outcome of problems in the accumulation/institution relation, with over-investment and under-consumption leading to severe structural crisis (Kotz 1990). Resolution of long-term crisis requires a transformation of the accumulation/institution relation, with the evolution strongly influenced by the outcome of class and political struggles. While the basic institutions of capitalism remain, their specific form changes as the combination of mode of regulation with regime of accumulation gives rise to a distinctive mode of development. Thus, the new form of capitalism that emerged from the processes of restructuring and class struggle in the 1930s was quite different from the *laissez-faire* model of the pre-Depression era.

Fordism in Europe

The concept of Fordism has been used by regulation theorists to describe the mode of development that evolved in order to resolve the contradictions of the previous mode of development. This links mass production with mass consumption through an:

> ensemble of productive, institutional, social and political relations and practices that, in combination, regulate the accumulation process. (Schoenberger 1989: 101)

In a European context, the 1930s had represented a period of depression and protectionism and, against a backdrop of the Cold War and Marshall Aid, the strategies behind the implementation of the European Coal and Steel Community (1951) recognized the need for a new common structure to encourage the resurgence of heavy industries of the Ruhr, France, and other European countries. With a supra-national body responsible for policy relating to the coal and steel industries, its decisions were to apply directly to each country and, for Monnet, represented the first stepping stones to a European federation. Member states asserted themselves against the realization of the federal ideal, however. National sovereignty, nation-state identity and industrial profile remained prominent, reinforced by the Luxembourg Compromise (1961) enforcing unanimity in the decision-making process. Thus, the vision was one of a European economy big enough to accommodate the scale required for the contemporary technology of mass production and Taylorist techniques (Pinder 1991: 5). As Townsend has commented, "Fordism reigned at the heart of Community programmes" (Townsend 1991: 7), as it sought to challenge the USA as the world's economic super-power.

Fordist production combined the task fragmentation of "Taylorism" with intensive mechanization and the continuous flow principle of the semi-automatic assembly line. This resulted in gains in productivity, reduced relative cost, and increased sales, at the same time enabling the real incomes of the working class to rise without directly impinging upon capitalists' profits. Subsequent emergence of new forms of mass consumption or "ideological commodities", revolving around automobiles, consumer durables, and other standardized industrial products, permitted the realization of scale economies inherent to assembly line production and temporarily ensured a successful period of capitalist development. The Treaties of Rome (1957), establishing the European Economic Community (EEC), set about abolishing barriers of tariffs and import duties, creating a situation in which, according to Townsend, "prosperity could be guaranteed by extending the internal market to all members of the new club and by confronting countries outside with tougher conditions of trade" (Townsend 1991: 7). Thus, the Customs Union represented a central economic feature of the EEC facilitating larger markets for scale, higher investment, and faster growth (Pinder 1991).

New ways of working were accompanied and supported by other factors such as new forms of consumption, the development of domestic credit, and new types of welfare provision. The post-war period saw a commitment to full employment and universal welfare, as nation-states sought to maintain levels of consumption with intervention through social programmes (Peck & Tickell 1991). As Jessop (1989) has indicated:

> The Keynesian Welfare State system provided the political shell and the organizing myth in and through which a Fordist regime of sorts extended its hold over most parts of British society.
> (Jessop 1989: 267)

Thus, the linkage between production and consumption under the Fordist regime of accumulation was facilitated by the institutional framework, with the mode of regulation, in turn, providing the mechanism for channelling productivity increases into higher wages and ultimately into mass consumption (De Vroey 1984).

17

National variations

This is not to suggest that all countries are heading in a unilinear direction or to minimize the differences in developments in each country. Each nation-state will experience its own particular mode of growth, emanating not only from its specific political and industrial profile, but also from its own mode of insertion into the international economic system (Jessop 1989). Jessop highlights developments in Britain and Germany, where the nature of Fordism in both societies is different. German post-war expansion relied on an industry comprised of predominantly skilled workers, located within an export-oriented capital goods sector. The expansion of mass production industries, Taylorist modes of production and organization, and the development of the Keynesian welfare state became most prominent in the 1960s. Even then production processes were only partially Taylorised, and involved a high proportion of skilled workers with broad job classifications, in contrast with "continuous process" industries in Britain and France, which operated largely with specialized, semi-skilled workers (Lane 1988). In the US, Fordism was based on privatized consumption and the "suburban ideal" with a limited social contract between capital and labour (Florida & Feldman 1988).

Post-Fordism and the "New Europe"

The crisis of the 1970s revealed the declining effectiveness of the mechanisms established earlier. The boom of the 1950s and 1960s dissipated as rampant inflation disrupted the circulation process, wage demands lowered the rate of profit, and the oil shocks of 1974 and 1979 prompted austerity policies as the International Monetary Fund (IMF) imposed a new economic discipline throughout the world economy (Kotz 1990). As European economies adopted deflationary measures to correct the deficit and reduce inflation, large-scale unemployment was aggravated by increasing competition from outside Europe, particularly Japan. The introduction of new techniques and information technology threatened Europe's ability to compete in the world economy. Thus the dynamic phase of the 1980s in the EC can be seen as a response to these difficulties, and the Single European Act (1987) represented a trigger for the reassertion of the four freedoms of capital, goods, services, and people. The European barrier-free market will be larger than the USA, with a combined population of 350 million. The establishment of a European Economic Area (EEA), proposed for 1993, will combine the twelve EC nations with those of the European Free Trade Association. The EEA will be the world's largest free trade area, with 380 million consumers and 46 per cent of world trade (The Economist 26 October 1991, 105–6). Thus, Callinicos sees "economic logic" reflecting "the partly converging, partly conflicting interests of a bloc of capitalist states" (Callinicos 1992: 12). In response, the USA is also seeking to expand its free trade area by lowering barriers between Canada and the USA. There is also the possibility of a trans-Pacific free trade zone between the USA, Canada, Mexico, and Japan as a way of competing with the European Community.

Evolving regime of accumulation

New modes of capitalism have emerged that, with national variations, have seen the internationalization of capitalism opening up global markets and the establishment of a new international division of labour (Froebel et al. 1980). As Knight has highlighted, the

> international framework or organization is evolving to facilitate and govern transnational flows that weave national systems into the global fabric . . . Sovereign nation-state remains the basic organizational unit of the international system but new types of power centres are emerging to structure the global system.
>
> (Knight 1989: 32)

The nature of the successor to Fordism is a matter of fierce debate. However, an examination of the fundamental elements of regulation gives some indication of the direction of developments. The *restructuring of work processes and labour markets and a substantial change in the pattern of state intervention* are crucial elements in capital's response to workplace resistance to Taylorism and the crisis of productivity slow down in the core Fordist countries of Europe and the USA.

Labour market restructuring

Throughout the Community the impact of recent and prospective technological change has impacted on employment levels and has had a major effect on the nature and content of jobs. Similarly, the decline of manufacturing employment and the rise in service employment, in nearly all the developed countries, has severely altered the structure of opportunities.

According to the American Federation of Labour,

> Every industrialized nation is undergoing a scientific, technological, economic revolution every bit as significant as the industrial revolution of the 19th century. (Kassalow 1989: 44)

During the early period of assembly line production, one of the principal reasons for introducing new technologies was to reduce direct labour costs by achieving economies of scale and standardization of production. In contrast, the increase in pace of technological change over the past two decades has accompanied the objective of achieving a greater degree of flexibility (Piore & Sabel 1984) as management strategy has emphasized the customization of product and fast reaction times in terms of changes in specification, delivery times, and so on. The post-Fordist regime of accumulation appears to be based on flexibility in relation to labour processes, products, and patterns of consumption, but to be effective it must run parallel with labour market flexibility. Based on trends established over the previous decade, it was predicted that by the early 1990s non-traditional types of work would account for 40 per cent of the workforce in Britain (Hakim 1987: 37), with similar changes in the nature of employment relationships increasing in many countries.

Post-Fordist employment trajectories

Esping-Andersen attempts to identify post-industrial activities that are most closely associated with novel relations of consumption, production, and human reproduction (Esping-Andersen 1990: 196). He distinguishes between occupations that mainly belong to the traditional industrial world (skilled and unskilled production workers, craft workers, clerical and sales personnel) and occupations that epitomize post-industrialism (professionals, scientists, and technicians) and generally unqualified service workers engaged in leisure service production. Lindley (1991) has identified these trends as occurring throughout member countries.

Technological change and the growth of the service sector have had major influences on the structural change of the labour market, with a relative decline in employment in manufacturing in virtually every industrialized country (OECD 1984; Kuwahara 1989). The development of services is found not only in the tertiary sector, but also in the primary and secondary sectors. In the manufacturing industry, jobs categorized as "information related" or "service" jobs have been increasing. In his analysis of occupational trends in employment growth in Sweden, Germany, and the USA, Esping-Andersen (1990) recognizes that though the pace and mix vary, for all three countries, the post-industrial occupations dominate the growth profile. Within the European Community virtually all additional jobs created between 1985 and 1990 were in services, with trends indicating that the proportion of employment in this sector grew continuously from 42 per cent in 1985 to over 62 per cent in 1989. The share of the workforce in agriculture and industry has fallen, with the latter from 41 per cent in 1965 to under 32 per cent in 1989 (ComEC 1991: 9). This is likely to continue as manufacturing companies increasingly contract out service elements of their operations. This growth is particularly significant for women, as three-quarters of them already work in services.

However, just as there is nothing new about technological innovation, services as such are not revolutionary. What is important is not simply an increase in the numbers employed in this sector, but the significant intersectoral changes. At the beginning of the century, domestic service was most prominent. Later, the growing importance of financial services, retail, marketing, and advertising can be associated with the mass production and mass consumption of Fordism (Esping-Andersen 1990). New areas of expansion are concentrated in recreation and tourist activities, social services, and business services.

It is worth reasserting that these general trends do not imply unilinear developments throughout the advanced industrial nations. On the contrary, the use of comparative data highlights the divergence of developments occurring in different social formations. In Germany, for example, Esping-Andersen (1990) notes that while overall employment has declined, the share of manufacturing has remained constant since 1960. At about 40 per cent, this proportion employed in industry is by far the highest in the Community (ComEC 1991). The traditional industrial blue-collar worker remains important, as social welfare occupations and other service-worker jobs are vastly underdeveloped.

Wage relation

The increase in atypical or non-conventional and less secure types of employment (part time, temporary and fixed term, home based, and independent contracting) which is impacting on all employment sectors, can be seen to be accommodating greater flexibility while at the same time creating difficulties for union organization and influence. Patterns in the USA are indicative of developments in other countries. It is those occupations in which the unions have their greatest strength that have weak employment prospects, while those where unions tend to be weak are projected for strong growth (Kassalow 1989: 45). As Castells (1989) has indicated, organized labour in most capitalist countries is at the lowest point of its power and influence in the last 30 years. While British trade unions have heralded the arrival of the

European Community's Social Charter (signed by eleven countries but not Britain) as representing a new form of bargaining power and promising new rights for workers, according to John Stirling "the Social Charter is the result of political compromises rather than a commitment to workers' rights" (Stirling 1991: 8).

Emanating from the spirit of the Single European Act, it could be anticipated that the Social Charter derives from a concern to ensure the effectiveness of European capital in world markets. Draft directives on temporary and part-time work and working time have been met with opposition from Britain, as John Major attempts to maintain a low wage economy with relatively low social costs (Callinicos 1992). In other European countries, where working arrangements are more regulated, there is likely to be little gain from the legislation. However, as Stirling points out, unlike the Council of Europe and the International Labour Organization, the European Community has the potential power of forcing member states to change their laws, which may offer some hopes for the future.

The changing nature of power relations between employers and organized labour, and the introduction of flexible working practices as a response to the crisis of Fordist accumulation, has obvious implications for the wage relation. Esping-Andersen (1990), commenting on developments in Germany, has predicted a scenario whereby collective negotiations are conducted solely on behalf of those with jobs, pursuing wage maximization at the expense of job expansion for the "outsiders". He points to the implicit relations between business, trade unions, and government that have influenced the German trajectory.

In Britain, the apparent polarization between polyvalent skilled workers and unskilled workers would seem to represent "a recomposition of the collective labourer", and a move towards new dominant forms of wage relation, emphasizing enterprise or plant level collective bargaining and new forms of social wage. For workers, casualization impinges upon the social relations of production. A study by Morris (1988) indicated that possible subcontracting out of work was used as a bargaining tool for management, who threatened that such a policy would be extended if labour did not agree to greater productivity agreements, wage restraint, the introduction of new technology, changed working practices, etc. Burawoy (1983) has referred to a new balance of economic forces arising from the greater mobility of capital. No longer is the fear of being fired paramount. Instead the fear of capital flight, plant closure, the transfer of operations, and disinvestment become the main issues in the exercise of control.

Exclusion in the post-Fordist state

In the remainder of this chapter, I intend to link the impact of restructuring with the changing relations of the welfare state, and to examine the future relationship between member states and EC institutions. The hegemonic discourse within the EC is centred around "integration", "freedom" and "cohesion". Deconstruction of this discourse reveals that for particular social groups within the "New Europe", exclusion and discrimination on the grounds of unemployment and homelessness are on the increase.

Tsoukalis (1991) has identified a general shift to the right in terms of economic policies in most countries of western Europe, irrespective of their political stance. For example, the French socialist government moved towards more market and European-oriented policies in 1983. Spanish socialists, after 1981, pursued a path of economic orthodoxy with a strong market orientation (Tsoukalis 1991: 48) which has been strongly and consistently supported by the European Commission. For Mellor (1989), the reversal of Keynesian policies, which had provided the foundation of post-war economic policies in western Europe, represented a shift from the hegemonic collective norms and values associated with the development of the Keynesian welfare state consensus. Major changes in the structures of welfare states have represented a definite strategy intended to reorient the emphasis within the welfare state away from the sphere of reproduction and towards the sphere of production.

The early stages of European integration coincided with the rapid expansion of the rôle of the state in the social policy field, with modest internal redistribution and reduction of the impact of loss of income as one of the main aims.

> social policies were aimed at the incorporation of the working class in the political and economic systems and the achievement of a wider consensus for the growth policies of the 1950s and 1960s.
> (Tsoukalis 1991: 152–3)

More recently, the debate surrounding the "harmonization" of social policies has been influenced by the fear of "social dumping", a situation in which dependent groups move to states where social security is more generous. Alternatively, labour-intensive industries are attracted to regions where labour is cheap and plentiful, and social expenditure levels are low (Abrahamson 1991: 240), thus upsetting the balance of competitiveness within the EC. Intervention by the EC in areas of social policy has thus been concerned with the establishment of a "level playing field".

The concept of "subsidiarity" has become prevalent in the EC, particularly in relation to social policy, and supports the notion of "a decentralised organization of responsibilities, with the aim of never entrusting to a larger unit what can be realized by a smaller one" (Delores 1989 in Spicker 1991: 4). Spicker has suggested that the use of the principle of subsidiarity is being used to limit Community activity in a range of areas and that the "role of the Community must of necessity be minor in relation to that of other providers of welfare" (Spicker 1991: 8).

Titmuss (1968) distinguishes between the residual welfare state in which the state assumes responsibility only when the "family" or the market fails, thus limiting its commitment to marginal and "deserving" social groups, and an institutional welfare state, representing a universalistic commitment to welfare extended to all areas of distribution vital for social welfare. Developing Marshall's (1950) thesis, Esping-Andersen (1990) suggests that social rights, given the legal and practical status of property rights, and granted on the basis of citizenship rather than performance, will entail a decommodification of the status of individuals in relation to the market and thus an erosion of the commodity status of labour in capitalist society. He refers to these processes of decommodification as: "the degree to which individuals, or families, can uphold a socially acceptable standard of living independently of market participation" (Esping-Andersen 1990: 37).

Thus, it is the extent to which social rights will apply to all citizens that will define the nature of the welfare state. Greater decommodification exists if access is easy and if rights to an adequate standard of living are guaranteed, regardless of previous employment, needs test, or financial contribution. For Esping-Andersen (1990), "both social rights and social stratification are shaped by the nexus of the state and market in the distribution system" (Esping-Andersen 1990: 4). His analysis becomes of particular significance, given the "work incentive logic" (Abrahamson 1991: 246) incorporated within recent EC recommendations to combat poverty in the face of rising unemployment and growing disparities between income and welfare (Ferge & Miller 1987; Townsend 1991).

The sharp increase in unemployment in the early 1980s represented a worldwide phenomenon from which few countries escaped. In the European Community, unemployment has declined from its peak of 11 per cent in 1985, though it still represented an average of over 8.7 per cent in 1991, or 12 million people. Some 4 per cent of the Community labour force, or around 6 million people, were classified as long-term unemployed and had been out of work for more than a year (ComEC 1991: 8). The forecast was for continued increases throughout 1993.

The more extensive forms of social protection have favoured workers with regular and stable employment, with a growing but poorly protected and neglected group of the welfare state largely reliant on national or local assistance measures. In Britain, changes in social security have made it much more difficult to get benefits as of right (Labour Research 1990). In Germany, it is local government that is responsible for the administration of social assistance; thus the impact of the rising numbers of claims, combined with retrenchment in general city revenues, and various programmes in social policy transfers, has increasingly relegated municipalities into institutions "of the last resort". Those who are dependent on local means-tested social assistance were more severely affected by the social expenditure cuts than were most social insurance beneficiaries, as the basic rates of social assistance have failed to keep pace with inflation.

The growth of recurrent and long-term unemployment has thus been associated with dependence on more basic forms of social assistance, often providing poverty line benefits. Results of an EC study carried out in 1987 indicated that the number of people living in poverty had shown a sharp increase (Teekens & van Praag 1990). It was those receiving social assistance because of loss of employment who showed the most dramatic increase, rising from 0.7 per cent to 26.4 per cent. In the Netherlands in 1979, 2.7 per cent of persons receiving social assistance were unemployed, compared with 66.7 per cent in 1985. In contrast, during the same period 28 per cent of elderly people were in receipt of social assistance, compared with 1.5 per cent in 1985 (Laczko 1990). In the UK the percentage of unemployed families on social assistance rose from 15 per cent to 35 per cent between 1979 and 1983. Demographic changes involving the rise in divorce and the increase in the number of lone parent families can be seen to be contributing to another group at risk of poverty (Millar 1989). Room et al. (1989) identified the increase in the reliance by single parent households on social assistance in both Germany and the UK, with a large proportion of them being in poverty.

So far, the EC has offered only limited proposals to deal with the issues of either regional or personal poverty. Structural Funds have been made available for infrastructure investment, and the Social Fund supports training and employment creation. In March 1990, the Commission of the European Communities launched "Poverty 3" – described as a "medium-term" Community action programme to foster the economic and social integration of the least privileged groups. The Commission is also sponsoring an "Observatory on Policies for Combating Social Exclusion". Abrahamson (1991) surmises that the aim of these programmes is to "mobilise private and voluntary networks and institutions" in a welfare mix combining market, state, and community (Abrahamson 1991: 244–5). The Commission has also discussed the introduction of a guaranteed minimum income representing "a differential allowance, means-tested, in principle available to all citizens, and in general linked to labour market re-insertion for people of working age" (Peters 1989: 4, in Abrahamson 1991: 246). It is clear that the fight against poverty has been relegated to the domain of individual nation-states at a time when the current system of income transfers is under stress and fails to provide adequate resources for those dependent on it.

Homelessness as marginality

The increase in the number of marginal households has been accompanied by a rise in the most extreme and visible form of poverty and exclusion. The escalation in the numbers of people dispossessed and homeless has been recognized throughout the industrialized nations. While the exact number of homeless people in a country is difficulty to quantify, it is evident that numbers are rising, as various studies have shown (EC member states see National Campaign for the Homeless 1985; Schuler-Wallner 1986; Ferrand-Bechmann 1988; FEANTSA 1992).

Gentrification and the rapid increase in the number of affluent non-family households and childless couples in the 1970s raised the demand for older urban housing. Rather than passing to households with lower incomes, it had become common for housing to filter up to higher income groups (Smith & Williams 1985). As the demand for unskilled labour in the city centre is reduced, so the demand for central city locations from professional and managerial employees increases (Marcuse 1989). For Harvey (1989), the advent of "free market populism" has strongly influenced the reshaping of the urban environment. For the middle classes there is the

> enclosed and protected spaces of shopping malls and atria, but it does nothing for the poor except to eject them into a new and quite nightmarish postmodern landscape of homelessness.
>
> (Harvey 1989: 77)

Increasingly, the housing environment and public areas of the inner city are tailored to the tastes of the new middle class as investment is focused on office building and luxury waterfront developments. Low-cost housing has become a low priority despite a recognition of the problems of affordability and availability of housing for low and moderate income earners. The crisis has resulted in growing waiting lists for public housing, overcrowding, and increasing pressure on the cheaper end of the private rental market, pushing up rents and increasing homelessness (Thorns 1988). In Germany, for example, the construction of low-cost housing is currently less than at any time since the Federal Republic was founded in 1949, when the need may never have been greater. In a country where renting is the rule, gentrification of inner-city areas has seen rents rising to such an extent that in Munich, for example, rents are now 53 per cent higher than the national average. Similar trends can be seen in other "global cities" as increasing pressure on the cheaper end of the private rental market pushes up deregulated rents, with crises in supply compounded as landlords pull out of the less profitable lower end of the market.

The specific social and economic conditions of the present represent a retreat from welfarism and a reorientation of the welfare state, with housing policy diverging between the well-housed majority and a disadvantaged, badly housed, or homeless minority. Government spending trends can be analyzed not only in terms of expenditure cuts, but as representing a change in the balance of public expenditure away from the public sector and direct investment to, for example, the support of owner occupation. This can be perceived as a general shift away from state welfare collectivism to "subsidised individualism (Forrest & Murie 1986). Privatization by subsidization is boosting consumption for those who can afford it.

The European Commission has had little to say in the housing arena, where an extension of competence in housing policy has been questioned on the grounds of the principle of subsidiarity. Instead, interest is growing as issues of exclusion, social cohesion, and a "two speed" Europe threaten to impair progress towards economic and monetary union. Kleinman (1991) has highlighted the contradictions evident for those interested in developing a "social space" as well as an "economic space" within the EC, when the "logic of economic and financial integration is pushing in the opposite direction – towards greater deregulation and less overall state involvement" (Kleinman 1991: 6). As European economies converge around counter-inflationary strategies, the likely outcome is further labour and class dislocations.

The direction of housing policy, then, has seen a concentration on the needs of those city residents who are considered to be promoters of economic activity with a promising future (Hausserman & Siebel 1990). Governments have modified their commitment from those based upon notions of equity and involvement, and instead have adopted attitudes based on the belief that the best remedy for an ailing housing industry lies in the "genius of the market", unfettered by government housing policies and regulations. As Kleinman has indicated,

> while policies in the earlier period were designed to preserve jobs and the existing social structure, policies now are aimed at promoting the adaptation of cities to economic change.
>
> (Kleinman 1991: 3)

The expanding group of homeless represents a more diverse population than the received image of the middle-aged white male. Young people, women, and those from ethnic minorities are now heavily represented among a section of society that is likely to experience more entrenched exclusion. Marcuse (1989) links the treatment of the homeless with economic restructuring and changes in the labour process. The emphasis is no longer on the production of goods, but is instead placed on increasing the appetite for consumption. Thus, the poverty of the homeless challenges the pursuit of wealth as an end in itself: greed becomes less acceptable in the presence of poverty (Marcuse 1989: 216).

This is particularly evident in the context of race and immigration, as a discourse is established around Europe's inability to absorb and integrate foreign populations. The increasing concern of EC governments regarding the "problem" of immigration has coincided with a growth in racial tensions, xenophobia, and neo-Nazi groups throughout Europe. The Social Charter contains no explicit reference to racial discrimination. The response instead has come from *ad hoc* and secret inter-governmental organizations emerging outside the formal apparatus of the EC. Most notable are the TREVI group of Ministers (1976), the Ad Hoc Group on Immigration (1986), and the Schengen Accord (1985 and 1990), established to address issues of immigration in the contest of law and order, terrorism, public order, and international co-operation on policing (Bunyan 1991). These new supra-national modes of capitalist regulation can be seen to be contributing to an ideological construction of a European identity involving "us" and "others". Thus, access to employment, labour monopoly, and social benefits seems to encapsulate increasingly a narrowly defined notion of EC "nationals", and excludes that part of the population considered unnecessary or unsuitable for the production process. Foreign workers, indispensable during the period of rapid economic growth after the Second World War, are now deemed "unnecessary".

Conclusion

While it would be true to say that the Keynesian welfare state and the associated modes of growth have been discredited, it is difficult as yet to determine the meaning of the "New Europe". So far, we can only hypothesize as
to the nature of the successor to Fordism, and the new types of social and
political regulation that will emerge. This chapter argues that the economic,
social, and political conditions of the present are different in many advanced
industrial economies from what they were in the 1950s and 1960s, and that
the transition to a post-Fordist society has involved momentous international
restructuring, creating massive labour and class dislocation. As Townsend
has commented:

> changes in the structure of both the global economy and the
> economy of the EC are leading to polarization in labour markets
> and more general polarization in some of the larger EC states.
>
> (Townsend 1991)

Societies with a commitment to social-democratic welfare are increasingly becoming fragmented and individualized. The Fordist "dream of ev-
erlasting prosperity" has evaporated as high unemployment, poverty, and
homelessness have become more acceptable with the advent of postmodern
culture. A new "common sense" about social policy has emerged throughout the Community. This appears to indicate that a more diverse and expanding group are likely to experience more entrenched exclusion from the
mainstream of civil society, as the "code of relief" is toughened and there is
growing reference to "workfare" rather than welfare. EC institutions appear
unable, or unwilling, to address the issues involved as the importance of the
nation state remains prominent. Developing structures of regulation would
appear to be promoting social relations based on the notion of Community
"insiders" and "outsiders". As rates of labour force casualization and
marginalization expands, it is those regarded as second class citizens for
whom second class solutions are prescribed.

For the 40 million EC citizens badly housed and the estimated three million homeless in the European communities, local initiatives are encouraged,
rather than an overall commitment to changes in standards throughout EC
countries.

References

Abrahamson, P. E. 1991. Welfare and poverty in the Europe of the 1990s: social progress or social dumping? *International Journal of Health Services* **21**, 237–64.

Aglietta, M. 1979. *A theory of capitalist regulation*. London: New Left Books.

Bunyan, T. 1991. Towards an authoritarian European state. *Race and Class* **32**, 3.

Burowoy, M. 1983. Between the labour process and the state: changing face of factory regimes under advanced capitalism. *American Sociological Review* **48**, 587–605.

Callinicos, A. 1992. Conflicting interests. *Socialist Review* (January), 12–15.

Castells, M. 1989. *The informational city: information technology, economic restructuring, and the urban regional process*. Oxford: Basil Blackwell.

Commission of the European Communities 1991. *Employment in Europe 1991*. Brussels: Directorate General Employment, Industrial Relations and Social Affairs.

De Vroey, M. 1984. A Regulation approach interpretation of contemporary crisis. *Capital and Class* (Summer), 45–65.

Dunford, M. 1990. Theories of regulation. *Environment and Planning D: Society and Space* **8**, 297–321.

Esping-Andersen, G. 1990. *The three worlds of welfare capitalism*. Cambridge: Polity.

FEANTSA 1992. *Report on activities: February 1991 to February 1992, The revision of the Treaties of the European Community*. Brussels: FEANTSA.

Ferge, Z. & S. M. Miller 1987. *The dynamics of deprivation: a cross national study*. Aldershot, England: Gower.

Ferrand-Bechmann, D. 1988. Homelessness in France: public and private policies. In *Affordable Housing and the Homeless*, Jurgen Friedrichs (ed.), 147–55. Berlin: Walter de Gruyter.

Florida, R. L. & M. M. A. Feldman 1988. Housing in US Fordism. *Policy and Politics* **12**, 187–209.

Forrest, R. & A. Murie 1986. Marginalization and subsidised individualism. *International Journal of Urban and Regional Research* **10**(1), 16–65.

Froebel, F., J. Heinricks, G. Kreye 1980. *The new industrial division of labour: structural unemployment in industrial countries and industrialisation in developing countries*. Cambridge: Cambridge University Press.

Hakim, C. 1987. Trends in the flexible workforce. *Employment Gazette* **95**, 549–60.

Harvey, D. 1989. *The condition of postmodernity*. Oxford: Basil Blackwell.

Haussermann, H. & W. Siebel 1990. The polarization of urban development in the Federal Republic of Germany and the question of a new municipal policy. *International Journal of Urban and Regional Research* **14**, 369–82.

Jessop, B. 1989. Conservative regimes and the transition to post-Fordism: the cases of Great Britain and West Germany. In Capitalist development and crisis theory: accumulation, regulation and spatial restructuring, M Gottdiener & N Komninos (eds). London: Macmillan

Jessop, B. 1990. Fordism and post-Fordism: a critical reformulation. Paper presented at a conference on Pathways to Industrialisation and Regional Development, Lake Arrowhead, California.

Kassalow, E. M. 1989. Technological change in the US: unions and employers in a new era. In *Current issues in labour relations an international perspective*, A. Gladstone et al. (eds), 18–56. Berlin: Walter de Gruyter.

Kleinman, M. 1991. *Housing and urban politics in Europe: towards a new consensus?* Paper presented at Housing Studies Association Conference: "Housing in Europe", Oxford University.

Knight, R. V. 1989. The emergent global society. In *Cities in a global perspective*, R. V. Knight & G. Gappert (eds), 24–43. California: Sage.

Kotz, D. M. 1990. A comparative analysis of the theory of regulation and social structure of accumulation theory. *Science and Society* **54**(2), 5–28.

Kuwahara, Y. 1989. New technology in the context of structural change with special reference to Japan. In *Current issues in labour relations: an international perspective*, A. Gladstone et al. (eds), 71–8. Berlin: Walter de Gruyter.

Labour Research 1990. A meaner means test (April), 12–14.

Laczko, F. 1990. New poverty and the old poor: pensioners' incomes in the European Community. *Ageing and Society* **10**, 261–77.

Lane, C. 1988. Industrial change in Europe: the pursuit of flexible specialisation in Britain and W. Germany. *Work, Employment and Society* **2**, 141–68.

Lindley, R. 1991. European integration and the structure and nature of employment. SYSDEM Papers: 4, *Euro labour markets: the prospects for integration*. Commission of the European Communities, 130–36.

Lipietz, A. 1982. Towards global Fordism? New Left Review 132.

Lipietz, A. 1985. New tendencies in the international division of labour: regimes of accumulation and modes of regulation. In *Production, work, territory*, A. J. Scott & M. Storper (eds), 16–40. Hemel Hempstead: Allen and Unwin.

Marcuse, P. 1989. Gentrification, homelessness and the work process: housing markets and labour markets in the quartered city. *Housing Studies* **14**, 211–20.

Marshall, T. H. 1950. *Citizenship and social class*. Cambridge: Cambridge University Press.

Mellor, R. 1989. Transitions in urbanisation: 20th century Britain. *International Journal of Urban and Regional Research* **12**, 573–96.

Millar, J. 1989. Social security: equality and women in the UK. *Policy and Politics* **17**, 311–19.

Morris, J. L. 1988. New technologies, flexible work practices, and regional socio-spatial differentiation: some observations from the United Kingdom. *Environment and Planning D: Society and Space* **6**, 301–19.

National Campaign for the Homeless 1985. *Homeless in the European Community*. Cork: EEC Commission Seminar on Poverty and Homelessness.

OECD 1984. *Employment outlook*. Paris: OECD.

Peck, J. & A. Tickell 1991. *Regulation theory and the geographies of flexible accumulation: transitions in capitalism, transitions in theory*. SPA Working Paper 12, University of Manchester.

Pinder, J. 1991. *European Community, the building of a union*. Oxford: Oxford University Press.

Piore, M. & C. Sable 1984. *The second industrial divide*. New York: Basic Books.

Room, G., R. Lawson, F. Laczko 1989. New poverty in the European Community. *Policy and Politics* **17**, 165–76.

Schoenberger, E. 1989. Thinking about flexibility: a response to Gertler. *Transactions of the Institute of British Geographers* **14**, 98–108.

Schuler-Wallner, G. 1986. *Homelessness in the Federal Republic of Germany – a contribution to the International Year of Shelter for the Homeless*. Darmstadt: Institute of Housing and Environmental Research.

Schumpeter, J. 1934. *The theory of economic development*. Cambridge, Mass.: Allen & Unwin.

Smith, N. & P. Williams 1985. *Gentrification of the city*. London: Allen & Unwin.

Spicker, P. 1991. The principle of subsidiarity and the social policy of the European Community. *Journal of European Social Policy* **1**(1), 3–14.

Stirling, J. 1991. This great Europe of ours: trade unions and 1992. *Capital and Class* **45**, 7–16.

Teekens, R. & B. M. S. van Praag (eds)1990. *Analysing poverty in the European Community*. Luxemburg: Eurostat.

Thorns, D. 1988. Who gets housed: the changing nature of housing affordability and access in advanced capitalist societies. In *Affordable housing and the homeless*, J. Friedrichs (ed.), 27–44. Berlin: Walter de Gruyter.

Titmuss, R. M. 1968. *Commitment to welfare*. London: Allen & Unwin.

Townsend, P. 1991. Hard times. *European Labour Forum* **6**, 5–9.

Tsoukalis, L. 1991. *The new European economy: the politics and economics of integration*. Oxford: Oxford University Press.

Chapter 2

Flexibilization and part-time work in Europe

Irene Bruegel & Ariane Hegewisch

Introduction

The growth in part-time employment in the face of high unemployment is one of the more distinctive features of labour market change in western Europe over the last 15 years. It has generally been associated with the increasing participation of women in the labour market and with the rise of the service sector. More recently it has also been linked to a drive towards "flexibilization". Discussion of part-time employment has increasingly been subsumed within an analysis of precarious work (Rodgers & Rodgers 1989) and the concept of the "flexible firm". This shift in the debate has come under challenge (Rubery 1989), and in this paper we seek to examine information from individual firms across western Europe to unravel patterns of employment of part-time labour in the late 1980s, with two questions in mind:

- How are differences in the scale and recent growth in part-time employment in different *countries* to be understood?
- How far do employers who make extensive use of part-time workers correspond to the model of the "flexible firm"?

Whatever the common trends, part-time workers are used to very different degrees in the countries of western Europe, reflecting the varying institutions of labour market regulation, of contract law, of social reproduction, and of income maintenance (Hakim 1991). While part-time work can broadly be described as a specifically gendered form of numerically flexible labour (Beechey & Perkins 1987), the distinction between part-time and "standard" or "normal" employment is differently constructed in different countries. Some kind of "societal effects" model has therefore to be incorporated in any comparative analysis of part-time labour (Michon 1990). At the same time, institutions are not immovable. Even the domestic division of labour can be changed, and the rising demand for more flexible working arrangements can be seen to have altered regulatory frameworks in many states (Kravaritou-Manitakis 1988). The feminization of the labour force has itself had at least some effects on the system of social reproduction. The pattern of utilization of part-time labour may not then, we suggest, simply be the outcome of the conjuncture of economic forces and institutional forms: the specific form of differentiation of the part-time workers from the rest or, more accurately, the gradations across part-time and full-time workers, may itself act as a societal effect, influencing wider forms of labour market differentiation.

The study

Much of the recent debate on part-time work has hinged on whether its increase stems from structural trends on the demand or supply sides or represents, instead, a conscious labour utilization strategy on the part of employers. Conceptually the "labour shortage" perspective can be distinguished from the "flexibilization" approach, though in practice the one may flow into the other. Empirical evidence for Britain points to a limited applicability of the flexible firm model (Wood & Smith 1989; McGregor & Sproull 1991; Pollert 1991), but much less is known about employers in other parts of western Europe.

In this paper we seek to examine the broader European picture, using material from the EC Labour Force Survey and the Price Waterhouse Cranfield Project (PWCS), a survey of 5500 employers across 10 countries, covering public and private sectors as well as services and manufacturing.[1] The PWCS allows us to examine trends in various forms of flexible employment across Europe, and their link to part-time employment, in the three years leading up to 1991. It also updates the last major British surveys on flexible labour use, the "Employers Labour Use Strategies" survey of 1987 (McGregor & Sproull 1991), and the Warwick Company Level Survey of large private sector employers in 1985 (Marginson et al. 1988).

The difficulties of undertaking a comparative analysis over such a wide range of circumstances are well documented (Michon 1990; Hakim 1991): part-time work has very different characteristics, connotations, and implications across the various countries in our study. Even if the definition of part-time work (employment at less than the normal working week) is relatively unproblematic, it can in principle vary from a casual couple of hours a week to work that is full time in all but name.[2] This study overcomes some of these problems by looking at the employment patterns for part-time workers in larger, well established workplaces, concentrating on a rather more homogeneous set of employers than would be the case, had smaller firms been included.

Gender and flexibility

A comparative analysis of part-time work and the flexibility it might offer to employers necessarily involves discussion of gender roles and relations in the different countries of our study. Any "flexibilization" of part-time work is to a degree both gender and country specific. It can be argued that part-time work was originally constructed to draw in a very specific labour force of married women, and that, far from gaining flexibility themselves, employers were forced by demand pressures and supply constraints to offer flexibility to women to enable them to fulfil their "double burden". The domestic duties of women who seek part-time work *limit* the flexibility offered to employers. Only in so far as employers face *regular and anticipated variations in demand* through the day or the week, can they gain flexibility from part-time women workers (Robinson & Wallace 1984). Thus the relationship between gender and employer-based flexibility is complex. The particular age and sex structure of the part-time workforce will then influence the form of its potential flexibilization. Paradoxically, perhaps, the ageing of the part-time workforce in Britain, which has resulted in a majority of the part-time workforce being without children under 16, may itself have increased employer-centred flexibilization, but this will depend on the degree to which these older women are constrained by other homecare responsibilities.

Increases in unemployment and reductions in union strength have enhanced employer-centred flexibility in Britain, with part-timers increasingly working to hours determined by employers (Walsh 1990). Thus part-time work in Britain can be said to have undergone employer-centred flexibilization, even if a shift towards part-time work in itself represents only a limited form of flexibilization. Indeed Horrell and Rubery note that male full-time workers may bear the brunt of new contractual requirements for (numerical) flexibility, quite apart from their vulnerability to functional flexibilization (Horrell & Rubery 1991). In sum, the potential flexibility of part-time workers from the viewpoint of the employer will turn on a complex of societal factors structuring the part-time workforce. The position of part-time workers will also depend on the flexibility of other workers. It is possible to see part-time contracts as a substitute for other moves to greater flexibilization and, as in Italy, other types of flexibilization may restrain the development of part-time employment (del Boca 1988).

In this paper we approach these issues as follows: Starting with a discussion of differences in the scale of part-time work in 10 European countries, we consider explanations from the demand side, the supply side, and in relation to institutional differences. We then consider the *patterns of change* in the use of part-time workers in the firms covered by the study, seeking to identify whether there are distinct *country* as against sector or demand trends. This takes us to an analysis of the degree to which the organizations covered in the study use part-time work as a *substitute* for other forms of flexible labour or alternatively the degree to which "flexibilization tendencies" cluster in a distinct set of "flexible firms", using part-time contracts as a complement to other forms of "precarious" labour.

Differences in the scale of part-time work across European economies

The degree to which labour is employed on a part-time basis, at less than a standard working week, varies across Europe (Figure 2.1), broadly in line with differences in the degree of feminization of the labour force and in the degree of service sector employment, though exceptions are common. Figure 2.1 gives both the Labour Force Survey/census information and the ratios in the PWCS. Differences between the two relate both to differences of definition (part-timers in the PWCS are as defined by the firms themselves) and coverage.

Grouping countries by the level of part-time work in the late 1980s, three groups can be distinguished:
- The "high" group, northwest Europe (UK, Netherlands, Norway, Sweden, and Denmark): here part-time work accounts for over 20% of the labour force; between 43% (UK) and 48% (Sweden) of all employees are women (except for the Netherlands);and service sector employment accounts for between 66% (UK) and 69% (Norway) of total employment
- The "middle" group, roughly central western Europe, where part-time employment lies between 10 and 20% of total employment; here women's employment accounts for between 37% (Belgium) and 42%

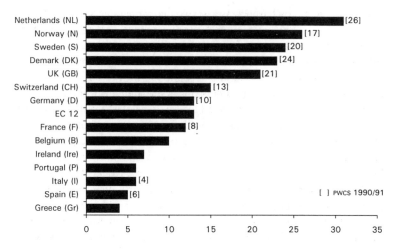

Figure 2.1 Proportion of labour force working part time, by country. National/EC statistics and PWCS. Sources: Eurostat Labour Force Survey 1989; Recensémenet Fédéral, Berne 1985; Statistical Abstract Stockholm 1991; Statistik Årbok Oslo 1991.

(France) of all employment; and between 54% (Switzerland) and 64% (Belgium) of the workforce are employed in the service sector

- The "low" group, mainly in the south (Ireland, Spain, Portugal, Italy, and Greece), where despite some growth, part-time employment remains below 10%; women's share of the labour force ranges between 31% (Spain) and 35% (Greece), except for Portugal. In these countries, service employment levels are apparently on a par with the more central countries, at between 52% for Portugal and 63% for Ireland. The uncertain status of part-time work in some of these countries, together with the high level of family and self employment, makes for some uncertainty about the comparability of the figures.

Our broad grouping into a high, medium and low group of countries on each of the measures of part-time work, feminization and service employment still leaves a fair variation between countries in each group. There are also some important differences within each group of countries in the sex and age composition of the part-time labour force and in the legal status and employment rights for part-time workers.

Among the "high" group – countries such as Sweden, Norway, and Denmark – part-time work has long been an important component of women's employment; in the Netherlands, by contrast, the importance of part-time work in the economy has increased very much more rapidly in recent years. This growth has been attributed to specific measures taken by the Dutch government to counter growing unemployment (Neubourg 1985). As a result, part-time employment is rather less concentrated on women than in Sweden, Norway, and Britain. Indeed almost a third of part-time workers in the Netherlands are men. Reductions in the standard working hours in the public sector are also considered to have generated a demand for part-time cover in traditionally male as well as female jobs (Thurman & Trah 1990). There are also important differences within the "high" group of countries in the status of part-time work, and in the scale of the differential between part-time and full-time work. In Sweden, Maier (1991) suggests workers have far more control over whether they do their job on a full or part-time basis. Parents of children under the age of eight have the right to reduce their working hours to 75 per cent of the norm and hence to work a six-hour day (Sundström 1991). As a result part-time work is spread across a much wider range of occupation groups than elsewhere. In general, part-time workers in Denmark and Norway also appear to be working rather longer hours than is the norm in Britain and the Netherlands (Thurman & Trah 1990). Indeed the growth of employment at regular but very short hours seems to be a feature of these two labour markets alone.

In the "medium" group of western European countries, part-time employment increased particularly fast in recent years. There are still important differences between Germany and Belgium in the degree to which part-time work is voluntary; Marshall (1989) suggests that as many as 35 per cent of part-time workers in Belgium want full-time jobs, but only 10 per cent in Germany. In both Germany and Belgium, part-time work is highly concentrated on married women, especially when compared to France. Relatively few mothers in France work part-time, though part-time work is attractive for tax reasons to higher-paid married women (Dex & Walters 1989).

In the more southern economies, part-time work is both rare and tends to be spread rather more evenly between men and women, with married women accounting for less than half of part-time employees. It may well be that a high proportion of part-time work remains hidden in family based employment. Moreover, Kravaritou-Manitakis (1988) maintains that in both Greece and Portugal most of the registered part-time workers are in second jobs. In these countries the sector distribution of part-time work is less skewed towards services, with part-time family employment still found in agriculture.

Explaining variations in the scale of part-time work

Although much of the early British literature posed supply side (gender based) and demand side explanations against one another, taking the institutional framework largely as given, comparative studies have tended to concentrate on institutional differences, taking the structure of supply and demand rather more as given.

The degree to which the expansion of women's paid employment has relied on the growth of part-time work varies considerably between countries. Some economies operate with a far higher proportion of women working part-time than others, even allowing for demographic differences. Thus women's overall participation in paid work is far higher in Portugal than can be expected from the level of part-time employment (Figure 2.2). Conversely, part-time employment in the Netherlands is higher than that expected from women's relatively low participation. One factor accounting for these variations is the differences in the system of childcare provision and family structure, which influence the scope of women's choices. These are reflected in the substantial differences in the pattern of employment of mothers of young school-age children (Moss 1991).

Nor do differences in the level of part-time employment relate closely to differences in industrial structure. Earlier studies showed that the very wide-

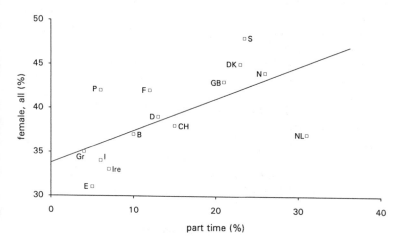

Figure 2.2 Proportion of labour force working part time by proportion of females 1987/9 and by country. Sources: Eurostat Labour Force Survey 1989; Recensément Fédéral, Berne 1985; Statistical Abstract Sweden 1991; Statistik Årbok Oslo 1991.

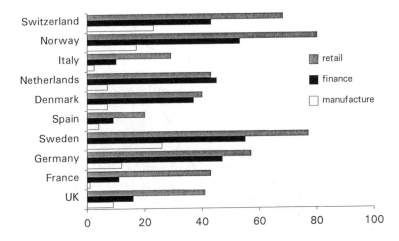

Figure 2.3 Proportion of firms with more than 11% part-time workers: by sector and country.

spread use of women as part-time workers in retailing in Britain is not found in France (Gregory 1991) or Germany (Schoer 1987). Both the EC Labour Force Survey (LFS) and PWCS indicate considerable variation across countries in the degree of part-time work within specific industries. Figure 2.3 shows the proportion of employers in each of the sectors of manufacturing, retail, and finance in the PWCS who we class as "part-time users" (i.e. with a workforce over 11 per cent part-time[3]) by country ranked by the overall proportion of part-time employment. Figure 2.4 shows the differences in high part-time use (employers with over 20% part-timers) in PWCS between the private and the public sector,[4] ranked similarly. There were insufficient public sector employers using part-timers in Italy and Spain to merit analysis. These results are in line with those for employees from the LFS and indeed reflect the findings of detailed British studies, which show a large variation between employers in the same industries in the degree to which they use part-time workers (Walsh 1990; Horrell & Rubery 1991).

Institutional differences

Although the public sector in every country makes more use of part-time workers than the private, Figure 2.4 also shows quite stark differences between public administrations in their propensity to use part-timers, reflect-

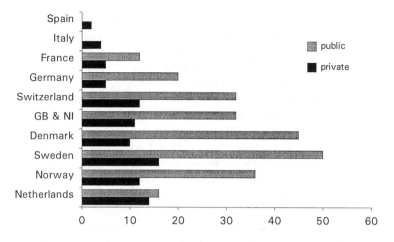

Figure 2.4 Proportion of firms with more than 20% part-time workers: by sector.

ing different employment norms in different countries. A number of researchers have looked to such institutional factors as forms of labour regulation and labour law to understand national differences in part-time work and its relation to flexibilization (Rubery 1989; Hakim 1991; Marshall 1989). Some aspects of an "inverse rights law" can be demonstrated in differences between countries. The high rate of part-time employment especially in jobs for very short weekly hours in Britain and the Netherlands can be attributed to the fairly substantial cost advantages to employers (and short-term advantages of higher net earnings for employees working below tax and/or national insurance thresholds) (Maier 1991). That said, quantification of the value of the various dispensations available to employers of part-time labour is by no means simple. Indeed full exploitation of these may incur large management costs, for example in complex shift systems (Walsh 1990). Nor is it clear how precisely employers do calculate such costs. As Hakim suggests, perceptions of the advantages of employing part-timers may diverge from reality, and the degree to which rights established in law are operational depends very much on the legal and industrial relations systems. In most countries, differences in employment status and rights depend on certain threshold levels of hours or earnings, and only in very specific circumstances on part-time status as such. This creates important differences *between* part-time workers that are frequently ignored in the discussions of flexibility and part-time work.

41

The distribution of part-time workers across such divisions differs greatly from country to country. Schoer shows for example that part-time workers in Germany are less likely to fall below the rather lower threshold required for national insurance benefits than in Britain (11 per cent compared to 29 per cent). They are also less bunched into low-level occupations (Schoer 1987). Dex and Walters' comparison of France and Britain shows that, in most occupations, French part-time workers' hourly earnings are closer to full-timers' (Dex & Walters 1992).

The impact of the legislative framework on the use of part-time work in different countries is complex. It may impact most on the range of differences *between* part-time workers, rather than on the overall level of part-time employment. Changes in the framework have been important in raising the level of part-time employment in specific circumstances, notably in the Netherlands and Spain (Fina et al. 1989), otherwise the effects may be more indirect: in the degree to which alternative forms of flexibilization are available.

Changing levels of part-time employment

The last three years of the 1980s (1987–90/1) were largely characterized by economic expansion, skill shortages, and generally tight labour markets,

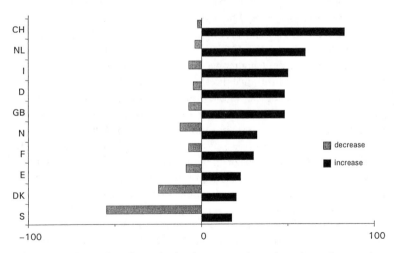

Figure 2.5 Proportion of organizations by country: decreasing or increasing part-time employment in the last three years.

42

though Britain and the Scandinavian countries were moving into a recession at the time of the PWCS. In that period, nevertheless, differences in the proportion of organizations in each country that increased or decreased part-time work were marked. Almost every Swiss respondent increased his or her utilization of part-time employment, and yet the proportion of enterprises cutting part-time work in Denmark and Sweden outstripped those increasing it (Figure 2.5). While the differences bear some relation to national employment trends, increases in part-time employment can be expected while full time employment is falling. A rise in part-time labour can come as a policy response to rising unemployment (Berg 1989), or may anticipate future falls in employment. Blanchflower and Corry suggest that when firms are unsure of the durability of any upturn, they look to part-timers as a flexible workforce (Blanchflower & Corry 1987).

To elucidate these contrary trends, respondents to the PWCS were asked whether they had increased part-time employment and whether they themselves had experienced a growth in product demand and/or in employment in the three years. Figure 2.6 contrasts expanding and contracting firms in each country, showing that in many countries (Denmark, France, GB, the Netherlands, and Switzerland) the proportion of each group that increased part-time work in the three years is broadly similar. In other countries (Italy, Norway, Spain, and Sweden), expanding firms were more likely to have increased part-time employment. In practice, some organizations or types

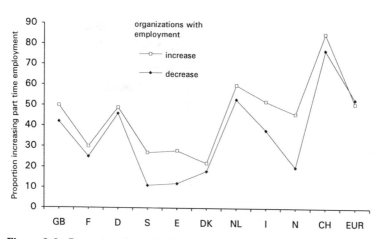

Figure 2.6 Proportion of organizations increasing part-time employment: by recent employment change.

of organizations may increase part-time work against an overall trend of employment stagnation, while others increase part-time work only with rising demand. There is a third group of organizations, found mainly in Sweden and Denmark, that *reduced* part-time work, while increasing employment as a whole.

The shift to a part-time workforce

We looked first at those enterprises in the PWCS that increased part-time work at the same time as cutting employment overall, as the clearest cases of "substitution", though a shift in the proportion of workers who are employed on a part-time basis can occur in other circumstances. Substitution in our analysis refers not only to cases where work done by full-time workers is reorganized on a part-time basis, but also to changes in the pattern of production and employment that result in an increased proportion of part-time workers in the organization's labour force when the overall employment level is falling. Given that the respondents to the PWCS were medium-sized and large employers (200+), some with a number of establishments, some of this substitution may well arise from the closure of some units when others expand. Substitution at an organization level is then distinct from that at an enterprise or "shop" level, and could be a result of changes in product mix, in occupation mix, etc.

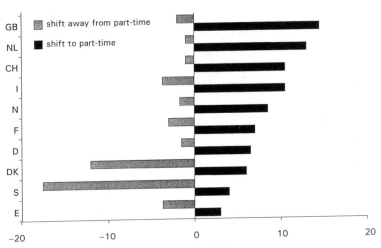

Figure 2.7 Proportion of organizations "shifting" to or from part-time employment.

Defined in this way, Britain had the largest proportion of firms shifting towards part-time work, followed by the Netherlands. In both countries such shifts may be related to deregulation and other policy measures promoting flexibility, and may reflect rising unemployment and increased part-time work among men. In contrast, in Spain, Sweden, and Denmark, shifts *away* from part-time work were more common than shifts towards in the period in question (Figure 2.7).

Overall the public sector accounted for a disproportionate share of organizations shifting towards part-time employment. In GB twice as many public sector organizations had increased part-timers while cutting employment or keeping it static than would be expected on the basis of their numbers. In the Netherlands the concentration on public sector institutions is lower, but still very evident. The possible reasons for this sector split are discussed further below, alongside a consideration of its longer-term significance.

The association between part-time employment and other "non-standard" contracts

One of the major themes of debates in the discussion of part-time employment and the rise, or otherwise, of the flexible firm has been the association between part-time employment and the use of other forms of "non-standard" employment. The flexible firm model has been criticised for failing to distinguish between different forms of non-standard employment and for not recognizing the rôle that part-time or temporary employment has for a long time played in production (see for example Pollert 1991; Walsh 1990). These employment forms may affect very different groups of employees. Thus the question of how far *individual* part-time workers are in temporary or fixed-term jobs is distinct from that of whether a set of firms operate with strategies to extend flexibility across an array of dimensions. It is interesting to note how the overlap between part-time and temporary workers varies between countries (Marshall 1989). Part-time workers are rather more precarious in Belgium (where 23 per cent were in temporary contracts in 1985) than in France (with 9 per cent). Even so, in every country a large majority of part-time workers have permanent contracts.

Blanchflower and Corry's work examined the degree to which British *employers* of part-time workers used other types of atypical contract. They found that in the early 1980s a majority of firms using part-time workers in Britain used at least one other type of atypical contract, with over one quarter of manufacturing firms using a variety of types of contracts (Blanchflower & Corry 1987). Our analysis of the "flexible firm" in western Europe cannot draw out all the sector and country differences in all the variants of non-standard labour, and instead we concentrate on analysing the concurrence of temporary, fixed-term and part-time work among respondents to the PWCS, since changes in these types of work are the most prevalent in the period. Our analysis is in four sections: following a discussion of the overall pattern of change, we consider the overlap between organizations with a high incidence of each of the three forms of non-standard contract and then look at how far organizations that made changes in the use of one type of non-standard contract made parallel changes in the use of other types. Finally we consider how the public sector differs from the private, recognizing that the distinction between the two also varies between countries.

Fixed-term and temporary employment in western Europe

Fixed-term and temporary employment is by no means as common as part-time employment in western Europe, though it reaches quite substantial levels in more southern economies. Fixed-term and temporary employment are both means of adjusting the size of the workforce to meet changing needs, and are substitutes to an extent. One response to persistently high levels of unemployment in several West European countries in the mid-

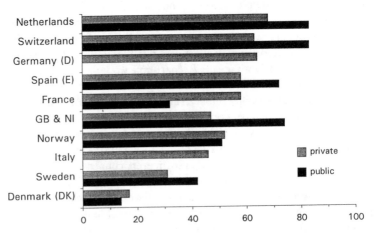

Figure 2.8 Proportion of organizations increasing non-permanent contracts: by sector.

46

1980s was a deregulation of employment legislation, permitting a wider use of fixed-term contracts in the belief that employers would recruit more readily as a result (Brewster et al. 1993). While the job creation effects of such measures are disputed (Büchtemann 1991; Deakin & Wilkinson 1991), employers in countries such as Germany, France, Spain, and the Netherlands are increasingly using non-permanent contracts as a means of screening recruits. In Britain, where dismissal is relatively easy in any case, much less use is made of such contracts. In Sweden, fixed-term contracts remain restricted, and use is correspondingly low (Söderström & Syren 1992).

While most employers in the PWCS survey made some use of non-permanent contracts, fewer than 15 per cent, outside Spain and the Netherlands, were "high users", that is employing over 10 per cent of their workforce on either type of short-term contract. In general employers in most countries used one or other of such non-permanent contracts, rather than mixing them.

There were significant increases in the use of such contracts in almost every country in 1987–90/91. In the period in question, these were far more common than increases in "traditional" ways of extending the working day, such as overtime, weekend working or shift work. In all, at least six in ten of firms in most countries increased their use of one or other non-permanent contract (Figure 2.8).

The co-incidence of non-standard contracts

In looking at the joint use of part-time and non-permanent contracts, we include only those employers whose workforce contains a significant number of workers on non-standard contracts: for part-time employment this is defined as those organizations with at least 20 per cent of part-time workers. Figure 2.9, which examines whether such high part-time users are also high users (10 per cent+) of non-permanent labour, suggests that only a small minority of firms make widespread use of both types of labour. Only in the Netherlands and Sweden do more than five per cent of all respondents make "high" use of both part-time and non-permanent contracts. In the case of the Netherlands, this stems from the almost universal use of non-permanent contracts of one form or other. Elsewhere, except in Spain, where high part-time use is extremely rare in any case, employers tend to concentrate either on part-time workers or non-permanent staff, once over the threshold of "high" use.

We also investigated Blanchflower and Corry's finding that the public sector (in Britain) had a particularly marked joint use of short-term temporary

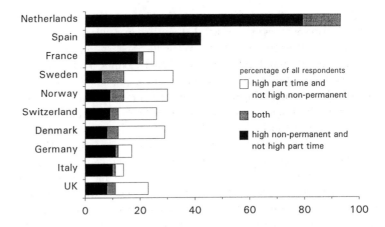

Figure 2.9 The concurrence of high use of part-time and non-permanent contracts.

and part-time contracts (Figure 2.10). For the five countries that had sufficient numbers of firms in both sectors, our results were mixed. In Britain, Sweden, and Norway, the public sector employers were rather more likely to make significant use of both types of contract than the private sector, while in the French public sector there was no joint use at all. The Dutch results were again swamped by the widespread use of fixed-term contracts.

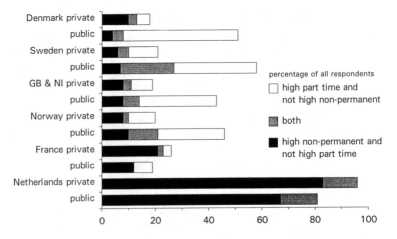

Figure 2.10 The concurrence of high part-time and high non-permanent employment: by sector (selected countries).

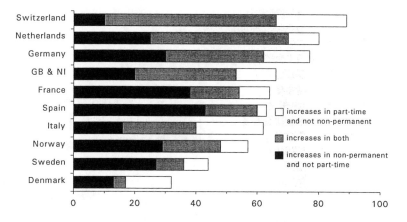

Figure 2.11 The concurrence of increases in part-time and non-permanent contracts.

Turning now to *changes* in part-time employment and its association with *changes* in use of such non-permanent contracts, our analysis indicates an important association. Figure 2.11 shows that, in contrast to the static picture, there is a substantial overlap between firms, except in Denmark, Sweden, and France. It is not clear how far firms that increase both types of work did so in the context of employment growth and how far we are seeing concurrent *shifts* towards part-time and non-permanent contracts. When a distinction is made between non-permanent contracts, we find that increases in *temporary* employment, but not in fixed-term employment, tend to be associated with increases in part-time employment. This difference is likely to be associated with institutional differences and the tendency for temporary employment to be white-collar office work and fixed-term employment to be more a feature of manual work and manufacturing. Thus the association between the growth in part-time and temporary work appears to be linked to the relative growth of non-manual work in the service sector in the period in question.

The position of the public sector

A number of recent commentators have identified the public sector as the growth area of flexible employment practices (for example Marshall 1989; Horrell & Rubery 1991; McGregor & Sproull 1991; Pollert 1991). In line with this we found that "shifts" towards part-time employment and the ex-

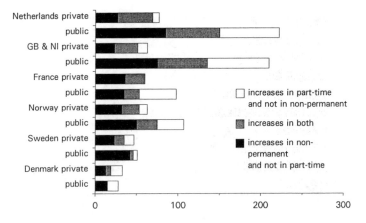

Figure 2.12 The concurrence of increases in part-time and non-permanent contracts: by sector.

pansion of non-permanent employment occurred more frequently in the public sector in a number of countries (Figure 2.12).

In Britain, differences in non-permanent employment between the private and public sectors may be an artefact of the public sector's *good* employment practices (see Rubery 1989). Smaller, private firms can fire people on permanent contracts almost as readily as those on temporary or fixed-term contracts, so that there is little need to make temporary status explicit from the outset. This is much less true of the public sector in Britain, and does not apply in other countries for the reasons discussed above. Outside Britain, any tendency for the public sector to increase the use of non-permanent contracts indicates that policy decisions with real effects have been implemented. When we look at the co-incidence of growth in non-permanent and part-time labour by sector (Figure 2.12), there is evidence of such a public sector effect in Britain and the Netherlands, and less so in Norway. Given the limited numbers of public sector employers that increased employment in the period in these countries, this reinforces our view that shifts towards "flexibilization" may well be a response to public sector budget cuts across Europe. In France, fixed-term contracts had increased rapidly in the public sector in the early 1980s; since then policy towards non-permanent employment in the public sector has been reversed, making for a lower rate of increase in the public sector than the private sector. The Danish exception may relate to continued strong trade union organization in the public sector, but we are not in a position to test this.

Managerial strategies and recruitment targets

Despite the attention given to the need for strategic and integrated policy making in the human resource management literature, it has been difficult to identify *any* shift in practice among British employers, particularly once investigation moves from the formulation of strategies to their implementation (Marginson et al. 1988). Increased employment of "flexible" labour is characterized by *ad hoc* responses to changes in the supply and demand conditions, and evidence of "a purposeful and strategic thrust to achieve flexibility" (Hakim 1990) remains elusive.

The approach taken to this issue in the Price Waterhouse Cranfield Survey was to ask whether organizations had a written human resources/personnel strategy or not. Again, a written personnel strategy is not necessarily evidence of purposeful action in relation to flexibility: one would need to know far more about the contents of the strategy to draw any such conclusion. However, those employers who increased their use of part-time, temporary or fixed-term employment were not in general more likely to have a written personnel strategy than employers who did not change their labour use. The only exceptions are Denmark and Spain, where an increase in fixed-term contracts co-incides with a higher use of a written strategy, and Italy, where the same positive relationship holds for both part-time employment and fixed-term contracts.

Purposeful, directed behaviour by employers may also be evident in the degree to which they specifically *introduced* part-time work as an aid to recruitment and the degree to which they targeted women as a specific group. Such considerations may well have been important to managers anticipating recruitment difficulties in the face of a "demographic time-bomb". In this light it is interesting to note that over 60 per cent of employers in Britain, Germany, Italy, the Netherlands, and Switzerland who increased their employment of part-time workers also saw part-time employment as a recruitment incentive. In the Scandinavian countries this proportion was far lower: not only were organizations shedding part-time workers, the high overall level of part-time employment made it an unlikely recruitment incentive for individual employees.

Differences in the degree to which employers associated part-time work as a recruitment incentive with the targeting of women in recruitment are also evident. The association between the two was particularly strong in Britain, Germany, and Switzerland, but was also seen among Danish and Dutch employers. This did not necessarily translate into a greater incidence

51

of actual growth of part-time employment. Indeed in Norway, Spain, and Sweden, employers who increased their use of part-time employment were *less* likely consciously to target women, possibly because the scope for increasing women's employment might have been seen to be limited.

Conclusion

A large-scale international survey of employers can offer insights to the comparative study of labour markets, usefully augmenting published statistics and labour force surveys. At the same time, the inevitably broad brush form of such surveys allows only for tentative conclusions. This study of variations between employers in the utilization of part-time work confirms that historical and institutional differences between countries continue to exert an influence across a number of dimensions, including:

- The extent of part-time work
- Employers' propensities to increase part-time employment
- The degree to which part-time work forms part of a wider move away from standard employment contracts.

Differences between and within industries remain important, too. The divide between the public and the private sectors has become particularly evident. This suggests that public expenditure policies may have a more immediate effect on part-time work than changes in the regulative environment for private firms, though the two are often implemented at the same time.

The degree to which specific jobs are done on a part-time basis varies from country to country; there is nevertheless a consistent tendency for part-time work to be associated with service employment, and with the public as distinct from the private sector. Differences within sectors between countries can be quite large and are not immediately explicable in terms of high national levels of part-time employment, nor a high female share of the labour force.

Employers vary in their propensity to increase part-time employment. In part this relates to differences in growth patterns, but substitution of full-time by part-time employment (and vice versa) is also evident. Such shifts in employment composition again vary both between countries and between sectors. The Scandinavian countries, Sweden in particular, have seen some reductions in part-time employment, some of it alongside increases in overall employment. How far this is a result of women choosing full-time over part-time employment, and how far a response of employers to changes in the relative advantages of part-time employment, can only be answered with more detailed study, but it could suggest that the expansion of part-time work may reach limits: once participation rates for women have reached male levels, labour shortages can be met only by shifting *from* part-time to full-time employment.

Such a concept of demographic limits to the expansion of part-time work implies that part-time work has been developed to tap a specific labour force and that flexibilization gains are not important. Where the accent is more specifically on flexibility, the development of alternative forms of flexibility may limit the importance of part-time employment.

We found that organizations that operate with high levels of part-time employment are more likely to make use of non-permanent contracts, though such "flexible firms" remain a small minority of the labour market. There is some evidence of private sector organizations taking different tracks; those going down the part-time route being distinct from those taking either the overtime/shiftwork route or alternatively the temporary/fixed-term and subcontract route. This may well reflect the distinction between manufacturing and services, detailed industrial differences and sex segregation of jobs, rather than a strategic choice of alternatives at the organizational level. The public sectors of most countries polarize somewhat differently: while some public sector organizations operate a variety of flexibility strategies (including part-time work), others operate none at all. In both sectors, such differences may reflect the fitting of such strategies to the gender of each particular workforce.

The pattern of uptake and expansion of different forms of flexible labour across Europe over the years 1988–91 is then quite complex, and its relation to changes in part-time work more complex still. In every country it is possible to discern elements of two opposing explanations for the expansion (or contraction) of part-time work: the one emphasizing anticipated labour shortages and attempts to tap a latent reserve of married women's labour, and the second flexibility perspective, emphasizing employers' efforts to pare down overheads. In practice, even at the level of the organization, these distinctions may be blurred, with both types of benefit sought at one and the same time; so differences within countries should come as no surprise. At any one time, different organizations, operating in different markets, may emphasize one aspect of part-time work over the other, though rarely, as we have seen, is this posed as an explicit strategy. In no country can the changes in part-time work be put down exclusively to labour supply considerations or to a new drive for flexibility.

Countries such as Italy and Switzerland, with relatively low levels of female labour force participation and relatively high proportions of firms increasing employment, would seem to be cases where the expansion of part-time work could be best associated with a labour shortage perspective. However, a fair proportion of organizations in both countries increased part-time employment while cutting overall employment, suggesting that labour shortages were not necessarily the main issue. In Switzerland some shift towards flexibility was evident too, in the increasing use of temporary or fixed-term contracts, the expansion of subcontracting, and a tendency for employers who increased these types of labour also to increase part-time employment. Spain also experienced employment increases in the period, and the increases in part-time employment there might also be thought to reflect labour shortages. However, few firms viewed part-time employment in any way as a recruitment incentive; increases in full-time employment were sometimes at the expense of part-time work, and the overall context was one of high unemployment.

In the Netherlands and Britain, where government policies have raised employers' abilities to make more flexible use of part-time work, some of the increase in part-time work is due to market expansion in the service sector. Moreover it is the public sectors in these economies that come closest to the "flexibilization" model, with a high proportion of part-time employment increases occurring alongside increases in temporary work and overall cuts in jobs.

Outside Britain the public sector can also be seen to have played a propulsive role in the development of flexible forms of labour. The importance of public sector employment in the growth of the temporary workforce, highlighted for example by Marshall (1989), appears to be confined to a particular group of high part-time users in the public sector outside Great Britain and the Netherlands. The shifts towards part-time employment in western Europe as a whole in the period would seem to have been more strongly related to recruitment problems than outright flexibilization strategies, though no doubt cost cutting exercises also played a role.

Notes

1. This paper draws on the Price Waterhouse Cranfield Project survey of European human resource management. The survey was set up to establish a comparative European database on trends in human resource management practices. It is carried out annually, starting in 1989/90. Based on a standardized postal questionnaire, the survey includes *organizations* (not establishments) with at least 200 employees across all sectors of employment. This paper draws on the results of the second survey, including 5500 organizations in Great Britain, Denmark, France, Germany,

Italy, the Netherlands, Norway, Spain, Sweden, and Switzerland. In each of the 10 participating countries the distribution of respondents across sectors and by size in the private sector is broadly representative of the national distribution. (For a more detailed discussion of the survey methodology see Brewster et al. 1991.)

The survey covers a broad range of human resource management practices, of which the area of contracts of employment and flexible labour use is only one. Data on part-time employment and its link to other forms of employment is inevitably less detailed than national surveys solely concerned with flexible labour uses.

Using a postal survey covering the major areas of personnel management imposes certain constraints on survey design. Thus the survey relies on self-definition and in general asks "yes/no"-type questions without quantifying effects. The survey is directed at employers, particularly personnel managers, at corporate HQ; as others have noted, they are not necessarily the most accurate guides to the extent of change in employment over time (Casey 1991); the survey should therefore be seen as complementary to census data and more specific case studies of flexible labour use.

2. Part-time work is taken as employment for 30 hours a week (or less) in most official statistics; in employment law however, only some of such contracts are regarded as part-time. Social insurance may operate other threshold points.

3. This makes it broadly comparable with the definition of part-time users in the ELUS survey, of at least 25 part-time workers.

4. Public sector in this paper refers to public administration (central and local government, health, higher education, and quangos). PWCS has a representative sample of public sector respondents in the Scandinavian countries, Britain, and the Netherlands. The French public sector sample mainly represents local government and health services, with no responses from higher education or central government. In some countries, such as Italy, Spain, Switzerland, and Germany, where public and private sector personnel management practices and institutions are seen to diverge widely, public sector response has been low, and results for the public sector there are only illustrative. The size of public sector response is: Denmark: 147; France: 66; Germany (West): 20; Italy: 3; Netherlands: 43; Norway: 119; Spain: 20; Sweden: 96; Britain: 316.

References

Beechey, V. & T. Perkins 1987. *A matter of hours: women, part time work and the labour market*. Cambridge: Polity.

Berg, A.-M. 1989. Part time employment: a response to economic crisis? In *The state and the labor market*, S. Rosenberg (ed.), 221–31. New York: Plenum.

Blanchflower, D. & B. Corry 1986/7. *Part-time employment in Great Britain: an analysis using establishment data*. Research Paper 57. Department of Employment.

Boca, D. del 1988. Women in a changing workplace: the case of Italy. In *Feminisation of the labour force*, J. Jenson, E. Hagen, C. Reddy (eds), 120–36. Cambridge: Polity.

Brewster, C., A. Hegewisch, T. Lockhart 1991. Researching European human resource management. *Personnel Review*, **20**(6), 37–40.

Brewster, C., A. Hegewisch, T. Lockhart, L. Mayne 1993. *Flexible working practices in Europe*. London: IPM.

Büchtemann, C. 1991. Does (de-)regulation matter? Employment protection and temporary work in the Federal Republic of Germany. In *Towards Social Adjustment*, G. Standing & V. Tokman (eds), 251–69. Genève: ILO.

Casey, B. 1991. Survey evidence on trends in "non-standard" employment. In *Farewell to flexibility?*, A. Pollert (ed.), 179–99. Oxford: Basil Blackwell.

Dale, A. & C. Bamford 1988. *Flexibility and the peripheral workforce*. Occasional Papers in Sociology and Social Policy; No. 11: Department of Sociology, Surrey University.

Deakin, S. & F. Wilkinson 1991/2. Social policy and economic efficiency. *Critical Social Policy* **33**, 40–61.

Dex, S. & P. Walters 1989. Women's occupational status in Britain, France and the USA. *Industrial Relations Journal* **20**, 203–12.

Dex, S. & P. Walters 1992. Franco-British comparisons of women's labour supply and the effects of social policies. *Oxford Economic Papers* **44**, 89–112.

Fina, L., A. Meixide, L. Toharia 1989. Regulating the labor market amid an economic and political crisis: Spain 1975–86. In *The state and the labor market*, S. Rosenberg (ed.), 107–25. New York: Plenum.

Gregory, A. 1991. Patterns of working hours in large scale grocery retailing in Britain and France: Convergence after 1992? *Work, Employment and Society* **5**, 4.

Hakim, C. 1990. Core and periphery in employers' workforce strategies: evidence from the 1987 ELUS survey. *Work, Employment and Society*, **4**, 157–88.

Hakim, C. 1991. Cross-national comparative research on the European Community: the EC labour force surveys. *Work, Employment and Society* **5**, 101–77.

Horrell, S. & J. Rubery 1991. Gender and working time: an analysis of employers' working time policies. *Cambridge Journal of Economics* **15**, 373–91.

Kravaritou-Manitakis, Y. 1988. New forms of work: labour law and social security aspects in the EC. Luxembourg: European Foundation for the Improvement of Living and Working Conditions.

Maier, F. 1991. Part-time work, social security protections and labour law: an international comparison. *Politics & Policy* **19**, 1–11.

Marginson, P., P. K. Edwards, R. Martin, J. Purcell, K. Sisson 1988. *Beyond the workplace: managing industrial relations in the multi establishment enterprise*. Oxford: Basil Blackwell.

Marshall, A. 1989. The sequel of unemployment: the changing role of part time and temporary work in western Europe. In *Precarious work*, G. Rodgers & J. Rodgers (eds.) 17–48. Genève: ILO.

McGregor, A. & A. Sproull 1991. ELUS – *Analysis of a national survey*. Research Paper 76. Department of Employment.

Meudlers, D. & B. Tytgat 1989. The emergence of atypical employment in the European Community. In *Precarious work*, G. Rodgers & J. Rodgers (eds) 179–96. Genève: ILO.

Michon, F. 1990. The "European social community": a common model and its national variations? *Labour and Society* **15**, 215–36.

Moss, P. 1991. School age child care in the EC. *Women's Studies International Forum* **14**, 539–49.

REFERENCES

Neubourg, C. 1985. Part time work: an international qualitative comparison. *International Labour Review* **124**, 559–76.

Pollert, A. (ed.) 1991. *Farewell to flexibility?* Oxford: Basil Blackwell.

Robinson, O. & J. Wallace 1984. *Part time employment and sex discrimination legislation*. Research Paper 43. Department of Employment.

Rodgers, G. & J. Rodgers (eds) 1989. *Precarious work in western Europe: the state of the debate*. Genève: ILO.

Rubery, J. 1989. Precarious forms of work in the UK. In *Precarious work*, G. Rodgers & J. Rodgers (eds), 49–73. Genève: ILO.

Schoer, K. 1987. Part-time Employment in Britain and West Germany. *Cambridge Journal of Economics* **11**(1), 83–94.

Söderström, M. & S. Syren 1992. Sweden. In *European human resource management guide*, C. Brewster, A. Hegewisch, L. Holden, T. Lockhart (eds), 483–523. London: Academic Press.

Sundström, M. 1991. Part-time work in Sweden. *Journal of Economic Issues* **11**, 167–78.

Thurman, J. E. & G. Trah 1990. Part time work in an international perspective. *International Labour Review* **129**, 23–40.

Walsh, T. J. 1990. Flexible labour utilisation in the private services sector. *Work, Employment and Society* **4**, 517–30.

Wood, D. & P. Smith 1989. *Employer labour-use strategies*. Research Paper 63. Department of Employment.

Chapter 3

Gender and pensions in Europe: current trends in women's pension acquisition

Jay Ginn & Sara Arber

Introduction

Pensions have recently become the subject of concern and controversy throughout Europe due to the ageing of populations, the projected escalating cost of public pension provision, and alleged intergenerational inequity (OECD 1988; Johnson et al. 1989; Gillion 1991). But in the debate about how public pensions could be reformed, little attention has been paid to gender inequality of pension income and how this is related to the constraints of women's domestic roles on their paid employment. Women's employment is more often than men's "atypical", that is, temporary, casual or part-time (see Bruegel & Hegewisch, Chapter 3 this volume). In view of the fact that such employment is common, especially among women, we shall use the term "non-standard" instead. Pension systems designed for individuals who are continuously employed full time leaves women in most countries without an adequate pension income of their own, a situation that is increasingly serious as families fragment and diversify.

The balance between public and private pension provision is crucial to the financial well-being in later life of those with non-standard employment, particularly women. Whereas state provision usually incorporates to some extent the objective of meeting social need, private occupational pensions do not. Their original function as incentives to loyalty and long service (Hannah 1986) is reflected in the design of occupational pension schemes, particularly the vesting, transfer, and preservation arrangements, and in minimum service requirements for eligibility to join. Occupational pensions have served as "golden chains" (Schmahl 1991: 55) on employees, because their benefits are often reduced or lost on leaving. The "golden chains", however, are selective, intended primarily to bind the most highly valued and long-serving "core" employees, among whom women have been under-represented. This use of occupational pensions as a "personnel management tool" (Commission of the EC 1991: 11) effectively discriminates against women in so far as their employment is non-standard. A key question is whether, in different types of European welfare state, women are likely in the future to obtain an adequate pension income based on their own employment.

At their inception, a number of welfare states were founded on an assumed model of the family as a long-term unit, with breadwinner husband and dependent wife. For example, the British social security system based on the Beveridge Plan incorporated these assumptions, and has contributed to the construction of women's dependence on men in marriage (Land 1989).

Family forms and practices in industrial societies have increasingly diverged from this assumed model. Although there is variation among the countries of the EC, the following statistics give some indication of the changes over time in family formation in the EC as a whole. Over the last two decades, the marriage rate has declined from 7.8 to 5.9 per thousand population (Eurostat 1989). The decline in marriage as a *life-long* contract is greater than these figures suggest, due to the rising divorce and remarriage rates. The divorce rate, and with it the incidence of lone parenthood, has risen dramatically since the early 1960s in most European countries, and more slowly since the early 1980s. For example, in Britain a third of marriages are projected to end in divorce (Haskey 1989), a similar proportion in Denmark, and about a quarter in Germany (Eurostat 1988). The breakdown of cohabiting partnerships is harder to quantify, but is unlikely to be less. In the EC as a whole, the proportion of births outside marriage has increased since 1970 from 5 per cent to 17 per cent (Eurostat 1991a). In Britain it has risen from 12.5 per cent in 1981 to 28 per cent in 1990 (Craig 1992: 20). All these trends point to the greater likelihood of women raising children without a lifelong partner to support them financially.

The diversification of family forms, the expansion of women's paid employment and the EC aim of equal treatment for men and women have all made the characterization of women as family dependants increasingly unsatisfactory, and have generated debate as to how social security, especially pension systems, should adapt. Social security and taxation systems are beginning to treat women as individuals rather than dependants on men, and as responsible for providing for their own financial support, both during their working life and, through their pension contributions, in retirement. In particular, the removal of widows' pension rights derived from their husbands' employment has been mooted (International Social Security Association 1991). For example, in Sweden the widow's pension is to be phased out as part of reforms designed to "shift the system from family protection to more individually-based social protection . . . [E]ach spouse is regarded as an economically independent individual in the event of death [of their spouse]" (International Social Security Association 1991: 18).

However, the individualization of social security and equal treatment of women, while an advance in terms of women's formal equality, may leave elderly women worse off if their earlier handicaps as employed workers are ignored. Women's employment rates, especially married women's, have risen steadily in most European countries, but where state support for childcare and other services is lacking, those with domestic responsibilities are still heavily disadvantaged relative to men (Joshi & Davies 1992). As a result, women's jobs are often concentrated in the secondary labour market, and are more likely than men's to be low paid and to be part-time, fixed-term contract or temporary. The opportunity for women to provide for their retirement through their own state and private pension contributions depends on both their employment pattern and the extent to which the pension system discriminates against those with non-standard employment. If widows' benefits are eroded without policies to enable women to obtain their own pension, they are vulnerable to reliance on means-tested benefits in later life.

In this chapter we first outline three contrasting models of welfare state in terms of their social objectives, and assess the extent of poverty and gender inequality among elderly people in one EC country exemplifying each model: Denmark, West Germany (as it was), and Britain. We next examine women's employment patterns in these three countries and the extent to which the pension system in each country presents obstacles to women with non-standard employment obtaining a pension income in their own right. We argue that the risk of an inadequate personal income in later life for those with non-standard employment, especially women with domestic responsibilities, is greater the larger the private occupational sector. We finally consider the impact that some of the possible reforms to pension systems are likely to have on gender inequality of pension income.

Three models of pension systems in Europe

In most countries, pensions policy has in the past been guided by two main objectives: to reduce poverty in old age (social adequacy through a basic pension) and to replace income lost at retirement (individual equity through an earnings-related pension). The balance of the two elements (basic and earnings-related) of pension provision differs according to historical and political factors (OECD 1988). A third alternative would be to leave pension provision mainly to the private market, with a safety net of minimal means- tested public provision for those unable to earn an employment-related pension.

State and occupational pensions in each country interact in their effects on the distribution of income in later life and should therefore be considered together as a system (Schmahl 1989). The boundary between private and public is often blurred, with some occupational schemes (e.g. in France) being mandatory and so closely regulated by the state as to be quasi-public. Public and private sectors appear to be reciprocally related, in that countries with very different ratios of public to private provision nevertheless devote a similar share of GNP to old age transfers (Tamburi & Mouton 1986). Although public and private welfare provisions sometimes co-exist constructively (Rein & van Gunsteren 1985), they are in competition for finite resources, the growth of one restricting the growth of the other (von Nordheim Nielsen 1988). Where the state social security pension provides for a high proportion of earnings to be replaced in retirement, or where a flat-rate pension is well above the poverty level, there is less demand from workers and less incentive for employers to operate private supplementary schemes. Thus the development of the private sector of pension provision depends to a great extent on the type of welfare state.

Social policy theorists have constructed typologies of welfare states in terms of whether the balance of social objectives is predominantly poverty alleviation or income maintenance; whether the basis of entitlement to state support is citizenship, work-merit, or need; and whether provision for times of hardship is viewed as primarily the responsibility of the state or of the individual and his or her family (Palme 1990). Although the types so constructed are likely to differ considerably in their impact on women's welfare, gender has not been a factor in the construction of these typologies.

Three different models of welfare state were distinguished by Titmuss (1974): the *Institutional-Redistributive* model, in which services were universally available according to need; the *Industrial Achievement-Performance* model, in which social needs were met in proportion to work performance; and the *Residual Welfare* model, in which the market and the family were expected to provide the bulk of welfare, with the state providing only a residual safety net. A typology of ideal types of welfare state in terms of their predominant ideology, which broadly coincides with that of Titmuss, has been described by

Esping-Andersen (1987): *social democratic or socialist* (Scandinavia), *corporatist or conservative* (European continent), and *liberal* (Anglo-Saxon). Four models of social security regime have been distinguished by Palme (1990) in terms of whether their main goal is to provide an adequate minimum income for all in old age (*basic security*), an adequate replacement of previous earnings (*income security*), neither of these (*residual*), or both (*institutional*). For the purpose of our analysis, we shall include Palme's "institutional" welfare regimes with those classed as "basic security", to give three groups that broadly correspond to Titmuss' (and Esping-Andersen's) three ideal types of policy regime: Residual Welfare (liberal), Industrial Achievement-Performance (corporatist), and Institutional-Redistributive (social democratic) (see Table 3.1).

The "residual" model of liberal regimes is characterized by minimal state provisions, allowing a great deal of scope for private (non-state) earnings-related pensions. There is no guaranteed income for non-earners, who must depend on an earner or rely on a means-tested safety net at a low level. Palme (1990) includes within this group countries where the minimum pension is inadequate and conditional on the contribution record, and the income replacement rate provided by the state scheme for a worker is less than half the average production worker's wage (APWW). Palme assigns Britain, Ireland, and Switzerland to this group.

Table 3.1 Typology of pension systems.

Political philosophy	Liberal	Conservative/ corporatist	Social Democratic socialist
Welfare policy orientation	Residual welfare	Industrial achievement performance	Institutional redistributive
	State plays a minimal rôle, family and market rôles emphasised	Social needs are met mainly according to work-merit	State support based on citizenship, as a universal right
Type of pension system	Residual	Income security	Basic security
	State provides a minimal safety net for those lacking an occupational pension	State ensures a high income replacement rate	State provides a universal benefit
Exemplar	UK	Germany	Denmark

The "income security model" of conservative, or corporatist, regimes is founded on earnings-related state social security that reflects stratification during the working life. Societies in this group are traditional and family-centred, and there is no income guarantee for non-earners, mainly house-wives. There is less incentive for the development of private occupational pensions than in the "residual" model. Pension systems which have no mini-mum citizen's pension and which provide an income replacement rate of at least half the APWW are assigned by Palme to this model: Germany, Belgium, France, Italy, Spain and Portugal.

In the "basic security model" of socialist or social democratic regimes, a basic pension is provided through the state to all citizens regardless of their work record, and funded from general taxation. Palme assigns countries to this model if the minimum pension replaces at least a third of the APWW and the link of earnings with pension income is weak. The Netherlands and Den-mark are approximate to this model. Palme's "Institutional" model, in which a basic citizen's pension is combined with an additional state pension replac-ing a high proportion of earnings, is represented by Sweden, Norway, and Finland.

We next turn to the effect on elderly people's income of the three differ-ent types of pension system, focusing on gender differences in the incidence of poverty. Germany (previously West Germany), Britain, and Denmark are used as exemplars of each type of welfare state.

Poverty and inequality among elderly men and women

Poverty among elderly people remains a persistent problem in the EC. Pov-erty is often defined as an income or expenditure level that is low relative to the average standard for the society (Eurostat 1990a). The measure of pov-erty used by Eurostat and adopted here depends on the relation of elderly people's average expenditure to that of the rest of the population in each country. Poverty rates among elderly people vary, with Britain having the largest absolute number of elderly people living below the EC's poverty line of 50 per cent of the National Average Equivalent Expenditure (Walker 1992).

Poverty in European countries is concentrated among elderly women, es-pecially widows living alone. For example, among those aged over 55 in four countries (Germany, Britain, Sweden, and Switzerland), single woman households have a substantially lower average income than couples or lone elderly men, after adjustment for household size. The disadvantage of lone elderly women is particularly acute in Britain, where their average income is only two-thirds of the average for all those aged over 55 in Britain (Kohl 1987).

Although data on the gender distribution of poverty as defined by Eurostat is not available for elderly people in the three exemplar countries, the percentages of elderly men and women receiving means-tested benefits provides an indication of gender inequality of poverty in Germany and Britain. In Germany from 1969–81, the proportion of elderly people receiving Public Assistance was very low, but elderly women were more than twice as likely as elderly men to be receiving it, 2.7 per cent compared with 1.1 per cent (OECD 1988: 46). In Britain in 1985, twice the percentage of women received Supplementary Pensions as men, but the proportions were much higher than in Germany – 15 per cent of women and 7 per cent of men (Ginn & Arber 1991). For widowed, divorced, and separated women, as many as a fifth were receiving Income Support in 1988/89 (Ginn & Arber forthcoming).

The majority of elderly people living alone are women, mainly because women live longer than men, and tend to marry men older than themselves, so that most wives outlive their husbands. In Britain in 1985–7 nearly half of elderly women lived alone, compared with a fifth of elderly men (Arber & Ginn 1991). Assuming similar demographic factors apply in the other two countries, this gender difference in living arrangements allows an indirect measure of gender inequality to be derived from Eurostat figures. If elderly women are substantially poorer than elderly men, this will tend to raise the poverty rate of elderly people living alone relative to that of other elderly households, in which the numbers of men and women are more evenly bal-

Table 3.2 Poverty rates of elderly people in Denmark, Germany and UK: by household type (percentage having weekly expenditure less than 50% of national average.

	Denmark	Germany	UK
Lone person aged over 65	17.0	14.5	41.3
	(1981)	(1983)	(1985)
Other households with head aged over 65	18.8	11.3	27.3
	(1981)	(1983)	(1983)
Ratio of poverty rate of lone elderly households	0.90	1.28	1.51
to poverty rate in other elderly households	(1981)	(1983)	(1985)

Source: Eurostate (1990a) *Poverty in Figures. Europe in the Early 1980s*, pp. 84–5, 105–6, 117–8.

anced. The poverty rates for lone-person elderly households and for other elderly households are shown in Table 3.2. In Denmark in 1981, the poverty rate (percentage spending less than half the national average) for lone elderly people was slightly less than the rate for other elderly households 17 per cent compared with 19 per cent, suggesting that elderly women suffered no financial disadvantage. In Germany in 1983, lone elderly households were about 25 per cent more likely to be poor than other households. But in Britain in 1985 the difference between lone elderly and other households was most striking: 41 per cent of lone elderly households were poor, compared with 27 per cent of other elderly households. The ratios presented in the bottom row of Table 3.2 summarize the data on poverty in the two types of household, and suggest that the concentration of poverty among elderly women is absent in Denmark, moderate in Germany, and highest in Britain.

In the next section, we consider how gender inequalities in financial resources in later life arise from interaction between women's employment pattern and the pension system in the three countries.

Impact of women's employment patterns on pension acquisition

Three patterns of women's employment in Europe have been distinguished by Joshi & Davies (1992): first, continuous full-time employment (typical in France), second, continuous employment with part-time work after childbirth (Scandinavia), and third, interrupted employment followed by part-time employment (Britain and Germany). These patterns are closely related to publicly provided childcare facilities. Joshi & Davies (1992) calculate that the employment pattern characteristic of Germany and Britain has the most serious effect on a woman's life-time earnings.

Low life-time earnings result from periods of economic inactivity, part-time work, and low pay, but the way each of these affects independent pension income depends on the structure of the pension system. Elements of pension systems that are crucial for those with a non-standard employment record include treatment of gaps in employment and job changes, coverage (such as whether part-time, low paid, new and temporary employees are eligible) and the formulae by which pensions are calculated (such as whether based on best years of earnings or on life-time average). The main features of the three exemplar countries' pension systems are described more fully elsewhere (Ginn & Arber 1992). We discuss in turn four aspects of women's employment in each country – overall rate of employment, age profile of employment, part-time work, and low earnings – and how these, in combination with each country's pension system, affect women's pension acquisition.

Overall rate of employment

Women's employment increased between 1950 and 1990 in most European countries, most rapidly after 1970 (OECD 1979, 1992). For example, in Denmark it increased from 58 per cent in 1970 to 78 per cent in 1990, while in Britain it increased from 51 per cent to 66 per cent over the same period (see Figure 3.1). Increases were less in Germany, France, the Netherlands, and Belgium. Comparing women's economic activity rate in the three exemplar countries in 1990, Denmark has the highest proportion in the labour force, at 78 per cent of the female population aged 15 to 64 (OECD 1992). The corresponding rate for Britain is 66 per cent, and Germany has the lowest rate at 55 per cent.

In Denmark, where women's employment rate is highest, the pension system provides an income in later life which is only weakly related to their rate of economic activity. There are three major components of the system. The first is a flat-rate state "Social Pension", which is universally paid from age 67 to all citizens, in full for those with 40 years' residence, and which replaces on average 40 per cent of the average production worker's wage (Palme 1990); the second is a compulsory employment-related scheme (the Labour

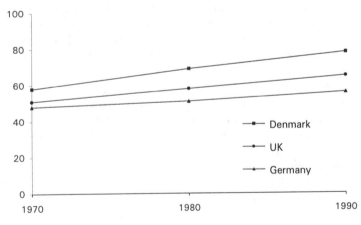

Figure 3.1 Percentage of women in the labour force (all ages) relative to female population aged 15–64, 1970–90. Source: OECD 1992, *Labour force survey*, 1970–90, Table II.

Market Supplementary Pension Plan, generally known as ATP) which pays a (small) pension linked to the years of contributions but not to earnings or hours of work; and the third is private occupational schemes, which, being earnings-related, modify the otherwise egalitarian structure of pension provision. About half of employers operate a pension scheme (Foster 1991), and membership is mainly confined to salaried employees, at present covering less than half of all employees. However, the private sector has seen a rapid expansion in recent years. Danish women's reproductive role has no apparent impact on their occupational pension scheme membership, and the membership rate of employed women is higher than men's until age 35. After this age it is lower than men's (see Figure 3.2a), but the gender difference is modest compared with Britain.

The British pension system links income in later life more closely to previous employment than the Danish. State provision is "residual", with a basic pension set below the level of means-tested benefits and a very low additional State Earnings Related Pension Scheme (SERPS). Those without an occupational pension, mainly women, have a pension income of their own that is close to the poverty level (Ginn & Arber 1991). Although women's employment rate is relatively high in Britain, the private occupational pensions sector is selective in its coverage, and membership is much less available to women than to men. Thus only 39 per cent of employed women, compared with 66 per cent of employed men, belonged to an occupational pension scheme in 1988/89 (Office of Population Censuses and Surveys 1989, authors' analysis). The effect of their reproductive role on employed British women's pension scheme membership is evident in Figure 3.2b, which shows a decline in their membership rates during the child-rearing years from age 25 to age 44. Employed men's membership rate in 1988/89 was 75 per cent for those aged 40–44 and women's 37 per cent, a gender gap of 38 per cent. Britain is unique in Europe in the size of its private sector of pension provision.

In Germany, more than in Denmark and Britain, married women are expected to confine themselves to a dependent domestic role (Allmendinger et al. 1991), and this is reflected in their lower employment rate (see Figure 3.1). The German "corporatist" welfare state provides a state earnings-related pension for all employees that replaces up to 45 per cent of earnings (Noble Lowndes 1991). This ensures near universal coverage of those able to work, including most part-timers, but does not enable those with low lifetime contributions to acquire a pension of their own above the level of means-tested benefits. The private occupational sector is smaller than in Britain, contributing 14 per cent of the gross income of households whose

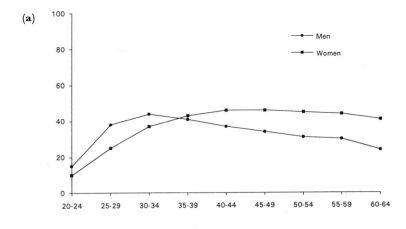

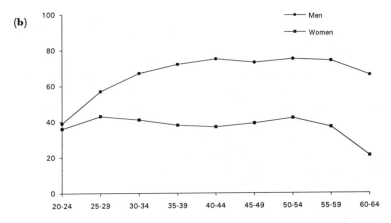

Figure 3.2 Percentages of men and women employees in occupational pension schemes: by group. (a) Denmark 1983; (b) Britain 1988–89. Sources: (a) Sociologisk Institut 1988; (b) General Household Survey 1989–90 (authors' analysis).

head is aged between 65 and 74 in Germany, compared with 22 per cent in Britain. As in Britain, German occupational pensions are selective in coverage, and are more available to men than to women. However, occupational pensions in Germany, unlike their British counterparts, are non-contributory for the employee. In 1982 only 14 per cent of women pensioners who had previously worked with a private company were receiving a company pension, compared with nearly half of men pensioners (Schmahl 1986:

264). Survivors' protections in the German state pension scheme are being reconsidered in the light of increased women's employment, but it has been argued that they cannot be dispensed with even when a widow has her own pension, because this is unlikely to be an adequate replacement of the couple's joint income (International Social Security Association 1991). The implication is that women are not generally expected to achieve an independent pension income comparable with men's in the foreseeable future.

Interrupted employment

Women's pension acquisition is influenced not only by their overall rate of economic activity but also by the age profile of their activity, which differs markedly among the three countries (see Figure 3.3). Women's age profile for economic activity approximates most closely to men's in Denmark, reaching 91 per cent among women aged 30–34, and showing no sign of decline during the child-rearing years. In contrast, women's age profile of employment in Britain has an M-shaped pattern, peaking at 76 per cent in the age group 20–24, falling to 68 per cent between ages 25 and 36, and peaking again at 77 per cent in the 40–44 age group. This bimodal employment pattern indicates interrupted employment and is clearly related to

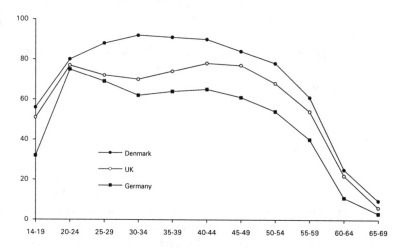

Figure 3.3 Percentage of women economically active: by age group – Denmark, UK and Germany, 1989. Source: Eurostat 1991b, *Labour force survey results, 1989*, Table 03, pp. 48–9.

women's childcare role in the absence of collective provision of childcare in Britain (Joshi & Davies 1991). In Germany, women's economic activity rate peaks in the age group 20–24 at 73 per cent and declines thereafter to around 60 per cent from the early 30s to the late 40s.

A bimodal or declining employment age profile reduces pension acquisition for several reasons; first, most pensions, whether state or private, depend on the number of years of pensionable employment. Secondly, earnings, especially for those in non-manual occupations, tend to increase with length of service. Contributions to earnings-related pension schemes are therefore potentially highest in the last years of a long career. Where there is a substantial private sector, with occupational schemes based on final salary as in Britain, earnings in the last few years before the normal retirement age have a disproportionate effect on the amount of pension income. Thirdly, in both Britain and Germany, career breaks have been shown to be associated with downward occupational mobility, reducing earnings. Fourthly, occupational pensions schemes, unlike state schemes, disadvantage those with interruptions in employment by requiring a minimum length of service before entry and by penalizing early leavers, that is, those who leave the pension scheme before retirement (Ginn & Arber forthcoming).

In Britain, a shorter average time served with an employer reduces the likelihood of belonging to an occupational pension scheme, mainly because of scheme rules requiring a minimum age or length of service (Green et al. 1989; Ginn & Arber 1993). Those who do join a scheme often lose their pension entitlement on leaving their employer. Vesting (the granting to the employee of a legal entitlement to the funds accumulated as a result of the combined employer and employee contributions) is not required by law until membership exceeds two years. Prior to 1987, the maximum period of membership before vesting was required was five years. This means that an employee who leaves with less than two years' membership of the scheme is entitled only to a refund of his or her own contributions. Even where an early leaver has vested rights, transfer of pension entitlements to a new employer has not usually been possible, and the option of preserving his or her pension rights in the scheme has been unattractive because of inflationary erosion of the pension. For these reasons, early leavers often withdraw their own contributions, relinquishing those of the employer. Because women's employment tends to be interrupted for domestic reasons, they are less likely than men to be able to join an occupational pension scheme and, if they do join but subsequently leave that employer, they are more likely than men to lose the value of the employer's contributions (Ginn & Arber forthcoming).

Occupational pensions in Germany have even stricter vesting conditions: vesting is required by law only when the employee reaches age 35, has 10 years' membership of the organization's pension scheme, or has 12 years' service with three years' membership. Women, if they have children, are far less likely to fulfil these conditions. The combination of these discriminatory conditions with a state pension scheme that depends on life-time earnings leaves the majority of married women dependent on their spouse's pension or on a widow's pension in later life.

In Denmark, the vesting requirements of occupational pension schemes could disadvantage women who left employment to have children. However, because Danish women are more likely than their counterparts in Britain and Germany to work continuously, they are less likely to lose rights through leaving an occupational pension scheme.

Part-time employment

The number of hours worked is also important to pension acquisition in Germany and Britain. Part-time employment of women is high in both Denmark (31 per cent of working-age women in 1989) and Britain (28 per cent), relative to the rest of the EC, but is only 17 per cent in Germany (calculated from Eurostat 1991b, and OECD 1991). In Germany and Britain, part-time employment not only reduces the pension income earned in state and occupational pension schemes, but has also resulted in exclusion from membership of the latter (Labour Research Department 1988; Schmahl 1991). In spite of a clear policy by the European Commission to end such discrimination against part-time workers, exclusion is still widespread. Neither the EC Court's judgement (the 1986 Bilka-Kaufhaus case), which ruled that exclusion of part-timers could be in breach of Article 119 of the Treaty of Rome, nor the German Supreme Court ruling that part-timers should not be excluded from retirement schemes (Hesse 1984), has had much effect. A draft EC Directive on so-called "atypical" workers would, if passed, require that most part-time workers have the right to join a scheme on the same basis as full-timers (TUC 1991). In the British public sector of employment in 1987, only 22 per cent of women employed part-time belonged to a scheme, compared with 91 per cent of those employed full-time, while in the private sector the corresponding figures were 7 per cent and 37 per cent (Ginn & Arber 1993).

Part-time employment in Denmark does not reduce pension income from the Social Pension or from the compulsory employment-related scheme (ATP), because the pension amount is based solely on years of employment, not on earnings. Income from occupational pensions is, however, diminished by part-time employment, because it depends on earnings.

Low earnings

Differences between men's and women's earnings, due to sex discrimination, occupational segregation, and the constraints of women's domestic roles, affect their pension contributions and hence their entitlements, in so far as these are earnings related. The ratio of men's to women's hourly earnings in manual occupations in industry is highest in Britain and lowest in Denmark, with Germany intermediate (see Figure 3.4). For non-manual occupations in distribution and finance, Britain has the highest ratio (over 1.8) of men's to women's earnings, of all EC countries (Eurostat 1990b).

In Britain and Germany, where occupational pension income is closely related to the final level of earnings, women's employment, even if continuous and full-time, generates a smaller pension than that of a man in a similar type of occupation. As a result, elderly women in Britain are not only less likely than elderly men to have an occupational pension, but they also receive lower amounts (Ginn & Arber 1991).

These four aspects of gender inequality in employment – overall employment rate, continuity of employment, hours of work and level of earnings – are all related to the unequal domestic division of labour in which women bear the bulk of the responsibility for child-rearing. The bimodal age pro-

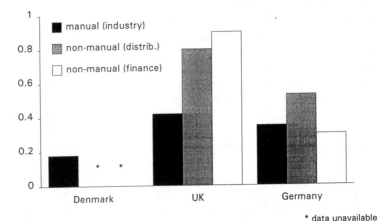

Figure 3.4 Ratio of male to female earnings, 1989 – Denmark, UK, and Germany.

file of employment in Britain and Germany suggests that a large proportion of women are unable to continue their employment through their child-rearing years (Joshi & Davies 1992). This is due, at least in part, to the lack of appropriate childcare facilities in these countries. For example, in Denmark three-quarters of working age women with a child under two years old are employed, but in Britain and Germany only a third of comparable women are employed (Joshi & Davies 1992: 39). Current responsibility for childcare is not, however, the only factor affecting women's work outside the home. The period when children are no longer dependent is potentially one in which married women can more easily undertake employment and en-hance their pension rights, but even among older women the economic activity rates differ among the three countries. For older women, aged 50 to 64, the economic activity rate is 54 per cent in Denmark, 48 per cent in Britain, and 36 per cent in Germany (Eurostat 1991b). The pensionable age for women differs in each country, being 67, 60 and 65 respectively, but this cannot account for the low rate of older women's employment in Germany. A more likely explanation is that the lack of suitable childcare during ear-lier years has a lasting effect on women's employment opportunities. The general prejudice against older workers (Laczko & Phillipson 1991) is exac-erbated for older women by the difficulty of maintaining or acquiring up-to-date knowledge and skills after a career break.

Women's independent and derived pension income

Our discussion of women's employment patterns in relation to three con-trasting European pension systems shows why higher employment rates of women will not result in a proportional improvement in their financial cir-cumstances in later life: the way pension systems interact with non-stand-ard employment is crucial. Those who are for any reason disadvantaged in employment, especially women with domestic responsibilities, are more likely to receive an adequate pension in their own right where the pension system approximates to the "basic security" model (such as Denmark) rather than the "income security" (Germany) or "residual" (Britain) model. Where occupational pensions are a major component of the pension system women are most disadvantaged relative to men, and most at risk of poverty and dependence in later life.

Germany provides a substantial state pension but only for those who are employed full-time for most of their working life. Because the social security system is founded on the concept of work merit, the lower employment rate, interrupted employment, and low earnings of married women are likely to result in inadequate pension income in their own right. However, two features of the German pension system do provide some help to women in building their own pension. First, on divorce the spouses' contribution records from the state scheme are split equally between them, and funds from any occupational schemes can also be split. Secondly, from 1992, contributions to the state insurance scheme are credited to a woman's record at 75 per cent of national average earnings during a career break or a switch to part-time work of up to three years per child. In Britain, where low state pension provision makes a good occupational or other private pension essential to avoid poverty in later life, women's employment pattern is inimical to obtaining such a pension. British women also lose any right to their husband's SERPS or occupational pension on divorce.

In Denmark, however, women's continuous pattern of employment and fairly equal earnings, combined with the egalitarian structure of state pensions, enables women to obtain a substantial state pension income of their own. Part-time employment does not place women at a disadvantage to the same extent as in the other two countries, because neither the Social Pension nor the employment-related scheme (ATP) depends on earnings. The low level of the ATP has given rise to a private occupational sector that is larger than in other Scandinavian countries (but smaller than in Britain), and as this sector grows it is likely to provide a substantial proportion of total pensioner income; such inequality need not lead to elderly women's financial dependence on men.

Denmark, as a social democratic regime, has moved furthest of the three countries in the direction of treating women as financially independent of men, providing childcare that facilitates continuous employment, and a relatively egalitarian pension system. However, Danish women's dependence on the state both as users of social services and as employees in these services has been seen as replacing private with public patriarchy, making women particularly vulnerable to cuts in state spending (Hernes 1988; Esping-Andersen 1990). Despite such criticisms, we would argue that state provision is more amenable than private relationships to collective action in defence of women's interests.

Pension income derived from a past husband's employment is still an important component of elderly widows' income in Britain (Bone et al. 1992) and in Germany. While the widow's pension from the state social insurance scheme in Germany is relatively generous, British widows' state pensions, from their husbands' basic and SERPS contribution, provide only a subsistence income. Further, from the turn of the century the amount of SERPS "inherited" by widows is to be reduced from all to half of their husbands' entitlement. Widows' income from their deceased husbands' occupational pensions are on average trivial amounts (Ginn & Arber forthcoming). With inadequate support as dependants, women in Britain need to earn their own pension. Yet they are handicapped by the combination of their employment pattern and the British pension system. They are neither protected from poverty in later life through derived rights as in Germany, nor are they enabled to obtain their own pension, as in Denmark, through childcare policies allowing continuous employment and a reasonably high level of state pensions for all.

The problem of having neither independent nor derived pension rights is particularly acute for divorced and separated women in Britain. They are likely to have experienced constraints on employment similar to those of married women, often spending many years caring for children at the expense of their own careers before and after the divorce. Yet they have no access to their ex-husbands' occupational pensions, and must rely entirely on their own employment to obtain an occupational pension. The introduction of pension splitting in Britain at the time of divorce, as is the practice in Germany, would be a gesture towards equity between divorcing spouses, but in the absence of improved state pensions it would not remove the risk of poverty for divorced elderly women, as Joshi & Davies (1991) show.

In Denmark and Germany there is some coherence in policy. In the former, social policy is directed towards maintaining high and continuous employment of women, with a generous state contribution to the caring functions, which are otherwise carried out as unpaid domestic labour. Benefits as dependants are minimal, but women are enabled to obtain a pension in their own right based on citizenship. In Germany, on the other hand, women are encouraged to care for young children at home and are relatively well protected as dependants. In Britain, however, policy appears to be contradictory. The deliberate withdrawal of state support services in the form of childcare and homes for frail elderly people, as "community care" is promoted, place the responsibility for providing unpaid care mainly on women, preventing them from pursuing continuous full-time employment. The gender gap in earnings is also greater in Britain than in other EC countries. Yet the British pension system heavily penalizes non-standard employment and low earnings, and, through the reductions in SERPs, is cutting back on women's already meagre entitlements as widows. Will the prospects for British women's acquisition be improved by current reform proposals in the EC?

The closer relationship of Britain with the EC has raised the possibility of a levelling up of social policy and of working conditions (as in the Social Charter and Equal Treatment Directives), which would benefit women if endorsed. Yet national governments' objectives, especially in the case of Britain, may conflict with EC policy. For example, a minimum wage, as formulated in the Social Charter, would raise more women's wages than men's, with consequent effects on their pensions. The British government, however, is moving in the opposite direction, having abolished the few remaining minimum wage councils in the early 1990s. Reforms aimed at removing obstacles to the mobility of labour across national boundaries and at promoting equality of treatment between men and women would facilitate pension acquisition for non-standard workers within the EC. But at the same time a perceived crisis of public expenditure has prompted governments to consider promoting private occupational or insurance-based schemes at the expense of state pension schemes, a development that threatens to worsen women's pension position still further. The likely effects of these divergent policies on women's pension income in the future are now considered.

Implications for women of proposed EC reforms in pension systems

Mobility of labour

A central aim of the EC is to remove all obstacles to the free movement of capital, goods, and labour within its boundaries (Commission of the EC 1991). Unrestricted mobility of labour is a requirement of capitalism at the macro level; "Freedom of movement for workers is one of the basic constituents of the common market" (Commission of the EC 1991: 15). In order to avoid losses of social security rights, which deter workers from migrating across national boundaries, public pension schemes have been "co-ordinated" according to a complex formula that allows all insured employment to count towards benefits, including a pension. But, as we have discussed in earlier sections, in different countries overall social protection is achieved by a varying mix of public and private (or supplementary) provision. Loss of occupational pension rights through inter-country migration is likely to be even greater than loss due to job change within each country.

The Commission of the EC is concerned to explore ways of ensuring better protection against loss of occupational pension scheme rights, and as a consequence addresses many of the disadvantages facing women and other

workers with interrupted employment patterns. "Such arrangements linking benefit entitlements to a worker's employment history with a particular
company will obviously make labour mobility more costly for employees"
(Commission of the EC 1991: 11). For these reasons, the Commission of the
EC views an expansion of private occupational pensions as threatening one
of the aims of the common market:

> Long vesting and waiting periods, calculations of transfer values
> which penalise scheme leavers and inadequate preservation of
> "dormant" rights are severe obstacles to labour mobility. In the
> presence of these obstacles the contribution of occupational pen-
> sions to the total retirement incomes of workers will depend on
> careers which are characterized by long uninterrupted periods of
> employment with the same company or employer. The social
> policy goal of guaranteeing an adequate retirement income will not
> be achieved for workers with a more mobile career profile . . . *women
> will be far more likely than men to receive insufficient occupational retirement
> benefits. This will be especially problematic in countries where occupational
> pensions are supposed to be a major source of retirement income.*
>
> (Commission of the EC 1991: 18–19, our emphasis)

The Commission (1991) recommends shorter vesting periods and easier
access to membership, choice of preservation or transfer without loss of entitlement, and full regular information to all scheme members as to the financial consequences of job change on retirement income. All these, designed to remove obstacles to migration of labour in the EC, would benefit
women if implemented.

The consequences for elderly women of minimal state provision and reliance on the private occupational pension sector are serious. Whether such
clear opposition by the Commission to occupational pension as they usually
operate will influence their discriminatory features remains to be seen, but
it seems unlikely that the British government, on its record so far, will be
willing to pay heed to the EC on this issue. The same observation applies to
the EC's objective of achieving equal treatment of men and women.

Equal treatment

Proposals by the Commission for directives concerning part-time, temporary, and interim employment are being considered. One of these directives
would require that such workers "will be afforded social protection under

statutory and occupational social security schemes in the same foundations and the same criteria as workers in full-time employment of indeterminate duration"(COM(90) 228) (Commission of the EC 1991: 13). If this were implemented, it would help women by increasing their access to occupational pension scheme membership, but it would not address the question of how those with low part-time earnings can obtain an adequate occupational pension.

Two "Equality of Treatment" directives (378(86) and COM(87)494) and the EC Court of Justice decisions in the Bilka-Kaufhaus and Barber cases concern occupational pension schemes (TUC 1991), but none of these has so far improved the position for women. The main effect of the Barber judgment in Britain has been to prompt many employers to equalize the age of eligibility for their occupational pension to 65, instead of 60 for women and 65 for men.

Reduction of state pension expenditure

We have argued that private (mainly occupational) pension provision is inherently discriminatory against those with non-standard employment patterns, whereas public provision can minimize the detrimental effects of the unequal domestic division of labour and childcare. Potentially, state pension schemes can enable women to obtain an adequate independent pension income and eliminate gender inequality of income in later life. Yet alarm at the increased public cost of pensions due to the ageing of populations and increased early retirement has led to proposals to cut public pension spending (Johnson et al. 1989; OECD 1988, Gillion 1991). Johnson et al. (1989) have argued that elderly people in industrialized countries are more affluent than ever before and that their generous pensions threaten the welfare of younger cohorts and could lead to intergenerational conflict. This "conflictual ageism" (Arber & Ginn 1991: 53) or "victim blaming" (Minkler 1986) predicts a fiscal crisis due to the rising ratio of elderly to working age people, but neglects the saving of state expenditure due to the unpaid caring work performed by elderly people, invisible to economists (Neugarten & Neugarten 1986; Greene 1989). It tends to overlook other factors that affect public spending such as high unemployment (Thane 1988) and military spending (Navarro 1984), and those that raise state income such as women's increasing employment (Falkingham 1989; Gibson 1989). Most important, depicting elderly people as an affluent interest group ignores the deep divisions by class, gender, and race and the persistence of severe poverty later in life, especially among women and the working class (Phillipson 1990; Ginn & Arber 1991).

Measures to reform pension provision that have been introduced or are being considered by EC countries include the following: reduction or means-testing of flat-rate benefits provided by basic statutory schemes; policies to emphasize the insurance principle, including placing more emphasis on the life-time "contribution profile" (OECD 1988: 12) in state, occupational, and private schemes; a stricter policy towards non-contributory periods; reduction of the accrual factor (maximum replacement rate) in state pension schemes; raising contribution ceilings at rates faster than inflation; limiting the indexing of public pensions, for example by delays or by linking to prices instead of wages; and raising the age of eligibility for full state pensions (including raising women's pensionable age to that of men), to reduce the number of years of pension receipt. This last proposal runs counter to the trend of earlier exit of men from the labour market (Kohli et al. 1991; Laczko & Phillipson 1991) and would raise unemployment rates.

The above changes would reduce benefit levels for all pensioners, but their effect would be felt disproportionately by those disadvantaged in the labour market, accentuating social inequality. In particular, women, because of their often non-standard employment, have more need than men for a redistributive state pension scheme. Gender inequality of income in later life is therefore likely to be increased by reforms that cut state provision.

A different strategy that has been proposed is to encourage further increases in women s employment. This would boost the funds of state pension schemes, and could in future entitle more women to their own pension. However, the net effect on the viability of public pension schemes is hard to estimate (Schmahl 1989: 154). As we have argued above, an increase in women s rate of employment would not substantially increase pension income if the employment were non-standard and the pension system discriminated against such employment.

Welfare states are not, of course, as static as typologies suggest, and the direction in which they develop depends on the economic climate and the balance of political forces. During this century, an increasing number of OECD countries have introduced citizenship-based old age pensions: there were none in 1930, two in 1950, and eight in 1980 (Palme 1990). Whether this trend will continue is doubtful, due to demographic trends and to the worsening economic situation in Europe. Indeed, Gordon (1988) claims that pension systems in industrialized societies are converging towards a two-tier model of public pensions, with insurance-based (i.e. earnings-related) pensions for workers and a means-tested minimum pension for those lacking an adequate insurance record. In this way the political tension between interest groups that benefit from earnings-related pensions (higher paid employees and sections of organized labour) and those that do not is built into the pension system (Overbye 1992). In this scenario, universalist "citizen's incomes" or flat-rate state pensions would decline, and those with non-standard employment would be at risk of having only a subsistence income in later life.

In Britain, means-testing access to the insurance-based but flat-rate basic state pension is being considered by both main political parties, arousing considerable opposition from the organized pensioners' movement due to the complexity of claiming, the stigma, and the invasion of privacy. Assuming means-testing continued to be based on joint income for couples, married women could lose the small state pension (the Wife's Allowance) that is often the only personal income they have.

Expansion of the private sector through tax incentives is an option that has been promoted by Conservative governments in Britain and that is being considered more widely in the OECD as a way of containing public expenditure (Holtzmann 1989). Where reforms of statutory schemes reduce the income replacement rate, supplementary (especially occupational) schemes are likely to fill the gap, especially for higher paid staff (Schmahl 1991). However, any saving of public funds through cutbacks in public pensions must be set against the public cost of tax concessions to occupational and private pension schemes, which is a substantial amount (Reddin 1985; Wilkinson 1986). Enlarging the role of the private sector is a development whose inegalitarian effect is recognized by commentators on pension policy (Commission of the EC 1991) but whose detrimental effect on women s pension income has been generally overlooked. Could occupational or other private pensions be regulated in such a way as to make them less hostile to those with non-standard employment and more compatible with social objectives?

The tax concessions available to private occupational and other pension schemes give governments a lever to influence them. Governments could in theory regulate schemes in respect of financial management, information disclosure, employee participation, revaluation formula, vesting periods, and eligibility rules (the latter three being crucial to women). Regulation of occupational pension schemes by the EC has been of limited effectiveness. The misuse of pension funds in Britain by Robert Maxwell has highlighted the vulnerability of pension funds and drawn attention to the need for some control by members and pensioners, backed by law. However, it is doubtful whether employers would voluntarily operate an occupational pension scheme that they did not control, or whether they would be willing to provide a scheme that covered all staff and did not penalize early leavers. For this reason, only mandatory occupational pension schemes could be so regulated by the state as to ensure that they provide an adequate pension for all, including women with domestic responsibilities.

Conclusion

The increased employment of women is unlikely, on its own, to have much impact on their income disadvantage in later life in European countries whose pension system discriminates against those with non-standard employment. Pension systems where the state provides minimal pensions, leaving private occupational pensions to play a major role, are particularly detrimental to women's acquisition of their own pension. Without state intervention, those with domestic responsibilities (mainly women) are substantially disadvantaged in their earning power and in their employment patterns, and hence in their ability to provide for their own retirement through pension contributions.

There are two ways in which the financial penalties in later life to those who undertake caring responsibilities could be reduced. Childcare and eldercare policies and employment practices could evolve to allow full-time continuous employment for everyone, but on present trends full-time employment for 40 years for everyone seems neither possible nor socially desirable. Alternatively, pension systems could adapt to provide adequate cover for workers with non-standard employment, that is, become less closely related to earnings and more universal in coverage. This also appears to run counter to current trends.

The reforms proposed to facilitate the mobility of labour throughout the EC would benefit women, as would Equal Treatment policies if these were implemented. The wider provision of a tax-financed flat-rate pensioner's income based on citizenship (as in the four Nordic countries) would minimize the disadvantage of women, especially if it were set well above the poverty level. However, it is worth bearing in mind that the EC originated as an economic grouping, the EEC, and that gender equality has not been a primary objective; the EC aim of levelling up social rights has been tacked on to an economic framework, and its main intended beneficiaries are not "citizens" but "workers". Improvements in social rights are evidently a great deal less popular among governments than the trading advantages of a common market. For example, Peter Lilley, the British Secretary of State for Social Security, has attacked the idea of levelling up social security provision to match the best in the EC, as "simply a road to bankruptcy" for Britain (Lilley 1992: 13).

European governments concerned at the public expenditure implications of demographic forecasts, and wishing to limit taxation, are unlikely to develop universalistic pensions farther. On the contrary, it seems more likely that the desire to contain welfare expenditure while responding to the preference of higher paid employees for earnings-related pensions will lead to erosion of the universalistic elements of state pensions, and further marketization of pensions. Such developments would increase pension income for the most articulate and powerful groups in society, exacerbating class and gender inequality in later life, and are opposed by most of the pensioners' organizations in Britain. It remains to be seen whether the European-wide organization of pensioners, and such events as the new annual Pensioners Parliament organized by socialist MEPs, and the European Year of the Elderly, and Solidarity Between Generations will be able to influence national governments towards more generous and egalitarian pension policies.

References

Allmendinger, J., H. Bruckner, E. Bruckner 1991. *Gendered retirement*. Paper presented at the Columbus meeting, August.

Arber, S. & J. Ginn 1991. *Gender and later life: a sociological analysis of resources and constraints*. London: Sage.

Bone, M., J. Gregory, B. Hill, D. Lader 1992. *Retirement and retirement plans*. London: HMSO.

Commission of the EC 1991. *Supplementary social security schemes: the role of occupational pension schemes in the social protection of workers and their implications*. Brussels: Commission of the European Communities.

Craig, J. 1992. Fertility trends within the UK. In *Population trends* 67, 17–21. London: HMSO.

Esping-Andersen, G. 1987. *State and market in the formation of social security regimes. A political economy approach*. Working Paper 87/281. European University Institute.

Esping-Andersen, G. 1990. *The three worlds of welfare capitalism*. Princeton: Princeton University Press.

Eurostat 1988. *Eurostat review 1977–86*. Luxembourg: Office for Official Publications of the European Communities.

Eurostat 1989. *Population and social conditions, rapid reports no.1*. Luxembourg: Office for Official Publications of the European Communities.

Eurostat 1990a. *Poverty in figures, europe in the early 1980s*. Luxembourg: Office for Official

Publications of the European Communities.

Eurostat 1990b. *Population and social conditions, rapid reports no.8.* Luxembourg: Office for Official Publications of the European Communities.

Eurostat 1991a. *Population and social conditions, rapid reports no.3.* Luxembourg: Office for Official Publications of the European Communities.

Eurostat 1991b. *Labour force survey results 1989.* Luxembourg: Office for Official Publications of the European Communities.

Falkingham, J. 1989. Dependency and ageing in britain: a re-examination of the evidence. *Journal of Social Policy* **18**, 211–33.

Foster, H. (ed.) 1991. *Employee benefits in Europe and USA.* London: Longman.

Gibson, D. 1989. *Advancing the dependency ratio concept and avoiding the Malthusian trap.* Research on Ageing **11**, 147–57.

Gillion, C. 1991. Ageing populations: spreading the costs. *Journal of European Social Policy* **1**, 107–28.

Ginn, J. & S. Arber 1991. Gender, class and income inequalities in later life. *British Journal of Sociology* **42**, 369–96.

Ginn, J. & S. Arber 1992. Towards women's independence: pension systems in three contrasting European welfare states. *European Journal of Social Policy* **24**(4), 255–77.

Ginn, J. & S. Arber 1993. Pension penalties: the gendered division of occupational welfare. *Work, Employment and Society* **7**, 43–66.

Ginn, J. & S. Arber forthcoming. Heading for hardship: how the British pension system has failed women. In *Beveridge: new challenges*, S. Baldwin & J. Falkingham (eds.). Brighton: Harvester Wheatsheaf.

Gordon, M. 1988. *Social security policies in industrial countries.* New York: Cambridge University Press.

Green, F., G. Hadjimatheou, R. Smail 1989. *Unequal fringes.* London: Bedford Square Press/NCVO.

Greene, V. 1989. Human capitalism and intergenerational justice. *The Gerontologist* **29**, 723–4.

Hannah, L. 1986. *Inventing retirement.* Cambridge: Cambridge University Press.

Haskey, J. 1989. Current prospects for the proportion of marriages ending in divorce. *Population Trends* **55**, 34–7. London: HMSO.

Hernes, H. 1988. The transition from private to public dependence. In *Welfare State and woman power: Essays in state feminism*, H Hernes, 31–49. Oslo: Norwegian University Press.

Hesse, B. 1984. Women at work in the Federal Republic of Germany. In *Working women: an international survey*, M. Davidson & C. Cooper (eds), 63–81. Chichester: John Wiley and Sons.

Holtzmann, R. 1989. Pension policies in the OECD countries: background and trends. In *An ageing world: dilemmas and challenges for law and social policy*, J. Eekelaar & D. Pearl (eds), 823–43. Oxford: Clarendon.

International Social Security Association 1991. What is happening to survivors' benefits under social security? Report of a research meeting. *Network News* **6**(2), 16–19.

Johnson, P., C. Conrad, D. Thomson 1989. *Workers versus pensioners: intergenerational conflict in an ageing world.* Manchester: Manchester University Press.

Joshi, H. & H. Davies 1991. *The pension consequences of divorce*. Discussion Paper 550. London: Centre for Economic Policy Research.

Joshi, H. & H. Davies 1992. *Childcare and mothers' life-time earnings: some European contrasts*. London: Centre for Economic Policy Research.

Kohl, J. 1987. Alterssicherung im internationalen Vergleich. Zur Einkommensstruktur und Versorgungssituation alterer Haushalte. *Zeitschrift für Socialreform* **33**, 698–719.

Kohli, M., M. Rein, A. Guillemard, H. van Gunsteren 1991. *Time for retirement*. Cambridge: Cambridge University Press.

Labour Research Department 1988. *The LRD guide to pensions bargaining*. London: LRD Publications.

Laczco, F. & C. Phillipson 1991. *Changing work and retirement*. Milton Keynes, England: Open University Press.

Land, H. 1989. The construction of dependency. In *The goals of social policy*, M. Bulmer, J. Lewis, D. Piachaud (eds), 141–59. London: Unwin Hyman.

Lilley, P. 1992. Beveridge and Europe. Address to the International Conference on Social Security 50 Years After Beveridge, York, September, DSS press release 92/44.

Minkler, M. 1986. "Generational equity" and the new victim blaming: An emerging public policy issue. *International Journal of Health Services* **16**, 539–51.

Navarro, V. 1984. The political economy of government cuts for the elderly. In *Readings in the political economy of ageing*, M. Minkler & C. Estes (eds), 37–46. New York: Baywood.

Neugarten, B. & D. Neugarten 1986. Changing meanings of age in an ageing society. In *Our ageing society: paradox and promise*, A. Pifer & L. Bronte (eds), 33–52. Ontario: Norton and Company.

Noble Lowndes 1991. *A guide to pensions in Europe 1991*. Croydon: Noble Lowndes.

OECD 1979. *Demographic trends*. Paris: OECD.

OECD 1988. *Reforming public pensions*. Social Policy Studies 5. Paris: OECD.

OECD 1991. *Labour force survey 1969–1989*. Paris: OECD.

OECD 1992. *Labour force survey 1970–1990*. Paris: OECD.

Office of Population Censuses and Surveys 1989. *General Household Survey 1987*. London: HMSO.

Overbye, E. 1992. *Public or private pensions? Pensions and pension politics in the Nordic countries*. Oslo: Institut for Sosialforskning.

Palme, J. 1990. *Pension rights in welfare capitalism: the development of old age pensions in 18 OECD countries 1930–85*. Swedish Institute for Social Research 14, Universitt, Stockholm.

Phillipson, C. 1990. *Intergenerational relations: conflict or consensus in the twenty-first century*. Paper given at the Welfare State Seminar Series, Suntory Toyota International Centre for Economics and Related Disciplines, London School of Economics.

Reddin, M. 1985. A view by Mike Reddin. In *Can we afford our future?*, M. Reddin & M. Pilch (eds). Mitcham: Age Concern England.

Rein, M. & H. van Gunsteren 1985. The dialectic of public and private pensions. *Journal of Social Policy* **14**, 129–49.

Schmahl, W. 1986. Public and private pensions for various population groups in the Federal Republic of Germany: past experience and tasks for the future. *Industrial Social Security Review* 258–76.

REFERENCES

Schmahl, W. 1989. Labour force participation and social pension systems. In *Workers versus pensioners: intergenerational conflict in an ageing world*, P. Johnson, C. Conrad, D. Thomson (eds), 137–61. Manchester: Manchester University Press.

Schmahl, W. 1991. On the future development of retirement in Europe, especially of supplementary pension schemes. An introductory overview. In *The future of basic and supplementary pension schemes in the European Community – 1992 and beyond*, 32–66. Baden-Baden: Nomos Verlagsgesellschaft.

Tamburi, G. & P. Mouton 1986. The uncertain frontier between private and public pension schemes. *International Labour Review* **125**, 127–40.

Thane, P. 1988. The growing burden of an ageing population? *Journal of Public Policy* **7**, 373–87.

Titmuss, R. 1974. *Social policy*. London: Allen & Unwin.

van Nordheim Nielsen, F. 1988. *Occupational pensions in northern Europe*. Copenhagen: Sociologisk Institut.

Walker, A. 1992. Integration, social policy and elderly citizens: towards a European agenda on ageing? *Generations Review* **2**(4), 2–8.

Wilkinson, M. 1986. Tax expenditure and public expenditure in the UK. *Journal of Social Policy* **15**, 23–49.

Chapter 4

Combining work and family: working mothers in Scandinavia and the European Community

Arnlaug Leira

The welfare state and the concept of motherhood

Different forms of the welfare state encourage different forms of motherhood. In Mary Ruggie's (1984) book *The state and working women*, it is argued that "social democratic" welfare states such as the Scandinavian are more responsive to the demands of workers than "liberal" welfare states such as Britain, and therefore more supportive of working women. For example, Ruggie shows that the provision of publicly funded childcare was far better in Sweden than in the UK. More recently, within the framework of a general welfare state typology, Gøsta Esping-Andersen (1990) also calls attention to different welfare state approaches to working women. Taking the different arrangements between the state, market, and family as a basis for his classification, he distinguishes between three main clusters or "ideal types" of welfare state regimes: "the social democratic", "the liberal", and "the conservative". The Scandinavian states are labelled as predominantly social democratic, although they also reveal "liberal" elements. The UK provides an example of the liberal, residualist cluster, while Austria, Germany, Italy, and France are identified as belonging to the class of conservative welfare states. Compared to the "liberal" welfare state, the "social democratic" welfare state is characterized by a large public sector labour market and a high labour market participation of women. According to Esping-Andersen, women's employment in Scandinavia is facilitated by the public take-over of the provision of education, health, and welfare services such as day care for children and services for the elderly.

However, if we deconstruct the concept of the family and take a closer look at the arrangements between mothers, fathers, state, and market, the relationship between the state and working mothers becomes more complex than outlined in Ruggie's and Esping-Andersen's analyses. Welfare states that in many respects are similar, for example, the Scandinavian ones, have adopted relatively different approaches to mothers who combine employment and childcare responsibilities. What different welfare state regimes imply for the political and social definition of motherhood obviously needs further examination.

The combination of wage work and childcare is a characteristic feature of motherhood in modern welfare states.[1] Focusing on the part played by the state in this redefinition of motherhood, I examine the relationship between the welfare state and working mothers. As an analytical tool, I introduce the concept that motherhood has both earner and carer aspects. The "earner" refers to mothers' economic activities and material provision, the "carer" to primary socialization, nurturing, and rearing. By this conceptualization of motherhood, I emphasize the need to transcend models of "work" and "family" that ignore or marginalize the interrelationship of production and social reproduction.

Conceptualizing mothers of young children as both providers and nurturers highlights an empirical fact often neglected in sociological theorizing of the family. Thus, my concept of mothers as earners and carers differs from that presented in much of the sociological literature, ranging from the structural-functionalism of Parsons to the domestic labour debate of the 1970s. Obviously, childcare and primary socialization are essential elements in welfare state motherhood. However, it is important not to underplay the material or economic aspects of mother as provider. In short, to capture central features of welfare state motherhood it is necessary to include both aspects, caring and earning, in the analysis.

Mothers' combination of employment and childcare responsibilities is at present most pronounced in Scandinavia, but is also gaining ground in the majority of EC member states. Although policies towards working mothers vary, the incompatibility of labour market and family organization is a common feature across western Europe (Pichault 1984; Moss 1990; Leira 1992). The ways in which working mothers are incorporated as citizens also vary. Utilizing recent statistical data on mothers' employment, childcare provisions, and opportunities for leave of absence for family reasons in Scandinavia and the European Community, the remainder of this chapter takes the following form: the first part examines the influence of two processes: "the modernization of motherhood", which refers to those mothers who have joined the labour market, and the "collectivization of childcare", referring to the introduction of public day care. In the second part, this data is used as a starting point for comparing different welfare state approaches to employed mothers and expanding what T. H. Marshall (1965) termed the social rights of citizenship. However, as Marshall emphasized, access to social rights is differentiated; social class generates processes of exclusion from benefits and entitlements. The concept of the employed mother also provides a perspective on processes of integration and exclusion in modern welfare states, and reveals an important premise of welfare state design across western Europe, namely the different citizenship status accorded to wage workers and carers. In conclusion, the paper examines this contradiction and the related gendering of citizenship.[2]

The core material for the paper is based on the Scandinavian experience. I use data from the EC member states more as a contrast than as a direct comparison, to illustrate both similarity and difference in policy approaches to the "new" labour, that is, those mothers who combine wage work and parental responsibility for young children.

Welfare states and working mothers – the Scandinavian model

The welfare state created in the post Second World War period in Scandinavia – the "Scandinavian model" – was shaped during a period of massive social democratic influence. Throughout the second half of the 20th century, Labour has remained Norway's largest political party, and was, like Sweden's Social Democrats, the ruling party for the greater part of the post-war period. The Scandinavian "model" is usually categorized as an institutional welfare state. According to the terminology developed first by Wilensky & Lebeaux (1958), this form of welfare state provides a wide range of services and benefits that are commonly universalist in orientation, and are perceived as citizenship entitlements. The Scandinavian welfare state aims not only to provide a safety net for the poorest. From early on, a commitment to the redistribution of resources in order to generate a more egalitarian society was also strong (Allardt 1986; Esping-Andersen & Korpi 1987; see also Siim 1987). The importance attributed to principles of universalism and equality also contribute to the legitimacy of this form of the state (Esping-Andersen 1990). Introduced in the wake of policies instituted to diminish differences between social classes and regions, the equal status policies developed from the 1970s may be seen as a late follow-up of the tradition of state intervention to promote egalitarian principles.

I do not want to underplay the considerable gains of the welfare state and its contribution to the general standard of living and well being in Scandinavia. However, the term "institutional" welfare state conveys an impression of a state generally setting generous standards for citizens' welfare. Even in well developed welfare states, such as the Scandinavian, policies are not equally well developed for all sectors and for all citizens (Leira 1990, 1992). Neither are the different distributive systems of the welfare state equally well institutionalized. This becomes evident if we contrast the policies to secure the replacement of income from gainful employment, i.e. the national insurance system, or "the social security net", which is generally well established, with the "caring net", i.e. the development of services to care for very dependent people, which is less firmly institutionalized.

The Scandinavian societies in the 1970s underwent remarkable social change. Women increased their attachment to the labour market, taking relatively short leaves of absence when children were born, and thereby changed the meaning and content of motherhood. In the 1970s, mothers of pre-school children became one of the fastest growing groups in the labour market. In the late 1980s, Sweden and Norway had a higher labour market participation among mothers of young children than had the EC member states, Denmark excepted. See Table 4.1.

What caused the change in women's relationship to family and employment has been much debated in Scandinavia. The supply of jobs changed, and so did women's practices. From the early 1960s in Sweden and Denmark, and the later years of the decade in Norway, adult women increasingly rejected the sequential "two roles model" envisaged by Myrdal & Klein (1957) and opted for both paid work and children. Women in the 1980s commanded a control of their own labour and of their reproductive capaci-

Table 4.1 Labour market participation of mothers with children aged 0–9 years[1] in Scandinavia and the EC member states (1988).

Country	Labour market participation (%)
Norway, Sweden , Denmark	70–80
Portugal	60–69
France, Belgium	50–59
United Kingdom, Italy, Greece	40–49
Germany, Netherlands, Luxembourg	30–39
Spain, Ireland	20–29

Sources: EC member states, Moss (1990), for details, see Appendix 1; Norway, the Equal Status Council (1990), Sweden (SCB 1990).

[1] Data from Norway and Sweden apply to mothers of children aged 0–10 years.

ties unparalleled in earlier generations. Access to oral contraception facilitated women's reproductive control. Fertility rates declined. Norms regarding family formation and parenthood changed. Divorce rates increased and cohabitation became popular, particularly among young people. In 1991, 41 per cent of children born in Norway were born out of wedlock, in Sweden and Denmark approximately every second child was born to unmarried parents. Smaller families and increased educational attainment facilitated women's employment.

From the early 1970s, legislation that embodied new images of women and motherhood was much debated. The revival of feminism and its incorporation or co-optation by the state, for example in equal status policies, added some political status to women's issues. Of particular importance to women was the legalization of abortion on demand, the passing of equal status legislation, and increased state support for childcare. Placed on the political agenda by the new women's movement, the Scandinavian countries passed legislation on abortion in the mid-1970s. The political institutionalization of equal status policies from the late 1970s charged the government with the responsibility of developing national policies and programmes to promote equality between women and men. In Sweden and Denmark, equal status legislation aimed at ending the discrimination in the labour market. Being more comprehensive in approach, the Norwegian legislation was in principle to encompass all spheres of society. However, in none of the countries did equal status legislation interfere with the private sphere of the family (Leira 1991). The women's movement from early on criticized the Norwegian legislation for not being sufficiently bold in design. While equal status policies aimed to facilitate sexual desegregation of the labour market, they did not include measures to transform or transcend the gendered division of labour in society. The policies were strikingly one-way, emphasizing the importance of recruiting women to the labour market, but leaving the question of childcare (and other forms of care) unresolved.

In Scandinavia the welfare state is usually considered to have promoted mothers' employment. In a sense, this is correct. But although the expansion of the welfare state created a large number of jobs, particularly in public sector employment, these were not specifically made for women. Nor was a quota system favouring women introduced. However, new jobs spread in areas commonly identified as typically "women's work": in education, health, and social welfare, in lower and middle level administration, and often in local labour markets. Women were recruited to welfare state wage work, not as a planned mobilization, but rather because they represented the only available reserve. Moreover, this entry of women was highly selective. It did not represent a serious challenge to men's traditional jobs, which may be one reason why women's employment was not more strongly opposed (Leira 1992).

Two features of the work/family relationship in modern Scandinavia are particularly interesting in a discussion concerning processes of social integration and exclusion. Firstly, the dual-earner family is not a dual-carer family. In Norway, Sweden, and Denmark the dual-earner family emerged as the predominant family form, even among families with very young children. But while mothers became more equal to fathers as providers, the asymmetrical division of childcare and domestic work remained a part of everyday life. Over the last 20 to 30 years, Scandinavian fathers have become more involved in childcare. However, in no way does this process of change correspond to the massive movement of mothers from full-time housewifery to labour market participation. Moreover, in none of the Scandinavian countries has public investment in childcare and other forms of vitally necessary care made the caring by family members superfluous. While in the European Community the promotion of equal opportunities for women provides the basis for the Commission's proposals concerning childcare policy (Moss 1990), equal status legislation in Denmark, Norway, and Sweden has not treated day care for pre-school children as a crucial issue.

Secondly, Scandinavian women's high participation rates have not resulted in integration in the labour market on equal terms. On the contrary, the labour markets of Norway, Sweden, and Denmark show a pronounced segregation by sex. In the upper segments of public and private bureaucracies, in finance and banking, in the top levels of trade unions and academic institutions, the representation of women is not impressive. Vertical and horizontal segregation remain strong.

Gender differences in the mix of paid/unpaid work are striking. According to time-use studies, women on average work as long a day as do men, but get paid for a smaller proportion of their work. Compared to the EC member states (Denmark excepted), part-time work appears as more significant in Scandinavian women's labour market participation. Part-time work is important in Scandinavian women's wage work, in men's it is not. Women's use of part-time work is generally considered as one way of dealing with the incompatible demands of labour market and family organization. Among Norwegian employed mothers of young children, part-time work still predominates, though in recent years more have been working full-time (Ellingsæter 1987). Part-time work is also an important feature of Danish and Swedish mothers' labour market attachment (Leira 1992). According to Norwegian studies, fathers of young children have longer working hours than other participants in the labour market (Ellingsæter 1990).

The prevalence of part-time work represents a mixture of supply and demand interests. Some branches and sectors offer mainly part-time or seasonal work. Some employees opt for part-time work, as witnessed among female teachers and nurses. It should be noted, though, that among part-time workers, the majority work more than half time. Women's organizations have been divided on the issue of part-time work. Arguably, some money is better than no money, and a small foothold in the labour market preferable to total exclusion. Among part-time workers in Norway, the majority work more than the number of hours (or income level) required for obtaining access to social insurance and benefits (for details, see Bjurstrøm 1993).

To date, the integration of mothers in the labour market has not been completed. So far, the integrative processes have not seriously challenged fathers' labour market participation, although they have led to a modest improvement in fathers' participation in childcare and household chores. Welfare state childcare policies, as I shall go on to show, may to some extent be interpreted as substitutes for paternal involvement. However, these measures have not sufficed to place mothers on an equal footing with fathers when access to social benefits and entitlements is the issue.

New models of motherhood

In the 1970s, the Scandinavian welfare states, acknowledging the parental status of workers – mothers and fathers – passed legislation instituting or expanding the working parent's entitlements. For employed mothers the following measures are of special importance: legislation concerning entitlements to leave of absence in connection with i) pregnancy, parturition and the early part of the infant's life, and when a child is sick, and ii) the provision of high-quality, state-sponsored childcare. The entitlements to leave of absence, while retaining job security and with wage compensation, are important not only for the practical support offered to employed parents, but also as evidence of an interesting shift in the conceptualization of "the worker", such that the demands of social reproduction take priority over those of production.

In the following section I shall comment in some detail on the legislation concerning maternity, paternity, and parental leave and increasing public support for childcare. These measures represent a direct state response to the situation of working mothers (and fathers), and an intervention to modify the structural problems posed by the incompatible organization of the labour market and the family. In terms of the possibilities offered for the sharing of childcare, the schemes for parental leave are the more "radical". The public provision of high-quality childcare may facilitate mothers' employment and offer children a safe and stimulating environment; it does not necessarily imply a more equal division between parents as regards responsibility for childcare. The plurality of entitlements are in principle related to parenthood. However, fatherhood has up to now interfered very modestly, if at all, with the labour market activity of men. In this chapter, discussion is therefore restricted to the working mothers.

Leave of absence

Among the Scandinavian countries, Sweden has introduced the most comprehensive system of leave of absence in connection with parenthood, with a set of entitlements that has attracted international attention. The entitlements established in Norway are less generous, but compare well with what the majority of the EC member states offer (Moss 1990; Leira 1992).

From 1989, the Swedish entitlement to parental leave following the birth of a child was 450 week days with income replacement. The mother might use sixty of these days before parturition. The rest of the leave could be split between the parents as they wished. It could be used to reduce working hours, for example, but had to be spent before the child was eight years old. Income compensation amounting to 90 per cent of the wage up to a maximum level was given for the first 360 days; for the remaining period at a reduced rate (Åström 1990). To come into effect from 1993, Norway's maternity/parental leave is to cover 52 weeks at 80 per cent wage compensation, or 42 weeks at 100 per cent. Twelve of the weeks may be used before giving birth. Of the leave to be used after parturition, six weeks are reserved for the mother. The parents can share the remaining period as they wish. How to get fathers more involved has been much discussed. The present Norwegian Labour government has proposed a "fathers' quota", which implies reserving four weeks of the parental leave for the father. In addition, fathers in both countries are entitled to two weeks' paternity leave, either with wage compensation as in Sweden and Denmark, or without, as in Norway (Knudsen 1990: 27–30). (Appendix 2 presents the details for the EC member states.)

Norway and Sweden, but not Denmark, have institutionalized the right of employed parents to paid leave in order to care for a sick child. In Sweden the entitlement in 1990 was for 120 days per year, per child for children under the age of twelve (Åström 1990). Norwegian parents were each entitled to 10 days' leave and single parents to 20 days per year, in order to care for a sick child aged 0–10 years old. Generous leave of absence in connection with giving birth and to care for sick children, with wage compensation and job security, certainly facilitates the combination of employment and childcare. However, in both Norway and Sweden, there is concern that if only women make use of these entitlements, their opportunities in the labour market may be impeded (Leira 1987; Åström 1990).

The state and childcare

The introduction of public day care is often interpreted as necessitated by the labour market participation of mothers, which at 70–80 per cent is considerably higher than what is seen in most countries in western Europe. However, when mothers in large numbers headed for the labour markets, public funding of childcare services was modest. Sweden and Denmark from relatively early on supported mothers' economic activity and introduced large-scale public investments in childcare to that end. Norwegian policies, however, show considerable ambivalence, even resistance, to the promotion of mothers' employment.

The provision of high-quality day care is now commonly regarded as a national concern and is incorporated as a part of the welfare state service system in all the Scandinavian countries. The development of national programmes for early childhood education and care with the explicit aim of providing state-funded services for all children represented an intervention by the state in matters that were traditionally considered a family or private matter. Moreover, the provision of extra-familial childcare offered new opportunities for women for involvement outside the home. For both reasons, legislation concerning day care for children was politically controversial in Norway in the 1970s, although much less so in Sweden and Denmark. In Sweden, as in Denmark, state-sponsored day care for children was conceptualized not only as educationally advantageous, but also as a means of meeting the economy's demand for labour.

Ruggie (1984) has argued that opposition to state intervention in social reproduction may have been less pronounced in "social democratic" Sweden than in a "liberal" welfare state such as Britain, given that the public–

private split is essential to the liberal conceptualization of the state. In the social democratic welfare state, the public–private distinction does not hold the same importance. In fact, Scandinavian vernacular does not always make a clear distinction between the terms "state" and "society". Scandinavians often refer to the welfare state as a "folkhem", literally "the people's home". The metaphor identifies – perhaps naïvely – the welfare state as "people-friendly", made by the people for the people. (I shall not dwell upon the historical processes from which this thinking about the relationship between the welfare state and its citizens emerged. It does, however, call attention to a conceptualization of the "welfare state" that may be unique to Scandinavia.)

However, as mentioned above, Ruggie's analysis does not account for the differences within Scandinavia regarding welfare state policies towards working mothers. Although the social democratic traditions have been strong in all three countries, having made a profound impact on the welfare state development, family policies do also reflect the influence of different family and motherhood values (see also Siim 1987; Leira 1992). For example, Scandinavian policies concerning early childhood education and care appear to aim at different family forms, and, moreover, to be grounded in different images of the mother–child relationship and of the relationship of the welfare state to mothers.[3] Preference for the gender-differentiated nuclear family was more pronounced in Norway, where this family form has attracted stronger political and popular support than in the neighbouring countries (Leira 1992). Throughout the post-war period, the Christian People's Party, one of the Norwegian political parties represented in the Storting (Parliament), has strongly advocated traditional family ideology and the support of traditional family forms. In Norway, the institution of a "caring wage" for those who care for young children at home, or provide informal care for old people, has been much discussed, but has not so far been instituted.[4]

The scope of public support of day care services for pre-school children may also be interpreted as evidence of difference in policy approaches towards working mothers; see Table 4.2.

As shown in Table 4.2, the Scandinavian countries have rather different profiles when it comes to public investment in childcare.[5] In all the three countries, the proportion of children admitted to public day care has been on the increase. However, in none of the countries has supply sufficed to meet demand (Leira 1987, 1992; see also Dahlerup 1987; Åström 1990). Sweden and Denmark have a much better supply of day care services for pre-school children than has Norway, particularly in respect of the under-threes. The Nor-

Table 4.2 Children in publicly funded childcare, Denmark, Norway and Sweden, 1990. Per cent of all children in age group.[1]

Form of childcare	Denmark Age of child		Norway Age of child		Sweden Age of child	
	0–2	3–6	0–2	3–6	0–2	3–6
Family day care	28	7	1	1	10	18
Centre care (full-time)	19	51	9	31	19	46
Centre care (part-time)	0	8	2	26	–	15

Source: Yearbook of Nordic Statistics 1992, NORD 1992: pp. 316–17.
[1] These figures are not directly comparable because of differences in entitlements to maternity and parental leave, and some differences in registration procedures.

wegian case does not show an impressive welfare state involvement. In 1990, when more than 70 per cent of the Norwegian mothers of under-threes were in the workforce, only 12 per cent of the children in this age group had access to public child care.

A striking feature of Norwegian policies in the 1970s and 1980s is the lack of co-ordination between economic policies on the one hand, and family and social policies on the other. The provision of childcare was not conceptualized as an element in "women's policies", nor as part of equal status policies (Leira 1991). Denmark and Sweden gave employed mothers and student mothers priority in access to childcare services, and the provision of services was specifically oriented towards their needs (Leira 1987). In Norwegian policies, the concept of the employed mother who is both earner and carer made only a slight impact. Childcare policies were more exclusively oriented towards the socialization of the child. The universal ambition of day-care policies, that is, to provide publicly funded services for all children whose parents wished for them, was a long-term objective. The Norwegian public day-care system was not in practice developed to accommodate labour market demands, nor the working mothers' demands for childcare. Danish and Swedish policies in this field appear as comparatively similar, while Norway's policies have a different "profile". Denmark and Sweden, the two countries in which reproduction policies were more closely co-ordinated with labour market policies, were more successful with regard to meeting the employed mothers' demand for childcare than was Norway, where childcare policies were introduced as in the "best interests" of the child.

The "collectivization" of social reproduction, often considered a characteristic of the Scandinavian welfare state, seems to apply more to Sweden and Denmark than to Norway (Leira 1987). Swedish and Danish policies favoured the employment of women and of mothers, and provided public day care to that end. For Norway, I have argued that welfare state policies played a very modest part in facilitating the economic activity of mothers. The problems of working mothers resulting from the structural incompatibility of employment and family organization were largely defined as private problems to be solved on an individual basis. The lack of attention paid to the problems of the employed mothers made private and informal labour markets in childcare much more important in Norway than in Sweden and Denmark. Up to the late 1980s, informal child-minding in Norway provided more services for working mothers than did the state system (Leira 1987, 1992).

Thus, my analysis does not show the Norwegian welfare state as the principal driving force in introducing new models of motherhood. Welfare state expansion meant jobs for women. Norwegian economic policies in the 1970s and 1980s apparently assumed that labour was free and mobile. When mothers joined the labour market in large numbers, the incompatibility of labour market participation with responsibility for the care of children was not given much attention. The resolution of working mothers' problems was not provided by the welfare state, but was rather generated by women's everyday practices. Facing a non-interventionist state, Norwegian women enhanced their economic opportunities, acting as change agents in the demand of opportunities for part-time labour and in establishing informal labour markets in caring. An examination of the Scandinavian welfare state policies towards employed mothers shows that the notion of a "Scandinavian model" of welfare states needs qualification (Leira 1992).

A comparison of publicly funded childcare services across western Europe also modifies the image of the Scandinavian welfare states as particularly interventionist as regards early childhood education and care. Similarities and differences in public support of childcare for pre-school children in the EC member states are presented in a recent report from the European Commission's Childcare Network (Moss 1990; see also Pichault 1984; Thayer et al. 1988), while the Scandinavian provision of publicly funded childcare is analyzed by Leira (1992). Tables 4.3 and 4.4 present an overview of the proportion of pre-school children accommodated in publicly funded day care in the EC member states and Scandinavia.

In the late 1980s, Denmark and Sweden provided for a larger share of the under-threes than did any other state in this region. Norway's record is not impressive, but rather on a par with what is offered in the majority of EC member states. As has been pointed out by Scandinavian researchers, in its services for the under-threes, the "social democratic" Norwegian welfare

Table 4.3 Places in publicly funded childcare services as per cent of all children aged under three.[1]

Country	Children 0–3 years in publicly funded daycare (%)
Denmark	48
Sweden	31
France, Belgium, Iceland, Finland	20–29
Norway, Portugal, Italy	5–10
Germany (West), Netherlands, Luxembourg, Ireland, UK, Greece	2–4

Source for the Scandinavian countries: NORD 1991: 1.

[1] Source for the EC member states: Moss 1990. For details, See Appendix 3. Please observe that data refer to different years in the period 1986–9.

Table 4.4 Places in publicly funded daycare as per cent of all children form three to compulsory school age.[1]

Country	Children age three to school age (%)
France, Belgium	95+
Italy, Denmark	85
Germany (West), Greece, Spain, Sweden	60–70
Netherlands, Luxembourg, Ireland, (Finland), Iceland	50–59
Norway	49
UK, Portugal	35–40

[1] Sources: see Table 4.3 note. Because of different registration procedures, the figure for Denmark in Table 4.4 differs from the one shown in Table 4.2.

state is more similar to the "liberal" British state than to its social democratic neighbours (Borchorst & Siim 1987). Table 4.4 also shows that several EC member states compare favourably with the Scandinavian when it comes to the proportion of children aged from three to the beginning of formal schooling accommodated in publicly funded services.

The drawing of boundaries between state (local and central) and family responsibility as regards early childhood education and care implies not only a reconceptualization of childhood, but potentially also of motherhood. Across western Europe policy-making as well as public debate show that the political institutionalization of the concept of "the employed mother" is controversial in many countries. Policies towards working mothers – as providers in single-earner or dual-earner families – vary, but, as noted above, the problems imposed by the incompatibility of labour market and family organization is common to most countries. Few countries combine high levels of labour market participation among mothers and generous public funding for childcare provisions for the under-threes.

In the late 1980s and early 1990s, political conflict over state support for childcare has increased in Sweden and Norway. Although state support for families with young children is commonly accepted, political parties disagree over the content of support, whether as cash transfers or as provision of childcare services. Put differently, the question concerns whether the public purse should be used to facilitate the wage work of mothers with young children, or to support the families where the mothers remain at home. A high proportion of women in the national assemblies of the two countries has not produced broad, cross-party agreement on the interpretation of women's best interests when the organization of childcare is at issue (Leira 1992). Parties to the centre and right in Norway and Sweden in the 1990s advocate an increase in economic subsidies to families with young children, in order to promote parental care in the home, and to lessen the demand for public childcare. Although usually formulated in gender-neutral language regarding parental choice as to the form of care, this proposal favours gender-differentiated roles within the family. The social democratic parties and other parties to the left generally have argued more strongly in favour of women's rights to economic independence and in favour of state-funded childcare.

The gendering of citizenship

In retrospect, the post-war welfare state experiment in Scandinavia shows a period of profound change in mothers' relationships to work, family, and the state, but also a remarkable continuity in the structure of gender relationships. The sex of a person still makes a difference to opportunities and therefore to welfare outcomes, for example, in regard to citizenship entitlements. Processes of change are highlighted in the striking shift in women's and particularly mothers' economic activity. The concept of the employed mother, referring to wage workers who also have caring responsibilities, transcends the traditional division of labour by gender, and challenges the concept of labour as free and mobile. Evidence of change is also seen in women's participation in politics and public life.

As women enter some previously male-dominated arenas in the labour market and in politics, the significance of equality and difference takes on new meanings. Considering the Scandinavian commitment to equal status between women and men, the continuity of sex/gender as an organizing principle in society is quite striking, though it appears as less pronounced than in other forms of the welfare state. After almost 20 years of active welfare state intervention to promote gender equality, the division of labour between women and men remains a feature of the Scandinavian societies in the early 1990s. This is clearly evident when the distribution of paid and unpaid work is considered, or when the employment and family responsibilities of mothers and fathers are assessed together. As some of the work of social reproduction was collectivized, what was formerly unpaid work was transformed into paid employment. The sexual stereotyping of this kind of work proved resistant to change. Some of the "old" equal status issues are still important in the 1990s, for example, questions concerning the division of time, money, power, and care that remain unresolved. Violence by men in the family directed towards women and children persists. If equal status policies neglect the private sphere, gender inequality will remain.

This is not to say that the Scandinavian welfare state was not important for women. On the contrary, the welfare state set the general frame within which women developed new approaches to womanhood and motherhood. Welfare state reforms increased women's "property in their persons", to use Pateman's (1988a) formulation, in two fundamental ways: women gained control over fertility and biological reproduction, and women's economic dependence on individual men was substantially decreased. Both as wage workers in public sector employment, and as pensioners receiving a state-guaranteed income, women came to depend more on the state for their personal income. However, unless women behave like men do, they are not integrated into the welfare state on equal terms. Citizenship entitlements remain differentiated.

Pateman (1988b) has argued that classical political theory has regarded the concept of "women" as separate from "worker" or "citizen". From the beginning, the welfare state, which expanded on citizens' entitlements, denied women full citizenship. Even advanced welfare states, such as the Scandinavian ones, have not granted women full citizen status. Expansion of citizenship entitlements, even when formally gender-neutral, has different consequences for women and men. The importance accorded to waged work when access to entitlements is decided means that paid employment is the more important basis of citizenship. Hernes (1987, 1988) emphasizes that Scandinavian citizenship was modelled on the worker. The more generous and more institutionalized benefits are reserved for the citizen as wage worker while, in comparison, the citizen as carer is excluded from access to a series of welfare state benefits. The welfare state relationship to mothers, therefore, has to be analyzed within a general context that makes explicit the different approaches of the welfare state to employment and caring respectively.

Welfare state legislation and provisions define much of childcare as a private concern and the responsibility of family members. In everyday practice this means that the mother is most often the parent to whom the main responsibility for children's upbringing, nurturing, and caring is ascribed, even when the mother is also employed. An examination of the social rights of employed mothers shows processes of integration and exclusion in operation side by side. Of particular importance in excluding mothers from access to some social rights is the interplay of three processes, presumed in the welfare state basic design:

- The importance accorded to paid work over other forms of work
- The definition of essential parts of social reproduction as a private responsibility and private concern
- the division of labour by gender, which ascribes the greater part of time-consuming unpaid care to women.

Employed mothers who are both earners and carers experience and give evidence of a contradiction inherent in the welfare state structure: welfare state policies acknowledge the need of citizens for material provision as well as for care, yet more comprehensive and generous benefits are accorded to those who participate in wage work than do those who engage in vitally necessary but unpaid care. In interplay with the gendered division of labour, this form of differentiation produces an exclusion of carers from some of the social rights of citizenship, and a gendering of citizens' entitlements. The social construction of motherhood is set within this framework, which clearly expresses a preference for formal employment over informal care and thus for men's traditional activity patterns over women's.

The state and working mothers

Different forms of the welfare state have instituted different approaches to working mothers. The integration of working mothers as citizens also varies. As I have shown, contrary to popular belief, social reproduction is not completely "collectivized" in Scandinavia. A considerable share of the socially useful and vitally necessary care for the very young and old persons remains in the private sphere of the family. In fact, state-funded services are sometimes modest. Conceptualizations such as "the public family" (Hernes 1984; Wolfe 1989), exaggerate the image of an interventionist welfare state and underplay the importance of individual management and responsibility in the provision of everyday care.

The inequalities witnessed in employed mothers' and fathers' parental responsibilities are part of the processes that generate a gendering of access to citizenship entitlements and an exclusion of women from certain kinds of entitlements. This situation is not unique to Scandinavia. Processes excluding women from some of the social rights of citizenship may well be more characteristic of "liberal" and "conservative" welfare states as opposed to the "social democratic" welfare state. More detailed examinations are necessary if we are to get a better picture of the ways in which new forms of mother/ father/market/state relationships function in different welfare states. Moreover, analyses of welfare state policies need the supplement of studies of everyday life (Leira 1987, 1992).

As my analysis also shows, introducing generous systems of leave of absence and investing in the funding of extra-familial childcare, the social democratic welfare states in Scandinavia have made considerable efforts to bridge the gap between the demands of the market for labour and the demands of children for care. Providing entitlements to maternity and parental leave and funding of childcare services, welfare state policies improved the situation of working mothers and contributed to an equalization of the situation of women and men as regards labour market participation. In several respects, the Scandinavian welfare states compare well with other welfare states when it comes to meeting the demands of working mothers and fathers.

Notes

1. This chapter is based on a paper prepared for the BSA 1992 conference, "A New Europe?". I much appreciated the discussion following my presentation. I am grateful to Joan Acker, Phil Brown, Anne Lise Ellingsæter, Janet Finch, and Mariken Vaa for comments on an earlier version, and to the Norwegian Research Council for Applied Social Science (NORAS) and the Institute for Social Research for grants that supported the research.

2. This chapter does not deal with all dimensions of welfare state motherhood, nor with all of the consequences of welfare state policies experienced by mothers across class and ethnic and socio-cultural background. I do not discuss the different experiences of single and married mothers, and barely touch on the biological aspects

or emotional qualities of the motherhood experience. I aim at clarifying the welfare state reconstruction of motherhood as manifested in two basic aspects, economic provision and primary socialization and care.

In my book, *Welfare states and working mothers. The Scandinavian experience*, Cambridge University Press 1992, I analyze the relationship between the welfare states and working mothers in greater detail.

3. Norway, alone among the Scandinavian countries, as part of the National Insurance Scheme offers a state-guaranteed income for single providers. Originally legislation was instituted to deal with the severe problems of single mothers. Even if the sum is far from generous, it does give single parents, of whom 90 per cent are women, an opportunity to opt out of employment while their children are very young. Sweden, on the other hand, like Denmark, has assumed that single mothers' problems are better solved through the labour market participation of mothers and the provision of state-funded childcare. Neither of these approaches takes into account, however, that single mothers are workers *and* carers. Measures that aim at supporting only one of these activities tend to handicap women in a longer-term perspective.

4. Since 1982, Sweden has offered the right to earn supplementary pension for persons caring for children under the age of three (SCB 1990). Since 1992, a change in the Norwegian National Insurance Act has enabled unpaid carers to earn entitlements to supplementary pension if they care for children under seven, or for old, sick, or handicapped people not in institutional care.

5. In this chapter I do not discuss the merits of different forms of childcare, I do not go into the professionalization of childcare, and I do not consider the important questions concerning the effects on children and childhood of different regimes.

References

Allardt, E. 1986. Representative government in a bureaucratic age. In *Norden – The passion for equality*, S. Graubard (ed.). Oslo: Norwegian University Press.

Åström, G. 1990. Föräldraförsäkring och vårdnadsbidrag. *Kvinnovetenskapligt tidsskrift* **11**, 37–48.

Bjurstrøm, H. I. 1993. *Deltidsansattes rettigheter. En komparativ studie av Danmark, Norge Storbritannia og Tyskland*. Oslo: Institute for Social Research.

Borchorst, A. & B. Siim 1987. Women and the advanced welfare state. A new kind of patriarchal power. In *Women and the state*, A. S. Sassoon (ed.). London: Hutchinson.

Dahlerup, D. 1987. Confusing concepts – confusing reality: a theoretical discussion of the patriarchal state. In *Women and the state*, A. S. Sassoon (ed.). London: Hutchinson.

Ellingsaeter, A. L. 1987. Ulikhet i arbeidstidsmønstre. In NOU 1987: 9b Vedlegg til arbeidstidsutvalgets innstilling.

Ellingsaeter, A. L. 1990. *Fathers working long hours. Trends, causes and consequences*. Working paper 2. Oslo: Institute for Social Research.

Esping-Andersen, G. & W. Korpi 1987. From poor relief to institutional welfare states: the development of Scandinavian social policy. In *The Scandinavian model: welfare states and welfare research,* R. Erikson et al. (eds). New York: M. E. Sharpe.

Esping-Andersen, G. 1990. *The three worlds of welfare capitalism.* Cambridge: Polity.

Equal Status Council 1990. *Minifacts on equal rights.* Oslo.

Hernes, H. M. 1984. Women and the welfare state. The transition from private to public dependence. In *Patriarchy in a welfare society,* H. Holter (ed.). Oslo: Universitetsforlaget.

Hernes, H. M. 1987. *Welfare state and woman power.* Oslo: Norwegian University Press.

Hernes, H. M. 1988. Scandinavian citizenship. *Acta Sociologica* **31**, 199–215.

Knudsen, R. 1990. *Familieydelser i Norden 1989. Tekniske rapporter 52.* Stockholm: Nordisk statistisk sekretariat.

Leira, A. 1987. *Day care for children in Denmark, Norway and Sweden.* Research report 5/87. Oslo: Institutt for samfunnsforskning.

Leira, A. 1990. Coping with care. In *Gender and caring. Work and welfare in Britain and Scandinavia,* C. Ungerson (ed.). London: Harvester Wheatsheaf.

Leira, A. 1991. Mor og far – stat og marked. Om den yrkesaktive mor og yngelpleien. In *Nye kvinner – nye menn,* R. Haukaa (ed.). Oslo: AdNotam.

Leira, A. 1992. *Welfare states and working mothers. The Scandinavian experience.* Cambridge: Cambridge University Press.

Marshall, T. H. 1965. *Class, citizenship, and social development.* New York: Anchor Books.

Moss, P. 1990. *Childcare in the European Communities 1985–1990.* Women of Europe Supplements, 31. Brussels: Commission of the European Communities.

Myrdal, A. & V. Klein 1957. *Women's two roles.* London: Routledge & Kegan Paul.

Pateman, C. 1988a. The patriarchal welfare state. In *Democracy and the welfare state,* A. Gutman (ed.). Princeton: Princeton University Press.

Pateman, C. 1988b. *The sexual contract.* Cambridge: Polity.

Pichault, C. 1984. *Day-care facilities and services for children under the age of three in the European Community.* Luxembourg: Office for Official Publications of the European Communities.

Ruggie, M. 1984. *The state and working women.* Princeton: Princeton University Press.

Statistiska Centralbyrån (SCB) 1990. *På tal om kvinnor och män.* Stockholm: SCB.

Siim, B. 1987. The Scandinavian welfare states. Towards sexual equality or a new kind of male domination? *Acta Sociologica* **30**, 255–270.

Thayer, P. P. et al. 1988. *Forms of childcare.* Strasbourg: Council of Europe.

Wilensky, H. L. & C. N. Lebeaux 1958. *Industrial society and social welfare.* New York: The Free Press.

Wolfe, A. 1989. *Whose keeper? Social science and moral obligation.* Berkeley: University of California Press.

Yearbook of Nordic Statistics 1992. Stockholm: NORD:1.

Appendix

Table 1 Parental employment, 1988.

	Employed – women with child under 10 (%)		Employed – men with child under 10 (%)		Employed – women aged 20–39, without children (%)		Change in percentage employed, 1985–88 – women with child under 10		Unemployed – women with child under 10 (%)	Unemployed – men with child under 10 (%)
Germany	38%	(21%)	94%	(1%)	75%	(15%)	+ 2.6%	(+2.5%)	6%	3%
France	56%	(16%)	93%	(1%)	75%	(11%)	+1.3%	(+1.9%)	10%	5%
Italy	42%	(5%)	95%	(2%)	55%	(4%)	+3.6%	(+0.7%)	8%	3%
Netherlands	32%	(27%)	91%	(9%)	68%	(30%)	+8.2%	(+7.7%)	8%	5%
Belgium	54%	(16%)	92%	(1%)	68%	(13%)	+2.8%	(+2.4%)	12%	5%
Luxembourg	38%	(10%)	98%	(–)	69%	(5%)	+3.7%	(+0.6%)	2%	1%
United Kingdom	46%	(32%)	88%	(1%)	83%	(20%)	+7.5%	(+6%)	8%	8%
Ireland	23%	(7%)	79%	(1%)	67%	(6%)	+5.1%	(+1.5%)	8%	17%
Denmark	79%	(32%)	95%	(2%)	79%	(6%)	+2.6%	(−1.5%)	8%	3%
Greece	41%	(5%)	95%	(1%)	52%	(3%)	+3.8%	(−0.2%)	6%	3%
Portugal	62%	(4%)	95%	(1%)	69%	(6%)	No information		6%	2%
Spain	28%	(4%)	89%	(1%)	44%	(5%)	No information		10%	8%
European Community	44%	(17%)	92%	(2%)	71%	(13%)	No information		8%	5%

Key: figures in bracket = percentage employed part-time.
Source: P. Moss 1990. *Childcare in the European Communities 1985–1990. Women of Europe Supplements*, 31. Brussels: Commission of the European Communities, p. 6.

Table 2 Maternity and parental leave.

	Maternity leave	Parental leave
Germany	6 weeks before birth, 8 weeks after (12 for multiple births) 100% of earnings	18 months. Low flat-rate payment for 6 months; payment then depends on family income, so higher-income family gets less.
France	6 weeks before birth, 10 weeks after (longer for third+ and multiple births). 84% of earnings.	Until child is 3. No payment unless 3 or more children; then low, flat-rate payment.
Italy	2 months before birth, 3 months after. 80% of earnings.	6 months. 30% of earnings
Belgium	14 weeks altogether; 8 weeks must be taken after birth, the other 6 weeks can be taken before or after. 75% of earnings (82% for first month).	None, but workers can take leave for family or personal reasons (see national report).
Netherlands	16 weeks altogether; 4–6 weeks can be taken before birth, 10–12 weeks after, 100% of earnings	None, but government proposal for part-time leave has been made.
Luxembourg	6 weeks before birth, 8 weeks after (12 for multiple births). 100% of earnings.	None.
United Kingdom	11 weeks before birth, 29 weeks after. 90% of earnings for 6 weeks, low flat-rate payment for 12 weeks, no payment for remaining weeks.	None.
Ireland	14 weeks altogether; 4 weeks must be taken before birth, 4 weeks must be taken after, and the other 6 weeks can be taken before or after. 70% of earnings (tax free). Mothers can request additional 4 weeks' unpaid leave.	None.
Denmark	4 weeks before birth, 14 weeks after. 90% of earnings (up to a maximum level).	10 weeks. 90% of earnings (up to maximum level).
Greece	16 weeks, to be taken before or after birth. 100% of earnings. 90 days altogether; 3 months per parent. Unpaid.	
Portugal	60 days must be taken after birth, and the other 30 days can be taken before or after. 100% of earnings.	24 months. Unpaid.
Spain	16 weeks altogether; 10 weeks must be taken after birth, and the other 6 weeks can be taken before or after. 75% of earnings.	12 months. Unpaid.

Source: P. Moss 1990. *Childcare in the European Communities 1985–1990*. Women of Europe Supplements, 31. Brussels: Commission of the European Communities, p. 8.

Table 3 Places in publicly funded childcare services as percentage of all children in the age group.

	Date to which data refer	For children under 3	For children from 3 to compulsory school age	Age when compulsory schooling begins	Length of school day (including midday break)	Outside school hours care for primary school children
Germany	1987	3%	65–70%	6–7 years	4–5 hours (a)	4%
France	1988	20%	95%+	6 years	8 hours	?
Italy	1986	5%	85%+	6 years	4 hours	?
Netherlands	1989	2%	50–55%	5 years	6–7 hours	1%
Belgium	1988	20%	95%+	6 years	7 hours	?
Luxembourg	1989	2%	55–60%	5 years	4–8 hours (a)	1%
United Kingdom	1988	2%	35–40%	5 years	6½ hours	(–)
Ireland	1988	2%	55%	6 years	4½–6½ hours (b)	(–)
Denmark	1989	48%	85%	7 years	3–5½ hours (a,b)	29%
Greece	1988	4%	65–70%	5½ years	4–5 hours (b)	(–)
Portugal	1988	6%	35%	6 years	6½ hours	6%
Spain	1988	?	65–70%	6 years	8 hours	(–)

Source: P. Moss 1990. *Childcare in the European Communities 1985–1990. Women of Europe Supplements*, 31. Brussels: Commission of the European Communities, p. 10.

NB. This table should be read in conjunction with the national reports, which contain important qualifications and explanations. The table shows the number of places in publicly funded services as a percentage of the child population; the percentage of children attending may be higher because some places are used on a part-time basis. Provision at playgroups in the Netherlands has not been included, although 10% of children under 3 and 25% of children aged 3–4 attend, and most playgroups receive public funds. Average hours of attendance – 5–6 hours per week – are so much shorter than for other services, that it would be difficult and potentially misleading to include them on the same basis as other services; however, playgroups should not be forgotten when considering publicly funded provision in the Netherlands.

Key: ? = no information; (–) = less than 0.5%; (a) = school hours vary from day to day; (b) = school hours increase as children get older.

Chapter 5

Some issues of race, ethnicity and nationalism in the "New Europe": rethinking social paradigms

Sheila Allen & Marie Macey

Introduction

The momentous political change in central and eastern Europe and the former Soviet Union from 1989 onwards and the less dramatic, but none-theless significant, changes taking place in western Europe associated with the completion of the Single European Market pose problems and challenges as to how these are to be analyzed and interpreted sociologically.[1] This chapter focuses on these problems and challenges in a number of ways. First, it examines the analyses of race and ethnic relations that have developed in Britain during the past 30 years. Secondly, it looks at the concepts of nation and nationalism and their relationship to ethnicity and the notion of ethnic origin. Thirdly, it raises the issue of gender as it relates to race, ethnicity, and nation, an aspect of social organization rarely mentioned in the current debates. Fourthly, it examines the role of religion in race and ethnic relations and the development of nationalism.

In each of these sections the emphasis will be on a discussion of sociological paradigms and the degree to which they may serve as a guide to coherent analyses of the apparently contradictory social forces and processes currently at work, as well as their inadequacies in these respects. Empirical evidence will draw on sociological and historical sources to illustrate the complexities of the issues being examined. Each of the matters we discuss is associated with strong sentiments that are expressed in a variety of forms in many parts of contemporary Europe. These range from the racialized and nationalist discourses of governments, political parties, military command-ers, and irregulars to the actual violence of physical assault, murder, and civil war. These problems are not confined to Europe, but are to be found in many areas of Africa, Asia and the Middle East. While acknowledging the significance of the global aspects of apparently similar phenomena, this chapter focuses largely on Europe.

Race and ethnic relations

The study of race and ethnic relations by sociologists in Britain is, in the main, a post Second World War phenomenon. Earlier work on national character and anti-Semitism (Ginsberg 1941, 1943) had raised these issues in a general way, drawing on insights from social psychology, psychoanalysis, social philosophy, and social and economic history. With a few notable exceptions (Little 1948; Richmond 1954; Banton 1955 1959; Freedman 1955; Collins 1957), it was not until the early 1960s that sociologists gradually began to give attention to race relations. By 1969, sufficient work had been undertaken for the annual conference of the British Sociological Association to take race relations as its theme. In organizing and then editing papers from the conference, Zubaida (1970) stressed the importance of the distinction between the social problem and sociological problem approaches to race relations. Over 20 years later this distinction is not always made, even by social scientists, including sociologists. Consequently, there is still evidence of an acceptance by researchers of "prevailing social and ideological designations of groups" that are sociologically inadequate. Ambivalence and confusion surround the vocabularies in current use, and there is no simple solution that can satisfy the politics of language and the need for analytical clarity. The use of the term "black" to refer to all people who share a common experience of racial discrimination is a case in point.[2] In addition to the conceptual and analytical confusion caused by its use as an all-embracing category, it is also used in a highly restrictive manner. Dummett comments:

> The term "black" is *de rigeur* in some circles for all victims of discrimination: the use of this term can lead, on the one hand, to calling the Chinese black, and, on the other, to denying that anyone who is not at least in part of African or Asian descent could be the victim of racial discrimination. (Dummett 1991: 172)

Zubaida emphasized the need for those groups and relationships designated as racial or ethnic to be analyzed within broader sociological theories. Theory was seen as contributing to "showing the way in which different components of structure are related together, and the way in which social groups are located within this totality" (1970: 1). The study of the interplay of political, economic, and ideological forces, in both contemporary and past societies, is essential to the analysis of race relations, whether at the interpersonal, community, national, or international levels. The necessity of integrating race relations into these broader theoretical concerns was well understood in the late 1960s by some sociologists. Though there was no uniformity of theoretical positions, there was an acceptance that theory was a crucial element in the analysis of social relationships, which were increasingly being defined in racial terms (Banton 1967, 1970; Rex 1970a, 1970b, 1973; Allen 1971; Cohen 1974). Discussing the role of the sociologist Bottomore insisted that:

> if the sociologist has a highly important intellectual role as a critic of society . . . He [sic] is not simply a critic, but a sociological critic; and the quality of his criticism will depend upon the quality of his understanding of the institutions and movements in present day and past societies . . . he has a duty to resist being swept off his feet by every passing wind of ideology. (Bottomore 1970: xii–xiii)

That the promise of the late 1960s was not fully realized is obvious from much of the current literature on both race and ethnicity as well as on sociological theory. There are many reasons why this is the case, and it is possible to refer here to only some of them. One, perhaps not the most significant, is the size of the task in relation to the resources available; there are few social scientists working in the field, a lack of research funding and, increasingly, a lack of time available.[3] Another is that despite the increasing attention paid to theory and theorizing in sociology from the mid-1960s, there was little attempt to integrate race and ethnic relations as part of it (Lockwood 1970; Parkin 1978). On a different plane there were other reasons, such as the politicizing of the area around such questions as who could legitimately define the issues to be researched, what methods and concepts were appropriate to pursuing them, and who was seen as having the right to undertake the work (Bourne 1980; Cherns 1987). At its most extreme, questions were (and are) raised about whether there is any value in academic work, that is in theory building and research carried out by academics, particularly sociologists. Issues that had emerged in confrontational debates in academia and in actual social conflict in the United States in the late 1960s became something of a battleground in Britain in the 1970s and 1980s, but with some marked differences. There was a much lower level of resources, of people or time, in British academia to deal adequately in intellectual terms with the questions being posed, some of which were, and remain, integral to social science theory and method. Nothing, for instance, to our knowledge, was produced in Britain to compare with the clarity and directness with which Genovese (1971) took up the challenges facing social science researchers in race and ethnic relations. It is not possible to examine all of these, and at some risk of simplifying the range of positions that were, and are, adopted in Britain we discuss only a few points that continue to be found, frequently implicitly, in much teaching, research, and writing.

Genovese tackled the intellectual, professional, and political dimensions of the attacks coming at that time from those who lionized relevance, political engagement, and organization rather than historical scholarship, writing, and teaching, and from those who deplored history being written by historians whom they deemed as outsiders. As a white American of Italian descent and a Marxist historian of slave societies, including the American South, he set his own work within the context of his socialist beliefs and his conceptions of historical research. He argued that "ideologically motivated history is bad history and ultimately reactionary politics"; that while pure scholarship and value-free social science were impossible, this did not free scholars from "the responsibility to struggle for maximum objectivity" (4). On the insider/outsider debates (see Merton 1972), Genovese remarks on the irony of an earlier presidential address to the American Historical Association in which the influx of non-WASP historians into the profession was bemoaned: "After all, how could Jews, Italians, and Irishmen possibly understand an American culture that was so profoundly Anglo-Saxon and Teutonic?" (viii). His conclusion from the "insider" arguments was that he was qualified to write only the history of Italian immigration, of which he knew nothing.

> I prefer, however, to wait until I can convince a black graduate student to undertake that task; he will, I think, do it in a more detached way than I, although, not having been raised on pasta, well-wrapped fig trees, and vendettas, he will certainly miss some important parts of the culture.   (Genovese 1971: viii)

His essays on the black experience were "consciously written from the outside" and their value "must rest precisely on the possibilities and in fact the necessity for writing the history of any people both from within and without" (ix). Such views were not only ignored by many, but towards the end of the 1970s and for much of the 1980s were increasingly unpopular. A form of intellectual paralysis was evident in Britain.

In a context of the increasing racialization of policies and of popular discourses, there was a polarization of approaches rather than debates. The pressures multiplied to narrow not only the field of enquiry and the questions to be raised, but the concepts and methods to be employed. It was not surprising that in such a politically charged environment some narrowing of intellectual endeavour ensued. Establishing the facts of racial inequality in Britain, and understanding the production and maintenance of these through the processes of institutionalized racism, was an important theoretical and analytical development (see Williams 1985; Loughlin 1986; Troyna & Williams 1986). The concept of institutionalized racism was developed first in the United States in the context of relations between African-Americans and white Americans. Briefly, it was a move away from explanations of social action and behaviour in terms of prejudice on the part of individual actors towards an analysis of the rules of normal, routine ways of acting in institutional contexts. It relied for explanation more on outcomes than intent, avoiding the attribution of motives and examining consequences instead. It explained the patterning of behaviour that led to the system where some categories were given priority over others in access to goods and services, to privilege and status, and in general to forms of exploitation and oppression. It identified a major social dimension in both the United States and in Britain, but in the latter was not given the recognition the authorities accorded to it in the former (National Advisory Commission 1968; Scarman 1981). The Gifford Report came much closer to identifying institutionalized racism as a major factor in British society, but this was an independent enquiry commissioned by the London Borough of Haringey following the Home Office's refusal to establish an official enquiry (1986).

The concept of institutionalized racism was not unproblematic. It raised the sociological questions of agency and structure and the inter-relationship between them. The span of individual discretion within the rules of any particular organization or social situation is a case in point. Discretion allows the highly prejudiced and those of lesser or no prejudice to act in opposite ways in applying the rules, but individuals cannot simply develop rules in an ad hoc way. Rules for social conduct are inherited from the past and constrain as well as facilitate behaviour. They may be compatible one with another as part of a relatively unified system, or there may be inconsistencies and contradictions between them. The task of identifying, describing, and analysing institutional racism as a pervasive social dimension throughout British social structure and culture required a recognition of the distinction between a racially prejudiced individual and institutionalized rules with racist consequences. The subsequent adoption in many discourses of the all-encompassing term "racism" fails to make this distinction.

The 1970s was an important decade for the development of theoretical positions in relation to migrant labour and around the articulation of race and class. Some of these dealt with groups of diverse origins, though most remained largely within a problematic of race relations designated by skin colour (Castles & Kosack 1973; Allen & Smith 1974; Miles 1982). There was an increased use of the terms ethnicity, ethnic relations, and ethnic minorities, but again these focused largely on skin colour, with ethnic and racial frequently elided within the discussion. The latter was due in part to the political designation in Britain of *black* groups as *ethnic* minorities, supplanting to some extent the earlier designation of all black people as *immigrants* – a manifestly absurd notion, but a powerful and pervasive one nonetheless. The relations of class and race were largely theorized within either Marxist/neo-Marxist or Weberian modes. These, it was claimed, had moved from a confrontational to a fruitful dialogue by the mid-1980s (Rex & Mason 1986). There remained, however, the question of whether racial and ethnic conflicts were to be theorized as interior to class location, class conflict, and struggle or as standing in a relationship of relative autonomy.

So far the development of adequate general paradigms has eluded social scientists, although there has been a considerable amount of work at the level of middle-range theorizing. There remains debate, controversy, and divergence among scholars in Britain, at times bitterly disputatious and accompanied by not a little ideological posturing. However, by the late 1980s the diversity of approaches was becoming more clearly stated, if not integrated (Miles 1980, 1984; Mason 1982; Rex & Mason 1986; Husband 1987a, 1987b; Solomos 1989). Moreover other issues were becoming central, and it was harder to sustain a narrow designation of race relations in terms of black and white, or a class analysis resting on restricted conceptions of the labour market given the imminence of closer western European integration. Before we turn to these issues and their implications for analyses of the interrelations among race, ethnicity, nationalism and religion, we wish to consider a major absence in most of the race relations literature over the period we have been discussing, that of gender.

What happened to the women?

It is not surprising that the sociology of race and ethnic relations failed to address the social divisions of gender, as mainstream sociology had paid little attention to these. Despite the growing literature on gender studies from the 1970s onwards there is a marked tendency to treat these as a sub-discipline rather than as centrally re-shaping sociology itself (see Maynard 1990 for a review of the trends and the literature). During the 1980s a critique of white mainstream feminism was developed by black women, who saw it as denying their existence. They argued not only for greater visibility, but for a recognition of the impact of racism on relations between women and between the genders (Davis 1981; Carby 1982; Hooks 1982, 1984; Amos & Parmar 1984). Attempts to theorize the relations of race and gender were undertaken, both in the United States and Britain, in the context of debates between feminists, and in some cases class divisions were also included (Joseph & Lewis 1981; Anthias & Yuval-Davis 1983; Bourne 1983; Hooks 1984; Barrett & McIntosh 1985; Bhavnani & Coulson 1986; Allen 1987; Ramazanoglu 1989; Anthias 1991). In addition there was a concern to formulate methodological approaches more in keeping with the insights and propositions arising from both empirical and theoretical work on women and gender (Roberts 1981; Finch 1984; Scott 1984; Cook & Fonow 1986; Harding 1987). There is no agreed position among feminist scholars on the alternatives put forward, and the debate continues in the journals (see for example Gelsthorpe 1992; Hammersley 1992; Ramazanoglu 1992).

Two issues arise out of the feminist literature that are of particular relevance for this chapter. One is the validity of personal experience in understanding the social world, and the other concerns the legitimacy of researching those who differ from oneself. Taking up the latter concern, we need only note here that there is a danger of infinite regression. Those who argue that only women (or black women, or working-class black women, or . . .) can carry out feminist/anti-racist/class-grounded research appear to conflate the need to ensure that differing experiences and perspectives are brought to bear on social science investigations and knowledge production with privileging particularistic truths. It is one thing to recognize that researchers are gendered, class located and racialized/ethnicized and as a consequence have diverse experiences, work with different assumptions, and may take different standpoints in their work (Harding 1987; Smith 1988). It is quite another to argue that any one position/characteristic validates, or conversely invalidates, knowledge or understanding. Standpoints are not static or fixed, but subject to change, through external events and reflexive processes, and in complex societies individuals (including researchers) occupy multidimensional statuses. The neglect of women and gender divisions in social science research, including the field of race and ethnic relations, has

114

produced very partial understandings of the social world; the theorizing was inadequate and much empirical work seriously flawed. Pointing this out has been one of the major contributions of feminist researchers.

A further contribution has been the opening up of the question of the status of personal experience as relevant to the understanding of the social world. From a researcher's viewpoint, what is at issue is how personal experience informs the research process, the assumptions made, the questions to be investigated, the methods used, and the knowledge produced. This is not a new problem, but it is one with which feminist scholars have engaged over several years and continue to do so. While recognizing the validity of the meaning of personal experience to every individual, and the insights this provides for researchers, the limitations of individual experience for understanding and explaining the social has also to be taken into account. The extreme position that privileges personal experience as the only valid knowledge, the only way of knowing and understanding, the only reality, is clearly absurd. This position may arise from the neglect of women's experience, and particularly from the invisibility of black, migrant, minority women in much of the literature of race and ethnic relations. In this context the stress on personal experience is understandable, but nonetheless it is inadequate.

During the 1980s, there was an increase in descriptive accounts of the situations and experiences of black women in Britain (see, for instance, Bryan et al. 1985; James 1985). At the same time there was increasing fragmentation in the literature on women in Britain as the diversity of experience in negotiating everyday life and the differences of structural location were recognized and celebrated. The commonalities shared by women of social, political, and economic marginality and their exposure to violence in the family, the household, and on the streets were researched and written about.[4] Since no clear theoretical articulation of the divisions of gender, class, race, and ethnicity was developed, there could be no clarification of the specificities of the different structuring of inequalities arising from these divisions; thus the social processes in which they were embedded were simply described but not theorized. This development was in contrast to the argument put forward at the end of the 1970s by three socialist feminists who grappled with a new approach to understanding theory, consciousness, and political organization (Rowbotham et al. 1979). Their concern was with the traditions of the male left, which had failed to listen to the insights and demands of socialist feminist women. Their concerns were therefore based within a different problematic, but one relevant to the issues of feminist social scientists researching personal experience and the fragmentation this

115

induced. However much their ideas may appear outdated and irrelevant in the context of changes in western, central and eastern Europe, their attempt to overcome the fragmentation is, we would argue, more relevant today than it was in the late 1970s,[5] as these changes have led to a retreat into other concerns where nationality, ethnicity, and religious affiliation are mobilized to create particularistic spaces against collectively held rights as citizens. It is to these issues that we now turn.

Ethnicity and nationalism

Discourses on nationalism and ethnicity, at times elided into ethno-nationalism, emerged in the 1970s and 1980s running in parallel with developments in race relations theories (Gellner 1983; Smith 1986, 1988). In his discussion of nationalism and myth, Smith sets out the dominant western conception of nations as modern social phenomena associated with industrialization. However, he maintains that:

> there is another conception of the nation which harmonises less well with western modernity. It sees nations as named human populations claiming a common ancestry, a demotic solidarity, common customs and vernaculars, and a common native history. Genealogy, demography, traditional culture and history, furnish the main resources for an ethnic view of the formation of nations.
>
> (Smith 1986: 9)

Smith argues that by including both concepts of the nation, we gain a "more comprehensive and sharper understanding of the nature and formation of nations and the role of nationalism in the process". This does not involve an acceptance of "primordialist" notions of nationality or ethnicity or the nationalist myth, but does allow us to explain "the durability and widespread appeal of nations, and the intensity of ethnic aspirations today" (1988: 10).

Among those studying race and ethnic relations in Britain, few took part in, or referred to, these discourses. Their paths crossed occasionally with regard to ethnicity and ethnic relations. Primordial and instrumental approaches were discussed in attempts to define and explain boundaries between groups and quasi-groups, not only labelled for administrative or classificatory purposes as ethnic, but where there was a combination of (real or imagined) common origins giving rise to some shared activities based on characteristics such as language, religion, a territorial homeland and a (real or imagined) common culture (Rex & Mason 1986; Douglass 1988). As ethnicity, however defined, always implies one or more other ethnicities, a crucial dimension of the analysis is a consideration of power relations and of ethnicity as a resource. The permeability of ethnic boundaries and the fluidity of ethnic group content are also important factors requiring analysis (Barth 1969; Wallman 1986), as is the resource aspect of ethnicity (Afshar 1989; Modood 1989; Lutz 1991). It should be noted that ethnicity is frequently used as a resource less in the interests of the members of an ethnic group than to serve the interests of those with power.

Stratification of ethnic groupings has been seen in Britain largely in terms of the minority status of black groups. The intersecting dimension of ethnic and class relations has been almost totally conceptualized as a black/white phenomenon, with a neglect of the salience of ethnic differentiation within both. This elision of ethnicity and skin colour, together with the all-encompassing use of the term "racism" and its restriction to black–white relations, has already been remarked on above. Set in a wider European context, it becomes clear that they are not just examples of particularistic uses of terminology, but are particularistic conceptions of divisions and boundaries shot through with confusion. Across Europe there are many minorities who are discriminated against in various ways. These include those of African, Asian, and Caribbean descent, religious minorities, especially Jews and Muslims, but also Christians, national minorities, migrants and their children, and gypsies. The criteria that define minorities are not necessarily discrete, so that religion, nationality, and skin colour may combine to define minority status (for a fuller discussion see Allen & Macey 1990; Macey 1992).

Rarely has the issue of nation and nationalism been located within the debates on race and ethnic relations. For instance, Barker (1981) does not refer to nationalism at all, and in the Rex & Mason collection there is only a brief mention of it, and that by an American scholar (Yinger 1986). Discussions of nation and nationalism have largely concentrated on the development of a British or an English nationalism since the 1950s and 1960s as an exclusionary force to deny the Black British a national (British/English) identity and equality of rights as British citizens (Gilroy 1987; Solomos 1989). Miles has taken a longer and more comparative historical view to examine the relation of nationalism and racism in the British context (1987a, 1987b). He does not regard them as independent ideologies, but argues that their formal characteristics overlap and contrast, the substantial difference being that the ideology of nationalism has a specified political objective (national self-determination) that racist ideologies lack. He states:

> My historical argument is that English nationalism is particularly
> dependent on and constructed by an idea of "race" with the result
> that English nationalism encapsulates racism. (Miles 1987a: 38)

Though he refers to historical sources and points to the supposed (Anglo) Saxon origins of the English nation and English nationalism, he frequently brackets English with British. He ignores the differences between nation and state, and elides the two.

It is necessary to examine the differences between nation and state. The intermeshing of these in popular language as ideological constructions and in the day-to-day lives of Scots, Welsh, English, and Irish requires historical and contemporary specification. These issues are being raised in constitutional terms in Britain, and the (re)emergence of nationalism following changes in central and eastern Europe and the former Soviet Union, together with the changes in western Europe, challenge sociologists to bring together the many discourses that up till now have run in parallel. The conflation of nation and state is rejected by many sociologists who argue that they refer to quite different social relationships. The British state is "one of the most centralised and unitary states in post 1945 Europe" (McCrone 1992), yet it is multinational, formed by the conquest of Wales, Scotland, and Ireland in the name of the English monarchy and maintained by legal and political union embodied in the parliament at Westminster.[6] The state has jurisdiction over territory, its laws are paramount, and it holds a monopoly of legitimate physical force over its citizens and against outsiders. The nation may be co-terminous with the state and legitimate its authority, but this is not the case for many states. Hobsbawm (1990) remarks that "nations do not make states and nationalisms, but the other way round" (10).

Carr (1945) points out that whereas nation was the term used in western Europe for the major political unit from about the 16th or 17th centuries, in central and eastern Europe it meant a racial (ethnic) or linguistic group and had no political significance before the 19th century.[7] He also remarks on the divisions between strata in both western and eastern Europe where not everyone was considered to be a member of nations. In revolutionary North America and in France the term "people" referred to property owners, and nationalism was a middle-class phenomenon. In much of eastern Europe, nation was restricted to the upper classes until well into the 19th century: "It was said of a Croat landowner of the 19th century that he would sooner have regarded his horse than his peasant as a member of the Croat nation" (Carr 1945: 3n). Much the same could be said of Poland. Carr discusses how nationalism spread across Europe but was managed and contained throughout three-quarters of the 19th century by the notion of the rights of man (sic), particularly the property rights on which full membership of the nation depended. These developed within an *ideological context*, that of *laissez-faire* economics, where goods and people could pass freely in an international economy and the economic and political systems operated independently. In reality those in control of the British market acted autocratically and effectively to develop and control the international market, and the uncontested supremacy of the British navy generated the political power on which to a large degree the political independence of nations was based. From the 1870s onwards, economic and political changes increasingly brought about a growth in the number of nations (in 1871 there were 14 independent European nations, in 1914, 24 and in 1924, 26) and a change towards populist and exclusive nationalism (Carr 1945: 17ff). He remarks that the political notion of national self-determination becomes an invitation to secession.

In a Europe that is undergoing profound change, nationalism is re-emerging and is being used to provide ideological justifications for ethnic conflicts being waged against those defined as "others". Along with ethnic identity and religion, nationalism may serve as a power resource to be mobilized for political purposes (Macey 1992). In the crisis in the former Yugoslavia, for example, Schierup (1991) contends that ethnic-nationalist mobilization is the dominant political factor. He argues, however, that a general "ethnification" of the political process is a characteristic product of the (post) socialist state system, rather than a perpetuation of past ethnic conflicts. Schierup also points to the growth of new class conflicts, which are fermenting under the cover of ethnic mobilization and national cohesion (125).

The link between nationalism and ethnicity is a crucial one; Allen (1991) points out that the *myth of origin* may play a central role in national allegiance and is a major mechanism by which nationalism survives. At its most extreme it is felt to be a matter of a common history that cannot be altered or shared by others, just because it is in the past. In this it shares some of the features not only of ethnicity but of racialized categories. In the re-unified Germany, for example, Wilpert (1991) relates how such thinking is being used to differentiate between ethnic Germans ("*Volksdeutsche*"), and foreigners. The former include many who were born and have lived outside German territory for generations. Proof of their being German with full rights of entry and citizenship is based on the concept of blood ties; in some cases the only proof of these that is available is that their forebears were members of the Nazi party (58). In contrast, the children born in Germany of migrant workers are, like their parents, deemed to be foreigners, are deprived of many rights, and are subject to routine harassment and to mental and physical assault.

Ethnicity and religion

We turn now to another neglected dimension in the study of race and ethnic relations, that of religion. Durkheim (1915) and Weber (1963) recognized the centrality of religion to sociological understanding, yet little attention has been paid to its contemporary relevance to mainstream sociology or to analyses of race and ethnic relations. Despite religion being viewed as a significant component of ethnic minority identity (Wagley & Harris 1958; Yinger,1986; Rex 1991), until the publication of *The Satanic Verses* (Rushdie 1988), it merited little more than a passing mention in analyses of ethnic relations. Part of the reason for this neglect is that much of the sociology of religion has traditionally conceived of religion as a kind of social glue, binding individuals and groups into the social and cultural order (Durkheim 1933; Parsons 1965) and simultaneously providing a symbolic universe, or sacred canopy, which gives meaning to a world of otherwise potential chaos (Berger 1969). The role of religion in Europe (and North America) was largely studied by sociologists as part of the process of modernity, with Protestantism (especially Calvinism) being viewed as the veritable seed-bed of this (Durkheim 1915; Weber 1963; Parsons 1965). The consequences for individuals and society of secularization as an integral part of the process of modernity were analyzed by Weber and Durkheim, both of whom highlighted the dilemma of anomie. Durkheim's concern was to consider alternative sources of moral authority once the Church no longer fulfilled this function, and he appraised the rôle of the nation in this respect. His observations of France during the First World War and the part played by patriotism in developing the collective conscience necessary for maintaining social cohesion, led him to see similarities between nationalism and traditional religion (Durkheim 1914).[8] However, as Turner points out, while nationalism as a surrogate religion may appear to fulfil the functions of social integration in certain crisis periods, it can be extremely socially divisive within an ethnically or culturally diverse political collectivity (Turner 1991).

Europe is just such a diverse entity in terms of culture, ethnicity, and religion, yet the dominant ideology maintains that Christianity is one of the most significant elements of the so-called European heritage (Haller 1990).

Such a view ignores both the historical and contemporary reality of religious diversity in Europe (Turner 1991; Modood 1992) and the major contributions made by Jews and Muslims to what is conceived of as European culture (Dummett 1991). The existence of religious diversity in Europe is not, however, ignored by right-wing ideologues, whose portrayal of this diversity stresses the threat to western values, culture, and identity posed by "fundamentalist" Islam (for a fuller discussion see Macey 1991), and indeed there are aspects of Islam to which social scientists need to pay attention. First, there are an estimated 5–6 million Muslims in western Europe, with Islam constituting a significant presence in Britain, France, Germany, Malta, Spain, Sicily, the former Yugoslavia, and the Balkans so that the growth in anti-Islamic feeling is a development of considerable concern (for a fuller discussion of this see Allen & Macey 1990; Macey 1991, 1992). Secondly, there is an apparently deep-rooted conflict between Christians, Jews, and Muslims, despite the fact that (see Hodgson 1974; Turner 1991) as variants of the Abrahamic faith, they have much in common in theological, historical, and sociological terms (for a discussion of the contrasted histories of pogrom and conquest between the Jews and the Muslims, see Yuval-Davis 1980). In terms of the relations between Christians and Muslims, both have been involved in processes of mutual colonization, having common traditions of *jihad* (holy war) and crusade (Turner 1991). Islam was a major colonizing force inside Europe and, from the 8th century onwards, provided the dominant culture of southern Mediterranean societies (Hodgson 1974). Thirdly, Islam as a religion that tries to put into practice the "whole life" philosophy underpinning all religions, can pose ethical dilemmas for Muslims living in secular societies. This can cause tensions between secular and religious law when there is a perceived conflict between the two.[9] Fourthly, it has been suggested that religion as a central part of Muslim identity is an important mobilizing force in Britain today (Rex 1991) and that the attitudes of Muslim youth are closer to their parents and, perhaps, their peers on the Indian sub-continent on a range of issues than they are to those of their British peers (Anwar 1986; Rex & Josephides 1987; Shaw 1988; Modood 1992;).[10] Thus it may be that as a consequence of historical and contemporary factors, in addition to structural discrimination on the basis of skin colour, Muslims will not follow the Herberg model of immigrant integration, which involves a combination of the weakening of religious ties and/or the transformation of the religion itself (Herberg 1960). One of these factors, and another reason for further sociological analysis of religion, is the increasing potential of Islam as a mobilizing force in Europe and other parts of the world, given its resurgence in global political terms and its establishment of international links (see Rex 1991 for a fuller discussion).

Historically, religion has had a significant influence on individuals, groups, and whole societies, and has been intimately involved in the construction of the world as we know it today, including the secular world. It has been the cause of, or been caught up in, civil and international wars and has been used to legitimize colonialism, slavery, and genocide. The role of Christianity in the processes of colonization and slavery needs no rehearsing (Macey 1989); it is less widely recognized that the Nazi regime believed in National Socialism as a religion of nature that was developed in opposition to traditional Christianity and was subsequently used to justify the genocide of the Jewish people. Pois (1986) suggests that the widespread appeal of National Socialism owed much to its being rooted in the fundamental existential concerns of 20th-century alienated people. He adds that though the content of National Socialism was German, "the form assumed could well prove to be congruent with the spiritual needs of all people who, rejecting Marxist solutions, have been unable to deal successfully with the necessarily alienating character of modern society" (Pois 1986: 11). Nawal Al Sadaawi points to the use to which religion may be put by politicians at the regional, national, and international levels. It is her view that neither Christianity nor Islam are the *causes* of oppression, but that religion as the servant of political systems, part of the ideological state apparatus, is used to legitimize injustice and oppression. She comments that "governments need God and religion to justify oppressive regimes" and that politicians use religion and authoritarian governments pursue fundamentalist positions for reasons far removed from theological ones (Al Sadaawi 1991).

It is interesting to note the discourse of the (currently ongoing) crisis in the former Yugoslavia, in which religious and ethnic designations are confounded and reference is made to Croats, Serbs, and Muslims, and not to Catholics, Orthodox, and Muslims. The actual rôle of religious affiliation and ethnic designation in this situation remains unclear. The use of a particular discourse, however, detracts attention from the fact that neither the religious nor the ethnic differences that are now purported to be reasons for people killing each other have not, since the Second World War, constituted a barrier to peaceful co-existence and inter-marriage in a country where no region is homogeneous in ethnic or religious terms.[11] Notwithstanding this, the current situation in the former Yugoslavia illustrates the use to which religion, linked to ethnicity and nationalism, may be put when mobilized in the context of a political project.

What any historical and comparative analysis shows is that religion may be used to divide and kill, but that it may also give strength and hope (Afshar 1989; Modood 1989; Lutz 1991; Rath et al. 1991; Turner 1991; Macey 1992). There is a long tradition in the sociology of religion that sees religion as fundamental to the emergence of utopian thought as a challenge to existing ideology and social practice (Mannheim 1936). Turner suggests that religion provides the ideas and mythology that act as major vehicles for the expression of social and political protest, especially against secular regimes (1991). Whatever the exact rôle of religion, its involvement in the politics of protest is undeniable, as is illustrated in such divergent countries as the former Soviet Union, Poland, Northern Ireland, Central and Latin America, Israel, Iran, Pakistan, Romania, and, of course, the former Yugoslavia. It may be that the strength and power of religion is intimately connected to the struggle against perceived inequality and oppression, but in such situations religion tends towards the extremes of the highly orthodox, reactionary (as in the Iranian revolution) or the radical, revolutionary (as in Central and Latin America). The speed and extent of social and political change also has a significant influence on the form taken by religion. Neilsen (1984) and Robinson (1988) have observed, with reference to Islam, that religious fundamentalism seems to flourish among people who are in a state of transition from one society to another (for instance some South Asians in Britain) or whose society is itself undergoing radical change (for example, Iran). Macey (1991) notes the tendency for fundamentalism to gain ascendency over more liberal variants of Christianity in situations of rapid change and/ or conflict, and Yuval-Davis, following Bauman, links the rise of fundamentalism across the world to the crisis of modernity (1991).

Religion is a major power resource, both for people who are struggling against oppression and for those in positions of power. It can be a source of social cohesion or provide the potential for conflict, the latter being more likely in situations of ethnic, cultural, and religious diversity, where power relationships are asymmetrical and act to prioritize systematically one ethnic group over others. Yet until recently, governments, political parties, policy makers, *and* social scientists have afforded religion little significance in the sphere of race and ethnic relations (Rath et al. 1991). Following the so-called Rushdie affair, however, there has been a pendular swing whereby the term "Muslim" has become all-encompassing and is now applied to a variety of groups in Britain formerly described by their, or their parents', national or regional origins, such as Pakistani, Mirpuri, Bengali, Punjabi (Yuval-Davis 1991). Nor is there any attempt to acknowledge the different branches of

Islam; while the majority of British Muslims are Sunnis (divided into Deobandis and Barelvis), there are also Sufis, Jamiat-Ahl-E-Hadiths, and Jamaat-i-Islamis (see Rex 1991 for a discussion of the social and political ramifications of the different branches of Islam).

Whatever the form taken by religion in specific contexts, it appears to be universally the case that it impacts disproportionately on women relative to men, not least because all religions are concerned with the custodianship and transmission of faith and culture to subsequent generations. We noted above that in situations of rapid change and uncertainty religion tends to develop in extreme ways, whether radical (as with Liberation Theology in Central and Latin America in the 1960s and '70s) or reactionary (as in Iran after 1979) and that there is a tendency towards fundamentalism at times and in situations of transition. It is not surprising, then, that many of the concerns of British Muslim males relate to women and questions of appropriate gender rôles, arranged/mixed marriages, female dress and family authority and honour (Anwar 1986; Rex & Josephides 1987; Shaw 1988; Modood 1992). Nor, perhaps, is it surprising that in situations of physical conflict and outright war the discourse centres so much around rape, whether in the metaphorical sense of the rape of a country or in the actual sense of rape of the enemy's women. The ongoing conflict in the former Yugoslavia is illustrative of this *and* of the association between religion, ethnicity, and women. If Macey (1991) and Sahgal & Yuval-Davis (1992) are correct in suggesting that there is a growing trend towards fundamentalism in many religions across the world, this has serious implications for ethnic relations in general and for women in particular. It is an aspect of social organization that requires investigation and analysis by social scientists.

Sociology and diversity

In 1981 Lange & Westin commented that "'the state of the art' as far as research on race and ethnic relations is concerned is best described as theoretical and empirical chaos". Some 12 years later, while there is little room for complacency, this statement requires some modification. The 1980s witnessed developments in different theoretical positions that we have discussed above. In rethinking sociological paradigms so that analyses of the social world become less partial, we began by examining the field of race and ethnic relations as it has developed in Britain. We pointed to the narrowing of the field to a concentration on black/white relations and its separation from parallel discourses on ethnicity and nationalism, its neglect of gender as a major social division and its lack of attention to religious diversity. In the light of the changes in Europe, especially since 1989, we argue for paradigms that include these dimensions and specify their interrelations.

This is not, however, a move on our part to the positions put forward in some postmodernist debates that fragment theoretical discourse and make claims about the social science project that we find unconvincing.[12] For instance, Seidman (1992) argues that the claims of science to value-neutrality and objectivity have been debunked by criticisms put forward by minority communities (in which he includes women, people of colour, the differently abled, and gays). This may be so, but only in a specific sense, for value-neutrality and objectivity have long been contested issues among social scientists (see for example Elias 1956; Hughes 1958; Bauman 1978). Linking postmodernism to the criticisms of Marxism in the 1970s, Seidman asserts that:

> A general theory of society and history that is centred on economically based class dynamics neglects and marginalizes social and political dynamics that revolve around gender, ethnicity, race, sexuality or age. (Seidman & Wagner 1992: 7)

These criticisms are in large part not new. From the mid-1960s the dominant sociological paradigm of Parsonian structural functionalism and Marxist interpretations of social structure and change were subjected to critical re-evaluations. The after-ideology, post-capitalist and post-industrial discourses were scrutinized in the context of ideas put forward by Sartre (1960), among others. The writings of Gramsci and of the "young" Marx were rediscovered, translated, and re-published. This period was one of intellectual ferment, breaking through, in a small way, the intellectual constraints imposed by the Cold War. Furthermore, many, including Schutz (1972), Laing (1968), Garfinkel (1967), Berger (1967), Luckmann (1967), Goffman (1956), Habermas and his colleagues of the Frankfurt School (1981), attempted to reconceptualize in phenomenological, ethnomethodological, symbolic interactionist, dramaturgical and hermeneutic terms, the approaches to understanding and explaining social relations.

In support of the postmodern claims that mainstream sociology neglects and marginalizes minority groups, Seidman refers to the social movements that emerged in the 1960s and 1970s, stating that "there is a close link between post-modernism and the new social movements" (1992). The nature of these links requires close attention, if we are to understand their impact on theory and research. In the analysis of race relations there can be no doubt that the Civil Rights and Black Power movements in the United States influenced the approaches to social theory and empirical investigation in the academy, little by little, and much more attention was paid to the situation of African-Americans and the effects of institutionalized racism on the whole of society. It is argued, however, that the reality of the social structural location of North American blacks (and many other minority categories) is understandable only if the economic structure (and the consequences of restructuring) and the organization of domestic politics are considered as central to that location (Tabb 1970; Wilson 1978, 1987; Killian 1990). In other words, a theory that includes the dynamics of the economy does not marginalize or neglect the dynamics around race, but is essential to explaining differential locations, including those of categories defined as racial. This position was espoused by both Martin Luther King Jr and Malcolm X shortly before their assassinations.

As far as postmodernist claims relate to gender, they offer little beyond descriptions of women's oppression. The re-emergence of a women's movement in the 1960s and 1970s in North America, western Europe and elsewhere was influential in social science, mainly through the work of women both inside and outside the academy, who produced cogent criticisms of social theory and methodology. Some of these have been incorporated into mainstream theorizing or into the research agendas of social science disciplines, and in total they constitute a formidable challenge to sociological analysis. However, there is no one indication of how theory is to develop on the basis of these challenges. It is quite possible to regard the consequences of modernity as more apposite for explaining women's location in structures of class, ethnicity, race, and nationality than those of postmodernity. The postmodernists who claim, or imply, that serious attention to gender necessarily involves an adoption of their position appear to us to be putting forward an untenable argument. They fail to take into account the work of feminist scholars (in particular, European socialist feminists), anthropologists, development economists, sociologists, and political scientists who have worked in many fields employing a social science approach, albeit with considerable and considered modifications. As we noted above, though these have not fully succeeded in integrating the class, race, ethnic, religious, nationalist, and gender dimensions, they have cleared much of the ground on which gender-blind and male-biased social science was based.

The postmodern critique of science brings out a number of issues that are important not only for the substantive fields with which this chapter is concerned, but also for the more general social science agenda. Perhaps one of the most significant is the claim that social theory is embedded in the socio-historical circumstances of its producers. Obviously much social theory is embedded in the circumstances of European, white, male, bourgeois heterosexuals. Hopefully, there are now few social scientists who would disagree with this. The question is not that this coloured the kind of theories put forward (this ground has been well covered), but what that means in terms of the validity of the knowledge outcomes so constructed. While giving due recognition to the partiality of all scientific knowledge, it serves little or no purpose to reject such knowledge out of hand. To move, as some post-modernists do, from this recognition to the general precept that social theory can be located only in local conceptualizations of situations and experiences is highly questionable. In embedded local situations and identities, people are gendered, racialized, ethnically encapsulated, and class specified. Social theory that takes all of this into account properly assumes that it can offer an analysis that goes beyond description, a history, and/or a classificatory account. If it does not, then it is not theory. We agree with Mason when he states "Only a social science free to develop categories and modes of analysis which are different from those embraced by everyday actors can have any claim to be more than common sense" (1990). We would also reiterate a point made earlier, that validating or invalidating knowledge simply on the basis of the characteristics of its producer is untenable, not only for social scientists, but for everyone. Pois' analysis of the links between religion and science reminds us that under the National Socialist regime the Nazis dismissed scientific objectivity and rejected "Jewish" science. He comments that relativism can be subject to radical misuse (1986).

We argue that existing sociological paradigms have much to offer in analyzing race and ethnic relations, gender, nationalism, and religion. Our approach is a commitment to social scientific analyses and the central rôle of theory in formulating questions and research designs that enable conflicting propositions to be measured against each other (Pawson 1989). None of this is unproblematic, but such an approach provides for the public scrutiny of assumptions and outcomes that is central to the scientific enterprise. This does not exclude reflexivity, but it is a guard against the kind of existentialism that Stern suggests characterized the Nazi regime, whereby authenticity, commitment, and personal truth usurped public, objective analysis (1975). The production of knowledge, as against opinion, is part of the question of validity central to all social science that we raised earlier. In the fields of race, ethnicity, and gender, as well as nationalism and religion, this question carries a strong political immediacy. In such cases it appears to us that there is a very clear case for caution in terms of clarity in conceptualizing the problems being addressed, rigour in pursuing their investigation, recognition of the difficulty of relating theoretical propositions and empirical data and also in acknowledging the tentative nature of any research findings. In our discussion of the commonality of the political and socio-economic marginalization shared by women of all ethnic, religious, national, and racial collectivities throughout Europe, we do not adopt the postmodernist approach. Our discussion raises the question of whether there can be a theoretical approach that encompasses all the divisions to which we refer, and this in turn raises the issue of whether the status of any one division is epistemologically privileged. Anthias suggests that:

> it is possible to consider the links [between ethnos, gender and class] in terms of the form of the modes by which subordination becomes constructed . . . The importance of the material reality of economic relations and other political and ideological relations will produce, however, different primary organizing principles at different times. Class formation though is a product not only of processes endemic within the sphere of production for it is historically constructed in relation to the history of race and of gender. Therefore an understanding of concrete class processes finds them intermeshed with those of social relations more broadly defined.
>
> (Anthias 1991: 44–5)

She does not privilege one formation above the others, but sees, rather, a need to distinguish them in analysis. Since they all intermesh in empirical situations, the task becomes one of understanding their various formations in terms of each other. There seems no reason why different propositions about their interrelations can not be made within specified historical periods and tested against one another in terms of their adequacy for understanding. The focus would be on social construction, not on a reified essentialism nor on reductionist models that conflate each into the other. Such a project would marry the canons of social science rigour with a recognition of the complexity and diversity of the human condition.

Notes

1. Europe is a highly problematic notion. Its geographical boundaries are unclear, particularly to the south and east, and change according to definitions of political entities and membership of supra-national bodies. Jordan (1988) maintains that "Eu-

rope is a human entity . . . its distinctiveness is to be sought in the character of the peoples who occupy it . . . Europe is a culture that occupies a *culture area*" (quoted in Haller 1990: 192). For a discussion of this, see Allen 1991.

2. It is only recently that the term black has been problematized, after more than a decade in which to challenge its analytical adequacy (whatever its political utility) was to be declared racist (Mason 1990; Goulbourne 1991). This is apart from the problems of a mutually intelligible vocabulary that arise among researchers in Europe. In Germany, for example, the term racism is used with reference to anti-Jewish sentiment (Dummett 1991), while in France there is a very different resonance to the words race and racism (Lloyd 1991).

3. There is still only one small funded research centre in the field; the CRE research budget is limited and can support only small projects, while government departments, in particular the Home Office and the Department of Employment, commission research that is restricted in terms of scope and time.

4. These include their shared experiences of low wages (for the majority of women below subsistence level); their widespread exclusion from full-time regular employment; the state's construction of them as being dependent on men while at the same time being responsible for most of the work on behalf of children, the elderly, the sick, and those with disabilities; their unequal treatment by the criminal justice system; and their poor representation in local and national politics.

5. Across Europe, the ground rules are now those of market forces, the drawing of boundaries against all defined as "outsiders", overlain by post feminism in the west and what can only be described as new feminine mystiques in the east.

6. There are, of course, differences in the relations between Scotland and the British state (the separate legal, education, and religious institutions, for instance), between Northern Ireland and, to a much lesser extent, between Wales and the British state. But the dominance of the British government is demonstrated by the Welsh, Scottish, and Northern Irish "offices" as part of Westminster's organization, where no English office is thought necessary.

7. It may be noted here that the question "what is your nationality?" in Russian means "what is your ethnicity/mother tongue?" Anthias & Yuval-Davis, following Shanin (1986), refer to the "missing term" in English that denotes a different and major set of social relationships and does not apply just to minorities or subordinate groups (1989: 3).

8. It should not, of course, be assumed that this implies nationalistic tendencies in Durkheim, whose leanings were towards a liberal, international socialism. For a discussion of the controversy that greeted Durkheim's publications on patriotism, nationalism, and the collective conscience, see Lukes 1973.

9. Examples of this include the "scarf" issue in France, the Ayatolla Khomeini's proclamation of a *fatwa* on Salman Rushdie, following publication of *The Satanic Verses*, and the demands for a separate Muslim parliament (and laws) in Britain.

10. There may, however, be a gender factor in youth attitudes to which the research literature does not refer. For example, one of the writers was recently involved in a discussion of racial discrimination in Britain with a group of Pakistani teenagers in a Bradford school. She noted a significant gender difference in that the girls' focus

was on institutionalized racism, whereas the boys rejected the term black, referred to themselves as Muslims, talked at length of the evil of Salman Rushdie, and differentiated between Muslims and people of Afro-Caribbean origin to whom they applied negative stereotypes. This group may, of course, be atypical, but the extent of such gender differences in attitudes raises questions that could profitably be researched.

11. The selection of a discourse may also, of course, serve to project a particular view of the situation. Kate Adie, a BBC news reporter, commenting on the reporting of the situation in the former Yugoslavia, said in an interview, "viewers like to identify with one side. Where are the good guys? Who are the bad guys? . . . . It's not that viewers are simplistic – it's just that in understanding any complex problem, people wish to look for what is right and what is wrong, what is good and what is bad. And if it's not clear, then people begin to lose either sympathy or interest" (*Guardian* 18 January 1993).

12. This is not to suggest that there is a single, unified, postmodernist approach, since different meaning stem from, for instance, different disciplinary locations; see Giddens 1990, Bauman 1991, Nicholson 1992.

References

Adie, K. 1993. When reporters go over the top. Interview with Ronald Keating, *Guardian* (18 January).

Afshar, H. 1989. Women and reproduction in Iran. In *Woman – nation – state*, F. Anthias & N. Yuval-Davis (eds), Ch.7. London: Macmillan.

Allen, S. 1971. *New minorities, old conflicts*. New York: Random House.

Allen, S. 1987. Gender, race and class. In *Race in Britain: continuity and change*, C. H. Husband (ed), Ch. 7 2nd edn. London: Hutchinson.

Allen, S. 1991. Diversity and commonality: building a dialogue. Paper presented at the conference Building a Europe without Frontiers: the Rôle of Women, Athens, Greece.

Allen, S. & M. Macey 1990. Race and ethnicity in the European context. *British Journal of Sociology*, **41**, 375–94.

Allen, S. & C. Smith 1974. Race and ethnicity in class formation: a comparison of Asian and West Indian workers. In *The social analysis of class structure*, F. Parkin (ed.), Ch. 3. London: Tavistock.

Al Sadaawi, N. 1991. Women in Islam. Paper presented at the Women in Society seminar series, University of Bradford.

Amos, V. & P. Parmar 1984. Challenging imperial feminism. *Feminist Review* **17**, 3–19.

Anthias, F. 1991. Parameters of difference and identity and the problems of connections. *International Review of Sociology* **2**, 29–54.

Anthias, F. & N. Yuval-Davis 1983. Contextualising feminism in gender, ethnic and class divisions. *Feminist Review* **15**, 62–75.

Anthias, F. & N. Yuval-Davis 1989. Introduction. In *Woman – nation – state*, N. Yuval-Davis & F. Anthias (eds), London: Macmillan.

Anwar, M. 1986. *Young Muslims in a multi-cultural society*. Leicester: Islamic Foundation.

REFERENCES

Banton, M. 1955. *The coloured quarter*. London: Jonathan Cape.

Banton, M. 1959. *White and coloured*. London: Jonathan Cape.

Banton, M. 1967. *Race relations*. London: Tavistock.

Banton, M. 1970. The concept of racism. In *Race and Racialism*, S. Zubaida (ed.) Ch. 1. London: Tavistock.

Barker, M. 1981. *The new racism*. London: Junction Books.

Barrett, M. & M. McIntosh 1985. Ethnocentrism and socialist feminist theory. *Feminist Review* **20**, 23–47.

Barth, F. (ed.) 1969. *Ethnic groups and boundaries*. Bergen: Universitetsforlaget.

Bauman, Z. 1978. *Hermeneutics and social science*. London: Hutchinson.

Bauman, Z. 1991. *Intimations of postmodernity*. London: Routledge.

Berger, P. L. 1967. *The sacred canopy: elements of a sociological theory of religion*. New York: Doubleday.

Berger, P. L. 1969. *The social reality of religion*. London: Pelican.

Bhavnani, K. & M. Coulson 1986. Transforming socialist feminism: the challenge of racism. *Feminist Review* **23**, 81–92.

Bottomore, T. 1970. Foreword. In *Race and racialism* S. Zubaida (ed.) London: Tavistock.

Bourne, J. with A. Sivanandan 1980. Cheerleaders and ombudsmen: the sociology of race relations in Britain. *Race and Class* **21**, 331–52.

Bourne, J. 1983. Towards an anti-racist feminism. *Race and Class* **XXV**, 1–22.

Bryan, B., S. Dadzie, S. Scafe 1985. *The heart of the race*. London: Virago.

Carby, H. 1982. White women listen! Black feminism and the boundaries of sisterhood. In *The empire strikes back*, Centre for Contemporary Cultural Studies (ed.), Ch. 5. London: Hutchinson.

Carr, E. H. 1945. *Nationalism and after*. London: Macmillan.

Castles, S. & G. Kosack 1973. *Immigrant workers and class structure in western Europe*. London: Institute of Race Relations/Oxford University Press.

Cherns, A. 1987. Paradigms in the sociology of technology and work. In *Ethnicity in the social sciences: a view and a review of the literature on ethnicity*, A. Bacal (ed.), 16. Research Paper in Ethnic Relations No. 3, Warwick: ESRC.

Cohen, A. (ed.) 1974. *Urban ethnicity*. London: Tavistock.

Collins, S. 1957. *Coloured minorities in Britain*. London: Lutterworth Press.

Cook, J. & M. Fonow 1986. Knowledge and women's interests. Issues in epistemology and methodology in feminist sociological research. *Sociological Inquiry* **56**, 2–29.

Davis, A. 1981. *Women, race and class*. London: Women's Press.

Douglass, W. A. 1988. A critique of recent trends in the analysis of ethnonationalism. *Ethnic and Racial Studies* **11**, 192–206.

Dummett, A. 1991. Europe? Which Europe? *New Community* **18**, 167–75.

Durkheim, E. 1914. Le dualisme de la nature humaine et ses conditions sociales. Paris: *Scientia* XV.

Durkheim, E. 1915. *The elementary forms of religious life*. London: Allen & Unwin.

Durkheim, E. 1933. *The division of labour in society*. New York: Macmillan.

Elias, N. 1956. Problems of involvement and detachment. *British Journal of Sociology* **7**, 226–41.

Finch, J. 1984. It's great to have someone to talk to: the ethics and politics of interviewing women. In *Social researching*, C. Bell & H. Roberts (eds), Ch. 4. London: Routledge.

Freedman, M. (ed.) 1955. *A minority in Britain*. London: Valentine Mitchell.

Garfinkel, H. 1967. *Studies in ethnomethodology*. New Jersey: Englewood Cliffs & Prentice-Hall.

Gellner, E. 1983. *Nations and nationalism*. Oxford: Basil Blackwell.

Gelsthorpe, L. 1992. Response to Martyn Hammersley's paper On feminist methodology. *Sociology* **26**, 213–18.

Genovese, E. D. 1971. In Black and red: Marxian explorations in southern and Afro-American history. London: Allen Lane.

Giddens, A. 1990. *The consequences of modernity*. Cambridge: Polity.

Gifford Lord, W. Brown, R. Bundey 1986. *Loosen the shackles: first report of the inquiry into race relations in Liverpool*. Liverpool Law Centre, London: Karia Press.

Gilroy, P. 1987. *There ain't no black in the Union Jack*. London: Hutchinson.

Ginsberg, M. 1941. National character. Inaugural address to the Social Psychology section of the British Psychological Society. Reprinted in *Reason and Unreason in Society*, M. Ginsberg 1947. London: Longmans, Green.

Ginsberg, M. 1943. Anti-semitism. Paper presented at the British Psychology Society. Reprinted in *Reason and Unreason in Society*, M. Ginsberg 1947. London: Longmans, Green.

Goffman, E. 1956. *The presentation of self in everyday life*. Edinburgh: University of Edinburgh Press.

Goulbourne, H. 1991. *Ethnicity and nationalism in post-imperial Britain*. Cambridge: Cambridge University Press.

Habermas, J. 1981 (originally published in Habermas 1970). Ideology. In *Modern interpretations of Marx*, T. Bottomore (ed.). Oxford: Basil Blackwell.

Haller, M. 1990. The Challenge for Comparative Sociology in the Transformation of Europe. *International Sociology*, 5, 2.

Hammersley, M. 1992. On feminist methodology. *Sociology*, **26**, 187–206.

Harding, S. 1987. *Feminism and methodology*. Milton Keynes, England: Open University Press.

Herberg, W. 1960. *Protestant, Catholic, Jew*. New York: Anchor Books.

Hobsbawm, E. 1990. *Nations and nationalism since 1780: programme, myth and reality*. Cambridge: Cambridge University Press.

Hodgson, M. G. S. 1974. *The venture of Islam*. Chicago: University of Chicago Press.

Hooks, B. 1982. *Ain't I a woman*. London: Pluto.

Hooks, B. 1984. *Feminist theory: from margin to centre*. Boston: South End Press.

Hughes, H. S. 1958. *Consciousness and society: the reorientation of European social thought 1890–1930*. New York: Knopf.

Husband, C. H. 1987a. "Race": the continuity of a concept. In *"Race" in Britain: continuity and change*, C. H. Husband (ed.), Introduction. London: Hutchinson.

Husband, C. H. 1987b. British racisms: the construction of racial ideologies. In *"Race" in Britain: continuity and change*, C. H. Husband (ed.). London: Hutchinson.

James, S. (ed.) 1985. *Strangers and sisters: women, race and immigration*. Bristol: Falling Wall Press.

Jordan, T. G. 1988. *The European culture area: a systematic geography*, 2nd edn. New York:

Harper & Row.

Joseph, G. I. & J. Lewis 1981. *Common differences: conflicts in black and white feminist perspectives.* New York: Anchor Press/Doubleday.

Killian, L. M. 1990. Race relations and the nineties: where are the dreams of the sixties? *Social Forces* **69**, 1–13.

Laing, R. D. 1968. *The politics of experience.* New York: Ballantine Books.

Lange, A. & C. Westin 1981. *Etnisk diskriminering och social identitet, En rapport fram Diskrimineringsutredingen.* Stockholm: LiberFörlag.

Little, K. L. 1948. *A study of race relations in England.* London: Routledge & Kegan Paul.

Lloyd, C. 1991. Concepts, models and anti-racist strategies in Britain and France. *New Community* **18**, 63–74.

Lockwood, D. 1970. Race, conflict and plural society. In *Race and racialism*, S. Zubaida (ed.), Ch. 3. London: Tavistock.

Loughlin, G. M. 1986. *Race relations training – the art of the state?* M.Sc. dissertation, University of Bradford.

Luckmann, T. 1967. *The invisible religion: the transformation of symbols in industrial society.* New York: Macmillan.

Lukes, S. 1973. *Emile Durkheim: his life and work: a historical and critical study.* London: Allen Lane.

Lutz, H. 1991. The myth of the "other": Western representation and images of migrant women of so-called Islamic background. *International Review of Sociology* **2**, 121–38.

Macey, M. 1989. Christianity and racism: rhetoric or reality? Paper presented at the annual conference of the British Association for the Advancement of Science, Sheffield.

Macey, M. 1991. Christian fundamentalism: the growth of a monster? Paper presented at the Women in Society seminar series, University of Bradford.

Macey, M. 1992. Greater Europe: integration or ethnic exclusion? *Political Quarterly* **63**, 139–53.

Mannheim, K. 1936. *Ideology and utopia.* London: Routledge & Kegan Paul.

Mason, D. 1982. Race relations, group formation and power: a framework for analysis. *Ethnic and Racial Studies* **5**, 421–39.

Mason, D. 1990. A rose by any other name . . .? Categorisation, identity and social science. *New Community* **17**, 123–33.

Maynard, M. 1990. The re-shaping of sociology? Trends in the study of gender. *Sociology* **24**, 269–90.

McCrone, D. 1992. *Understanding Scotland: the sociology of a stateless nation.* London: Routledge.

Merton, R. K. 1972. Insiders and outsiders. *American Journal of Sociology* **78**, 9–47.

Miles, R. 1980. Class, race and ethnicity: a critique of Cox's theory. *Ethnic and Racial Studies* **3**, 169–87.

Miles, R. 1982. Labour migration and racism: the case of the Irish. In *Racism and migrant labour*, R. Miles. London: Routledge & Kegan Paul.

Miles, R. 1984. Marxism versus the sociology of "race relations"? *Ethnic and Racial Studies* **7**, 217–37.

Miles, R. 1987a. Recent Marxist theories of nationalism and the issue of racism. *British Journal of Sociology* **38**, 24–43.

Miles, R. 1987b. Racism and nationalism in Britain. In *"Race" in Britain: continuity and change*, C. H. Husband (ed.), Ch. 16. London: Hutchinson.

Modood, T. 1989. Religious anger and minority rights. *Political Quarterly* **60**, 280–4.

Modood, T. 1992. British Asian Muslims and the Rushdie Affair. In *Race, Culture and Difference*, J. Donald & A. Rattansi (eds.), Ch. 12. London: Sage.

National Advisory Commission on Civil Disorders 1968. *The Kerner report*. Washington: US Government Printing Office.

Neilsen, J. S. 1984. *Muslim immigration and settlement in Britain*. Birmingham: Centre for the Study of Islam and Christian–Muslim Relations.

Nicholson, L. 1992. On the postmodern barricades: feminism, politics and theory. In *Postmodernism and social theory*, S. Seidman & D. G. Wagner (eds), Ch. 3. Oxford: Basil Blackwell.

Parkin, F. 1978. Social stratification. In *A history of sociological analysis*, T. Bottomore & R. Nisbet (eds), Ch. 15. London: Heinemann.

Parsons, T. 1965. Religious perspectives in sociology and social psychology. In *Reader in comparative religion: an anthropological approach*, 2nd edn, A. Lessa & E. Z. Vogt (eds), Section 2. New York: Harper & Row.

Pawson, R. 1989. *A measure for measures: a manifesto for empirical sociology*. London: Routledge.

Pois, R. A. 1986. *National Socialism and the religion of nature*. London: Croom Helm.

Ramazanoglu, C. 1989. *Feminism and the contradictions of oppression*. London: Routledge.

Ramazanoglu, C. 1992. On feminist methodology: male reason versus female empowerment. *Sociology* **26**, 207–12.

Rath, J., K. Groenendijk, R. Penninx 1991. The recognition and institutionalisation of Islam in Belgium, Great Britain and the Netherlands. *New Community* **18**, 104–14.

Rex, J. 1970a. The concept of race in sociological theory. In *Race and racialism*, S. Zubaida (ed.), Ch. 2. London: Tavistock.

Rex, J. 1970b. *Race relations in sociological theory*. London: Weidenfeld & Nicolson.

Rex, J. 1973. *Discovering sociology*. London: Routledge & Kegan Paul.

Rex, J. 1991. *Ethnic identity and ethnic mobilisation in Britain*. Monographs in Ethnic Relations 5: Warwick: ESRC/Centre for Research in Ethnic Relations.

Rex, J. & D. Mason (eds) 1986. *Theories of race and ethnic relations*. Cambridge: Cambridge University Press.

Rex, J. & S. Josephides 1987. Asian and Greek Cypriot associations and identity. In *Immigrant associations in Europe*, J. Rex, D. Joly, C. Wilpert (eds), Ch. 2. Aldershot: Gower.

Roberts, H. 1981. *Doing feminist research*. London: Routledge.

Robinson, F. 1988. *Varieties of South Asian Islam*. Warwick: Centre for Research in Ethnic Relations.

Richmond, A. M. 1954. *Colour prejudice in Britain*. London: Routledge & Kegan Paul.

Rowbotham S., L. Segal, H. Wainwright 1979. *Beyond the fragments*. London: Merlin Press.

Rushdie, S. 1988. *The Satanic Verses*. London: Viking.

Sahgal, G. & N. Yuval-Davis 1992. Fundamentalism, multiculturalism and women in Britain. In *Refusing holy orders: women and fundamentalism in Britain*, G. Sahgal & N. Yuval-Davis (eds), Introduction. London: Virago.

Sartre, J. P. 1960. *Critique de la raison dialectique*. Paris: Gallimard.

Scarman, Lord 1981. *The Brixton disorders, report of an inquiry by the Rt Hon Lord Scarman OBE*.

REFERENCES

London: HMSO Cmnd 8427.

Scierup, C-U. 1991. The post-communist enigman: ethnic mobilization in Yugoslavia. *New Community* **18**, 115–31.

Schutz, A. 1972. *The phenomenology of the social world*. London: Heinemann.

Scott, S. 1984. The personable and the powerful: gender and status in sociological research. In *Social researching: policies, problems, practice*, C. Bell & H. Roberts (eds), Ch. 9. London: Routledge & Kegan Paul.

Seidman, S. 1992. Postmodern social theory as narrative with a moral intent. In *Postmodernism and Social Theory*, S. Seidman & D. G. Wagner (eds), Ch. 2. Oxford: Basil Blackwell.

Seidman, S. & D. G. Wagner (eds) 1992. *Postmodernism and social theory*. Oxford: Basil Blackwell.

Shanin, T. 1986. Soviet concepts of ethnicity: The case of a missing term. *New Left Review* **158**, 113–22.

Shaw, A. 1988. *A Pakistani community in Britain*. Oxford: Basil Blackwell.

Solomos, J. 1989. *Race and racism in contemporary Britain*. London: Macmillan.

Smith, A. D. 1986. *The ethnic origins of nations*. Oxford: Basil Blackwell.

Smith, A. D. 1988. The myth of the "modern nation" and the myths of nations. *Ethnic and Racial Studies* **11**, 1–26.

Smith, D. E. 1988. *The everyday world as problematic*. Milton Keynes, England: Open University Press.

Stern, J. P. 1975. *Hitler: the Führer and the people*. Berkeley: University of California Press.

Tabb, W. J. 1970. *The political economy of the black ghetto*. New York: Norton & Co.

Turner, B. S. 1991. *Religion and social theory*. London: Sage.

Troyna, B. & J. Williams 1986. *Racism, education and the state*. Beckenham, England: Croom Helm.

Wagley, C. & M. Harris 1958. Minorities in the New World: six case studies. New York: Columbia University Press.

Wallman, S. 1986. Ethnicity and third world development: political and academic contexts. In *Theories of race and ethnic relations*, J. Rex & D. Mason (eds) Cambridge: Cambridge University Press.

Weber, M. 1963. *The sociology of religion*. New York: Beacon Press.

Williams, J. 1985. Redefining institutional racism. *Ethnic and Racial Studies* **8**, 323–48.

Wilpert, C. 1991. Migration and ethnicity in a non-immigrant country: foreigners in a united Germany. *New Community* **18**, 49–62.

Wilson, W. J. 1978. *The declining significance of race*. Chicago: University of Chicago Press.

Wilson, W. J. 1987. *The truly disadvantaged*. Chicago: University of Chicago Press.

Yinger, J. M. 1986. Intersecting strands in the theorisation of race and ethnic relations. In *Theories of race and ethnic relations*, J. Rex & D. Mason (eds), Ch. 1. Cambridge: Cambridge University Press.

Yuval-Davis, N. 1980. The bearers of the collective: women and religious legislation in Israel. *Feminist Review* **4**, 15–27.

Yuval-Davis, N. 1991. Fundamentalism, multiculturalism and women in Britain. *International Review of Sociology* **2**, 139–73.

Zubaida, S. (ed.) 1970. *Race and racialism*. London: Tavistock.

Chapter 6

Race, citizenship and "Fortress Europe"

Mark Mitchell & Dave Russell

Introduction

> The study of citizenship has to concern itself with all those dimensions which allow or include the participation of people in the communities in which they live and the complex pattern of national and international relations and processes which cut across these.
>
> (Held 1989, 176)

With the failure of the Citizens' Charters to make a significant impact in the 1992 British general election campaign, it remains to be seen whether the issue of citizenship will yet become "a Big Idea for the 1990s" (Taylor 1991). Arguably the ideological appeal of citizenship has not yet been truly tested by a set of Citizens' Charters based on a weak and limited concept of citizenship offering little more than consumer rights in the sphere of collective consumption. Such an approach to citizenship is far removed from the major concerns and issues that have been at the heart of the long-standing debate over race and citizenship in Britain and, more recently, in the New Europe. Throughout the post-Marshall period, when the concept of citizenship has drifted in and out of intellectual fashion, certain fundamental issues concerning the rights and duties of citizens with black or brown skins have continued to be addressed by writers on race in Britain and western Europe.

Most significantly, the concept of citizenship has long been associated with the issue of nationality and immigration control. Clearly systems of immigration control in the UK and elsewhere are designed to restrict access to citizenship rights. All forms of citizenship are ultimately dependent upon sets of policies and procedures that are both "inclusive" and "exclusive" and which involve a series of difficult and emotive issues concerning "who belongs?" to the nation, "who can participate fully?" in the life of the society and "who is a citizen?" and who is not. In reality, struggles over citizenship necessarily involve the limitation as well as the extension of citizenship rights, and all governments of whatever political persuasion are required to operate a series of measures – including immigration controls – that are designed to include citizens and exclude non-citizens.

For many years western European governments have operated immigration policies aimed at restricting the entry rights into Europe of black and third world migrants. Furthermore, the deliberate exclusion of individuals and groups from access to full citizenship rights has created a situation in which formal inequalities in civil, political, and social rights between people living in the same country have become a normal feature of western European societies (Castles et al. 1984). Strict control of immigration and restriction of access to welfare entitlements for non-citizens remain central policy concerns for all EC member states. Although a common European immigration policy has yet to emerge, similar trends are discernible in a variety of member states based on the tightening up of "influx controls", particularly against asylum seekers and illegal immigrants. It has for some time been recognized that one of the major challenges of an "open Europe" after 1992 will be the problem of how to close its borders to migrants and refugees from developing countries in the South (Sivanandan 1988; Paul 1991). More recently the expansion of migration from eastern Europe has contributed another dimension to this problem, though the major concern remains the prevention of an escalation in black immigration and the curtailment of access to citizenship rights for the increasing numbers of third world migrants arriving at Europe's door.

Of course, many EC countries already have substantial numbers of people with black or brown skins as permanent residents. However, the *de facto* settlement of minority ethnic communities has typically not led to the granting of full citizenship rights but to more restricted forms of entitlement involving some civil and social rights (Ireland 1991). Thus, EC countries such as Germany and Belgium, for example, still deny political citizenship to migrants and their descendants. Consequently their domiciled populations are in effect divided rigidly into citizens and denizens, with the latter comprising a significant minority within the population (Layton-Henry 1990). In the light of this, the UK remains something of an exception in terms of the high proportion of the black and minority ethnic population that enjoys entitlement to full citizenship rights.

Nevertheless, much British race research has found evidence of the differential access to citizenship rights that exists *de facto* for black and white citizens in the UK (Rex & Mason 1986; Gordon 1989; Smith 1989). For example, in the housing field substantial evidence has been accumulated showing the disproportionate allocation of the worst council housing to black and minority ethnic groups, and the extent to which they are required to wait longer than white citizens to be housed (Phillips 1987; Ginsberg 1992). Similarly, evidence of the relative under use of Social Services provision by black and minority ethnic communities and the "under policing" of racial violence illustrates the extent to which black citizens can experience citizenship entitlements unequally (Ginsberg 1989; Pearson et al. 1989; Butt et al. 1991). This in turn relates to the need to separate the entitlement to formal rights from the actual capacity that people have to enjoy those rights on a substantive basis (Giddens 1985; Held 1989). It also emphasizes the significance of sets of material constraints and obstacles that stand in the way of black and minority ethnic people enjoying full and effective rights of citizenship (Harrison 1991).

Finally, the race and citizenship debate in Britain raises the question of the extent to which cultural differences should be reflected within the overall framework of contemporary citizenship (Parekh 1991). An unresolved tension exists within British race policy and practice between assimilationist arguments that link citizenship rights to the duties of cultural conformity and multi-cultural arguments where the right to be culturally distinct and to have one's cultural traditions and practices recognized and respected is seen as an important prerequisite to the attainment of a wider range of citizenship rights. In the recent past, the sphere of education has provided the clearest battle ground for the contestation of these equally problematic assimilationist and multi-culturalist ideologies (Troyna & Carrington 1990; Coleman 1991). In the wake of the Rushdie affair[1] and following a series of highly publicized schooling controversies, reactionary assimilationist arguments have opened up profound questions concerning the integration of minority ethnic communities and the desirability of cultural diversity in Britain (Ball & Solomos 1990). In particular it has been Britain's Muslim communities who have been blamed for causing particular problems of social integration. Nevertheless, even the most beleaguered minority ethnic groups in the UK find themselves in a more favourable position with regard to the exercise of citizenship rights than many of their counterparts elsewhere in the EC.

Race and citizenship in the EC

There are some important international variations in the extent to which black and minority ethnic people across the EC can gain access to citizenship entitlements (Labour Research 1990; Wrench 1991a). These differences have lessened since they were at their sharpest in the early period of primary immigration during the 1950s and '60s. Most obviously the initial "open door" system, which allowed Commonwealth immigrants freely to enter into Britain with full citizenship rights as British subjects, has long since ended. The "guest worker" system that operated in West Germany and elsewhere in Europe as a system of migrant labour subjected foreign workers to much greater levels of control than in the UK. Typically, migrant guest workers had severe restrictions placed on their mobility, were denied rights of permanent settlement, and were prevented from bringing their dependants with them. In short, European guest workers had few if any citizenship rights. However, a process of convergence has since taken place whereby the differences over immigration policy that existed previously between EC countries have diminished amidst a general concern to develop tough immigration controls and to impose strict limits on access to citizenship entitlements. On the one hand, in the post-war period the UK has moved very substantially to a much less liberal position on entry rights and access to citizenship. Elsewhere in Europe, on the other hand, there has been a trend towards the gradual extension of citizenship for migrants (Layton-Henry 1990). In Germany and elsewhere, immigrants have undergone a transition from temporary foreign workers to permanent settlers with some limited rights (Castles et al. 1984; Ireland 1991). Regularizing the status of settled immigrants usually involves offering rights that stop well short of full citizenship. Most obviously, the right to vote in national elections is usually denied even to the most permanently settled "foreigners" and often also to their descendants. Less obviously, exclusionary processes incorporated into a divisive conservative-corporatist welfare regime still limit access to welfare for migrants (Esping-Andersen 1991; Pierson 1991). This social insurance model of welfare provision based on the contributory principle operates to the detriment of "alien" newcomers and other "undeserving" non-contributory groups.

There can be little doubt that UK immigration and nationality legislation has been primarily concerned to impose severe restrictions on black migration and to ensure that British policy is more closely aligned with that in the rest of Europe. As a consequence the status and citizenship rights of UK immigrants have been radically altered in the last 30 years (Gordon 1989). Nevertheless, some crucial and perhaps surprising differences remain between the UK and most other EC member states in terms of citizenship rights and the management of race-related problems. In particular, important differences exist across the EC with respect to anti-discrimination legislation and civil rights for minority ethnic groups. The EC itself lacks any legal framework for dealing with race discrimination, and the issue has hardly ever surfaced on the European political agenda. Within the EC, equal opportunities has been interpreted to mean gender equality and little else. Although a clause concerning race discrimination, was added to the introduction of the original EC Social Charter, predictably this involved no binding commitments or concrete proposals (Labour Research 1990).

As a result, the UK has some of the most advanced legislation for the elimination of race discrimination and at the local government level has arguably developed the most progressive race equality policies to be found anywhere in the EC (Wrench 1991b; Forbes & Mead 1992). This may be a claim that is hard to swallow for many critics of the UK legislation, especially given some of its obvious problems of implementation (Gregory 1987; Lupton & Russell 1990). Other member states have various constitutional and statutory provisions offering some degree of protection against discrimination, but typically these are toothless and ineffectual. Measure for measure the UK comes out best – or "least worst" – when its statutory provisions are compared to the other member states (Forbes & Mead 1992). Other countries to a greater or lesser extent lack detailed legislation to tackle race discrimination in its direct and indirect forms; nor are there enforcement agencies such as the Commission for Racial Equality (CCRE) to be found in most other EC states. Only the Netherlands can stand serious comparison with the UK in terms of its anti-discrimination measures and relatively progressive "minorities policy". However, although the Dutch strategy of using the criminal law appears to offer a more forceful lever against discrimination, there are grounds for believing that the British legislation is preferable (Bocker 1991). The strength of the far more elaborate UK legislation is that it addresses more explicitly the definitional problem of what is and what is not unlawful discrimination, covering indirect as well as direct discrimination. Nor do the Dutch have an enforcement agency with as much muscle as the CRE. Instead, responsibility for enforcing the criminal prohibition of race discrimination in Holland lies with the police – with all-too predictable consequences!

In addition to these differences in anti-discrimination legislation, it can also be argued that other differences exist in terms of race equality policy between the member states. To varying degrees, all member states seem to be committed to some kind of "integration" policy, however minimal, for legally settled black and minority ethnic communities. Like Britain, other member states have developed a dual strategy linking restrictive immigration controls with integrative measures. In the UK, from 1962 onwards, a political bipartisan commitment to this dual strategy has been maintained (Solomos 1989). Conservative and Labour governments have accepted the need for tougher immigration policies to be balanced by measures to bring about "integration" in areas such as housing, education, and social services. The stated aim of this aspect of government policy has been to increase the capacity of minority ethnic groups already settled in the country to participate more fully in society. Such a dual strategy has become common across the EC, although considerable variation exists over the terms on which minority ethnic communities are allowed to "participate" more fully and gain greater access to social citizenship rights. What have also become noticeably more common are the increasingly restricted "integration" measures and rights offered to asylum seekers (Sivanandan 1988; Layton-Henry 1990). Generally the harsh treatment of refugees and the intensification of immigration controls have overshadowed integrative measures right across Europe.

Although a strong case exists for UK race equality policies to be seen as the most advanced in Europe, little credit for this is due to central government, since the most progressive and far-reaching policies have emerged at a more local level. Race equality policy in the UK has long suffered from a serious degree of neglect by central government, which has declined to take a lead in this area. Nor have attempts been made by central government to make local authorities accountable for the special responsibilities given to them under the 1976 Race Relations Act to eliminate unlawful discrimination and to promote equal opportunities (Bulpitt 1986; Mitchell & Russell 1989a). Instead there has been an uneven development of local race equality policies and equal opportunities programmes, with significant variations existing not only between local authorities themselves but even between departments within the same authority (Ben-Tovim et al. 1986; Butt et al. 1991).

It was from the early 1980s onwards that local authority policy initiatives first secured a partial and progressive "racialization" of policy in the UK (Mitchell & Russell 1989b; Solomos 1989; Ouseley 1990). For the first time, service providers began to take a more overt stance on race and sought to make services more accessible to black and minority ethnic communities. Since then the geographical spread of service providers committed to some form of race equality policy has slowly widened beyond areas with sizeable black populations. Race equality has become much more widely accepted as a policy objective and has moved well beyond the confines of the local councils that first pioneered new race initiatives in the early 1980s. All this is not to deny the well known problems that race policy initiatives have encountered or the fact that race issues are still prone to marginalization. Too often policies have been adopted but not translated into an effective programme of action. However, significant progress has been made in advancing race policy and practice – albeit in a patchy and piecemeal way – with the result that race equality in Britain is some way ahead of most other European countries. Britain, therefore, is unable to look to Europe for a positive lead in progressing race equality. For once Britain does not seem to be dragging its feet in comparison to the rest of Europe, even though it has little reason to be complacent over the results of its race equality initiatives.

The legacy of past immigration and nationality policy partly explains why this is the case. From the outset, Britain's black and minority ethnic communities have been entitled to permanent settlement and citizenship rights, and this has placed them strategically in a different position to many other minority ethnic groups in Europe.[2] Of course, the political effectiveness of Britain's black population has been adversely affected by problems of exclusion and marginalization, which in turn have resulted in a significant under-representation of black interests within the UK political system. Nevertheless, in comparison with most other EC countries, it has been the relative strength of black political mobilization in the UK that has helped to advance the claims of black people to citizenship rights and to ensure that services are more accessible, more adequate, and more available to their communities (Goulbourne 1990; Solomos & Back 1991). For example, it was the serious urban unrest of the 1980s that precipitated new policy responses and catapulted race onto local political agendas. All in all, a broad range of black political strategies "from below" have been crucially important in demanding greater access to formal citizenship rights, which had been formally granted "from above" as a consequence of the commitment by successive British political elites to the idea of the British Commonwealth – itself a continuation of a deep-seated colonial ideology of trusteeship (Fryer 1984).

At the same time, it is vital to understand that differential incorporation into British society exists within the black and minority ethnic population, and that consequently black people have experienced citizenship in different ways (Harrison 1991). In this respect the greatest concern is for the position of the growing number of black migrant workers and asylum seekers inside Britain who, as aliens rather than citizens, enjoy very few rights indeed. The position of these groups in Britain is very similar to that of millions of black and third world migrants across the EC. The most power-less and vulnerable groups are the asylum seekers and illegal immigrants, who have been subject to an increasingly harsh clamp down and ever-more hostile treatment from Britain and other EC countries. These groups possess no political resources and are dependent on the efforts of voluntary agen-cies, churches, and community groups for support.

The asylum crisis

Currently, right across the EC, governments of all political persuasions are ac-tively seeking new ways to close Europe's doors to refugees from non-EC countries (Joly & Cohen 1989; Labour Research 1991; Webber 1991). The British government has been an all-too-willing partner in the efforts to inten-sify the policing of displaced people seeking asylum in the UK. However, there is nothing particularly new about these initiatives. They represent a further step along an already well trodden path that has been followed by every UK administration since 1962 in their attempts to intensify immigration controls over migrants of one form or another. In view of this, it was probably only a matter of time before refugees became the focus of race and immigration policy and practice. Nor is it accurate to blame these initiatives on the legacy of Thatcherism. The recent Conservative record on race and immigration does not differ substantially from that of previous Labour and Conservative administrations, and many of the changes that have taken place since 1979 represent an extension of earlier policies rather than distinctively "new right" initiatives (Mitchell & Russell 1989b; Cook & Clarke 1990).

Nevertheless, the period since the mid-1980s has certainly witnessed a new phase in the development of post-war European migration and in the attempts to police this through immigration control. In recent years west-ern Europe has been confronted by a growing asylum problem of a complex nature. In 1985 the number of asylum seekers coming to Europe exceeded the number of legally admitted foreign workers for the first time, and since then the number of refugees has continued to rise steeply, provoking a mounting wave of concern about "hordes" of unwanted aliens "flooding" into western Europe from various directions (Sivanandan 1988; Loescher 1989). However, the substantial growth in the numbers of asylum seekers in western Europe should not blind us to the fact that these numbers represent only a tiny proportion of the world's refugee population. The great majority of refugees both originate from, and remain in, the third world, with the biggest concentrations of refugees residing in the world's poorest countries. Thus Europe remains on the fringes of the refugee crisis and continues to receive a comparatively small proportion of the growing pool of refugees worldwide (Loescher 1989).

That having been said, it is obvious that the explosion of a global refugee problem during the 1980s, coupled with the collapse of communism in eastern Europe, has imposed immense strains on the liberal principles that initially framed European asylum policies in the early post-war period. The existence of severe labour shortages in the economy, and the fact that the overwhelming majority of refugees coming to western Europe were fleeing from political repression in the eastern European Soviet bloc, were major influences on these post-war policies. However, in the new configuration of Europe, East–West migration is driven more by economic motives and a desire for family reunification than by the need for political refuge, although increasing civil conflict and ethnic turmoil has also contributed to the upsurge in migration in recent years. At the same time, economic migration from the South, sometimes illegal in nature, has grown steadily, particularly in Italy, Spain, Greece, and Portugal – countries that have previously been substantial exporters of migrant labour to northern Europe. It is anticipated that these Mediterranean rim states will bear the brunt of the projected increase in the population size of the EC during the 1990s. In addition, there is a further concern over the apparent ease with which non-EC migrants can obtain entry to these states as a first step on the road north (Salt 1991). Certainly it is highly likely that there will be a continuing demand for cheap, flexible labour in the northern European, states which will continue to pull migrants from the South, often to work in the informal economy in the lowest-paid jobs. Faced with this flow of migrants and refugees from the South and the East, European governments have been increasingly concerned to draw a clear distinction between so-called "political" and "economic" refugees, "genuine" and "bogus" asylum seekers, and "deserving" and "undeserving" immigrants. In reality it is often difficult to make these distinctions, as the real divisions are less clear cut. A potent combination of geo-political, economic, ecological, and demographic factors is changing conditions in the world outside Europe and is precipitating unprecedented levels of migration of peoples who are in the main seen by European governments as "culturally incompatible" with the mainstream traditions and values of western Europe and who consequently pose major problems for future social integration. In the current circumstances, deciding between who is and who is not a "genuine" refugee becomes impossibly difficult.

These difficulties have been further exacerbated by the development of new forms of European xenophobic and racist hostility against the "hordes" of cultural aliens currently "invading" Europe. The recent re-emergence of the neo-Nazis in Germany and the rise of Le Pen and Le Front Nationale in French politics can be seen as important components of this process. Evidence of increased levels of racial violence against immigrants and of growth in political support for the organized racism of the far right has increased the pressure on European governments to pander to popular racism by taking a hard line on immigration. The clamp down on asylum seekers and "bogus refugees" is the most obvious manifestation of this, particularly in countries such as Germany and France where the number of asylum seekers is particularly high by European standards. Indeed, largely due to liberal laws drafted in the aftermath of the holocaust, Germany currently receives around half of all the asylum seekers who reach western Europe (*Guardian* 29 October 1991; *Economist* 15 February 1992). Around 500,000 asylum seekers are estimated to have arrived in Germany during 1992, twice as many as in 1991 and five times as many as in 1988, the year prior to unification (*Economist* 14 November 1992). It is widely believed within mainstream German political opinion that support for the neo-Nazis will rise and racial violence increase unless the influx of foreigners is effectively stemmed. It should come as no surprise therefore to find that it is Germany that has pressed hardest for the harmonization of asylum policy inside the EC, and that Britain, with much less acute asylum problems, has led the resistance to any erosion of its sovereign right to determine who should be permitted to cross its borders. There is a genuine need to develop a rational and humane European-wide policy with proper legal safeguards that will be capable of responding quickly to these intractable problems. However, the developments that have taken place to date give cause for real concern.

Towards a Fortress Europe?

In essence, the basic policy response to the refugee problem – both real and imagined – has been to erect new barriers around Europe in what can only be seen as a multi-lateral movement towards the creation of a Fortress Europe. By far the greatest effort has gone into strengthening the EC's external frontiers and to extending internal immigration controls, thus blurring the line between policing and immigration control. The Single Market will be a catalyst for the acceleration of a dual process that is already well established. One part of this process involves the lowering of border controls between EC member states to facilitate the "free movement" of labour across internal frontiers in an open European market. The second dimension of the process involves the progressive tightening up of "influx controls", both by restricting the flow of immigrants and refugees from the third world into Europe and through the closer surveillance of those who manage successfully to negotiate the European barriers to entry. In this situation, the acquisition of citizenship rights within a single member state is of crucial importance, since it will determine the ability of the individual concerned to become a "free mover" within the Single Market. In the run-up to 1992, efforts were made to clarify and in some cases re-define the legal status and citizenship entitlements of various categories of people within Europe's black and minority ethnic populations (Sivanandan 1988).

It should be stressed that as yet there is no common EC immigration and asylum policy, since both of these policy areas lie outside the competence of the European Commission. The development of Fortress Europe that has occurred to date is not the result of the imposition of a top-down supranational policy process. The British government in particular has resisted the imposition of any common policy on the grounds that this would represent a potential loss of sovereignty for the British state. Nevertheless there have been clear signs of convergence in policy and practice, as well as a growth of co-operation between member states in an effort to close Europe's doors. However, the Maastricht Treaty stopped some way short of passing responsibility to the European institutions. The drift towards a Fortress Europe has not been orchestrated from Brussels but has come about as the result of a combination of tougher measures introduced by individual member states and inter-governmental initiatives directed towards the harmonization of policy and practice. Before Maastricht the most important inter-governmental policy developments had occurred as a result of the deliberations of the Schengen and Trevi groups. Although these have often been taken as the pilots for an eventual common immigration and asylum policy across the EC, this still appears to be some way off.

At present, eight countries – all except Britain, Ireland, Denmark, and Greece – have signed the Schengen accord, committing them to the abolition of internal border controls and the harmonization of asylum policies with respect to visas, sanctions against airlines, etc. The accord also commits the participating member states to a progressive pooling of those national resources currently mobilized to restrict the flow of refugees and immigrants.

Most notably this involves the commitment to establish a computer system to share police information on criminals, refugees, and illegal immigrants (Jenkins 1989; Bunyan 1991). In part this overlaps with the work of the Trevi group (which takes its name from terrorism, radicalism, extremism, and violence!) of Justice and Home Affairs ministers, who have been meeting regularly since 1976 to discuss those matters of common concern that fall outside the EC's competence under the Treaty of Rome. The work of the Trevi group has expanded to incorporate problems presented by illegal immigrants and asylum seekers – a rather different agenda from the original concern with crimes such as terrorism and drug running. An important development from the inter-governmental co-operation established by these two groups is the agreement recently reached at Maastricht to set up Europol, an EC-wide system for exchanging information between European police forces. The Maastricht Treaty secured a consolidation of the inter-governmental rather than the federal approach to key European issues, with co-operation on immigration, asylum, and policing chosen as one of the three "pillars" of European union. The Maastricht Treaty in effect failed to strengthen the European Commission or the European Parliament. But with respect to justice and home affairs, the European Commission's powers were increased marginally, since it may now make proposals on visas (*Economist* 15 February and 14 November 1992). Otherwise Maastricht merely signalled the intention to extend the Schengen approach, with the aim of reaching agreement over the harmonization of certain aspects of asylum policy by the end of 1993.[3] It is unfortunate that the institutions of the EC will play little in the way of an active rôle in the formulation of a common immigration policy at European level. An unwillingness at Maastricht to accede to the German plan to pass responsibility to the European level will reinforce the current tendency to adopt the policies of the most restrictive states in the EC. In this area, no government wants to appear too liberal for fear of following in the footsteps of Germany and attracting increased numbers of refugees and asylum seekers. Although there is still a range of views across the EC about how best to develop policies in this area, it is nevertheless possible to identify a broadly similar European policy response based on deterrence and restriction (Loescher 1989). This has given rise to a wide range of increasingly authoritarian measures: tougher entry checks and more refusals; the imposition of visa requirements for individuals from an enlarged number of countries; sanctions against airlines; a stricter definition of who should count as a refugee; a growing trend to grant non-Convention refugee status rather than full asylum; the "criminalization" of refugees by putting them in unlimited detention on arrival and subjecting them to compulsory finger printing; and the removal of legal rights by allowing no appeal against entry refusals and denying legal assistance for asylum seekers. Clearly the aim of these restrictions is to make access to refugee recognition procedures more difficult and to speed the repatriation of asylum seekers. There is also an explicit use of certain measures that are designed to deter refugees from coming to Europe by ensuring that their treatment on arrival is harsh and inhumane. This is the New Europe at its worst! It illustrates well the impotence of European institutions in the face of a determination by individual member states to look after the interests of their own citizens and reveals just how far away we are from the idea of European citizenship.

Faced with these acute problems, there is an urgent need for a common European policy response that is both rational and humane. However, the attainment of such a project must necessarily imply a further diminution of national sovereignty through the transference of more decision-making powers to Community institutions and a loosening of the link between citizenship rights and the sovereign character of member states. It is beyond the capacity of any one country to effect these changes single handed or to prevent a downward spiral towards ever harsher and more restrictive policies. The problem is not a temporary one, and the pressures are likely to increase. Thus there is a need for a long-term European strategy.

The adoption of "open door" policies is clearly impracticable; but nor can a humane EC response be based solely on exclusion and deterrence. What is required is a selective system based on fairer and more effective adjudication (Loescher 1989). In addition, a more outward-looking European policy would involve foreign policy initiatives to address the refugee crisis and higher levels of development assistance for third world countries. More progressive Community policies would also grant a minimal set of "denizen rights" both for non-EC nationals and for EC nationals working or living elsewhere in the Community for any length of time (Layton-Henry 1990). However, the possibility of a more enlightened supra-national EC-led response on these issues remains remote at this point in time. This in turn has serious implications for the future of race equality policy in Britain.

Race equality policy in Britain: continuity and change

At the 1991 Conservative party conference, the Home Secretary Kenneth Baker accused the Labour party of "attempting to pander to ethnic minorities". At the same time there was an escalating furore in the tabloid press over the "flood" of immigrants into Europe from the South and East. Shortly afterwards, a spate of "bogus" refugee and illegal immigration stories accompanied the attempted passage of the Asylum Bill through Parliament (Le Lohé 1992). After the Bill was lost, with the dissolution of Parliament, the scurrilous tabloid offensive reached a new peak in a tightly contested 1992 general election campaign. According to the Conservative tabloids, a Labour victory threatened new floods of immigrants, which in turn would produce racial strife and the growth of extremism in Britain. As the campaign unfolded, increasing emphasis was given to the immigration issue by the Tory party. Arguably this "playing of the race card" tipped the balance towards the Tories and helped to secure their unexpected election success (Billig & Golding 1992). After the election the government predictably re-introduced another Asylum Bill with broadly similar provisions to its predecessor. In all probability, a Labour government would have done much the same! As things stand, a well established pattern is likely to prevail for the foreseeable future, in which the primary focus of state intervention in the area of race will be the control of immigration and the restriction of access to citizenship rights. This is likely to have serious knock-on effects for the successful implementation of race equality policies at the sub-central government level as well as for black citizens in their daily lives. Continuing references to the undesirability of more "cultural aliens" entering the country can only serve to foster greater levels of unequal treatment for those citizens who find their status queried by service providers and other state officials because of the colour of their skin. Hence it is likely that periodic press campaigns against the "migrant hordes gate-crashing our nation" will both reflect and reinforce the growing prominence of a reactionary assimilationist discourse in British public life. Thus the conflicts and tensions surrounding race policy and practice that emerged in the 1980s are likely to be further intensified throughout the 1990s – whatever the political complexion of the government.

As we have argued elsewhere, the most innovative developments that have taken place in race policy since 1979 have been at the level of the local state (Mitchell & Russell 1989b). Thus the 1980s saw the development of race equality policies by a range of local service providers and the emergence of anti-racist forms of professional practice to complement these. Together they represent the most serious challenge yet to the established patterns of control and restriction in a sphere of race. However, it is obvious that race equality and anti-racist policies have encountered serious difficulties in recent years. Many of the initiatives were developed in an environment that was becoming increasingly hostile to the advancement of anti-racism and to more radical equal opportunities programmes. One obvious dimension of this has been the emergence from the mid-1980s onwards of strident press hostility to all forms of anti-racism and multi-culturalism. In particular, certain local councils have been vilified for the high profile that they have given to race equality issues, and in general race equality work has undeservedly acquired a "loony left" tag. In this climate, various initiatives involving positive action to increase citizenship entitlements have been singled out – quite inaccurately – as evidence of "reverse racism" involving positive discrimination in favour of black and minority ethnic groups (Lewis 1988). In short, assimilationist arguments have reappeared with a vengeance, offering a strong critique of local efforts to advance race equality policies up and down the country. The effect of this ideological offensive has been to raise serious doubts over the possibility of the social integration of minority ethnic communities and the desirability of cultural diversity in Britain (Solomos 1990). It also appears that social authoritarian arguments in favour of the forcible assimilation of black citizens into the national culture have a close symbiotic relationship with the language of anti-immigration and Eurocentrism that has surfaced since the late 1980s (Balibar 1991).

Attempts by service providers to establish race equality policies to deal with the problem of racial differentiation in access to citizenship entitlements have also been critically affected by the changes that have taken place in the rôles and responsibilities of public service providers. Recent reforms of local government, the National Health Service, and social services have served primarily to promote a concern for managerial efficiency and cost effectiveness. In the new world of public sector management there remains a gap between a fashionable rhetoric about consumer choice and user empowerment on the one hand, and a continuing lack of accountability and responsiveness to black consumers on the other.

In this situation, central government has, in the main, continued to undertake a more limited promotional rôle in policy innovation, failing to go beyond a symbolic commitment to race equality. Recent legislation such as the Housing Act 1988, the Children Act 1989, and the National Health Service and Community Care Act 1990 have all placed legal obligations on service providers to take account of the needs of the black and minority ethnic population. However, much has been left to the agencies themselves to determine and deliver actual policy, all under the pressure of serious resource constraints. Furthermore, government race-related expenditure, such as the

Urban Programme grants and the Home Office grants made under Section 11 of the Local Government Act 1966, have failed to keep pace with the growing ambitions of service providers to pursue policies of race equality. Indeed, the recent curtailment of Section 11 funding indicates the determination of the government to control the growth of the "race relations industry". In general we can see that the government has paid little more than lip service to the notion of a multi-cultural and multi-racial society in its recent health and welfare reforms (Johnson 1991). Thus service providers attempting to pursue race equality policies must do so in difficult and trying circumstances brought on by the advent of the internal market and the new age of consumerism. Much remains to be achieved if black and minority ethnic people are to enjoy the full and effective rights of social citizenship. All of this qualifies our earlier view that Britain's race equality policies are relatively advanced in comparison to the rest of Europe. The existence of a framework of race equality legislation and the development of a range of progressive local policy initiatives are highly significant in a European context. But this should not blind us to the fact that much remains to be achieved in an increasingly hostile political climate.

Conclusion: racism, anti-racism and citizenship

This paper has argued that black and minority ethnic groups domiciled in the UK are in a comparatively privileged position when compared with those in other EC countries. Prior to 1973, migrants to the UK from the Commonwealth and colonies were virtually guaranteed formal citizenship rights in the civil, political, and social spheres. The consequence of this has been that the demands and struggles of black and minority ethnic communities in the UK have generally been of a qualitatively different nature in comparison with similar groups in other EC member states. This is because these groups have been able to use their more favourable status as full UK citizens to struggle for anti-racist policies that are generally unknown elsewhere in the EC.

These developments have brought about real – if limited – material changes that have benefited some members of these communities. The demands for race equality and equal opportunities policies, supported through ethnic monitoring and positive action, are gradually changing the employment practices of a significant number of organizations. Demands for more racially explicit and ethnically sensitive services in health care, social services provision and, more recently, policing are beginning to have an impact at the level of training and service delivery. This is not to deny the fact that much remains to be achieved; nor that there are hostile forces at work attempting to reverse these trends. Nonetheless, it is noticeable that the European social agenda is characterized by the virtual absence of the kind of anti-racist demands and policies that became relatively commonplace in the UK during the 1980s.

The clear differences between the UK and the rest of the EC over the development of anti-racist policies are much less discernible in the broad sphere of immigration policy. Here the trend towards a common set of highly restrictive and unjust regulations is already well underway, as illustrated by the work of the Trevi and Schengen groups. The contrast between the highly secretive nature of the proposals emanating from these intergovernmental groups and the more publicly debated provisions of the European Social Chapter is important. On the one hand, the Chapter contains no detailed provisions covering the specific rights of black and minority ethnic groups, and is little more than a symbolic and non-binding statement of intent concentrating largely on the rights of workers rather than citizens. On the other hand, precisely because it has been formulated and refined within the institutions of the EC, it does not pander to the lowest common denominator of the most reactionary forms of social provision among the member states. There is an urgent need for the issues of immigration control and asylum to be removed from the grip of assorted civil servants, security officials, and police officers and relocated firmly in the arena of the Commission and the European Parliament. This is not to run away from the fact that the dramatic increase in migration to Europe from the South and East in recent years has created real problems for EC member states, both collectively and individually. For the foreseeable future all governments of whatever political persuasion will have little alternative but to restrict the entry of migrants and to ration access to citizen entitlements across the EC. The advent of the Single Market makes this problem even more urgent and demands a much greater degree of harmonization of immigration and asylum policies. It also means that individual member states have a direct interest in how other EC countries resolve their problems of citizenship, particularly the question of how, when and under what conditions their settler populations can acquire citizenship rights. The granting of citizenship to Turkish settlers in Germany or the Netherlands or to settlers from the Maghreb in France or Spain would lead to the automatic entitlement to mobility across the EC. The possible enlargement of the Community to include the EFTA countries and even some of the former Soviet republics would inevitably make this difficult situation even more complicated.

The idea of citizenship has emerged as a recurrent theme throughout this paper. But of course citizenship itself is a concept that is highly contested. Brief mention has already been made of the debate in the UK between the assimilationist view of citizenship, which demands a high degree of cultural conformity from minority ethnic groups as a requirement for the conferment of citizenship; and the multi-cultural perspective, which sees cultural distinctiveness as a pre-condition for the enjoyment of civil, political, and social rights. In part this debate reflects different theoretical/ideological approaches to the concept of citizenship, in particular differences over whether citizenship is "granted" from above or "won" from below (Turner 1990). More importantly, this debate mirrors real racial tensions and cultural conflicts in UK society. On the one hand, substantial sections of the population still appear to be unwilling to accept as citizens minorities that are culturally distinct and visibly different from themselves. On the other hand, some elements within the black and minority ethnic communities apparently wish to live apart, rejecting the view that the internalization of some shared values and common commitments is the duty of every citizen. In our view it is only possible to begin to resolve these difficult issues by reworking both the concept and practice of citizenship.

Following Marshall, much of the debate over citizenship has been framed in terms of the progressive attainment of universal standards, whether in the legal, political, or welfare arenas. Thus ideas such as "the rule of law", "universal adult suffrage", and "equality" have generally been seen as the bedrock principles upon which forms of citizenship are constructed. However, some more recent contributions to the debate on citizenship have emphasized the importance of recognizing "difference" and the right to be different, not only in an individual sense but at the level of group activity, as an important component of citizenship in contemporary societies (Parekh 1991; Phillips 1991). Clearly the right to be different can never be unconditional and, in relation to the crucial dimension of cultural difference, it is important in attempting to reframe citizenship to avoid the more simplistic variants of multi-culturalism. One of the most fundamental problems with multi-culturalism is that it fails to address the difficult but necessary question of the boundaries and limitations that any modern society must impose upon culturally distinct groups. No society can maintain a position in which "anything goes" at the cultural level within its various communities. Multi-culturalists have generally failed to face up to the difficulties posed by the existence of certain reactionary and unacceptable forms of cultural practice within particular communities. This has made the defence of legitimate cultural difference far more difficult in the face of a sustained ideological onslaught by the supporters of cultural assimilation – particularly in the wake of the Rushdie affair. As the disenfranchised and disadvantaged settler communities throughout the EC begin to press their legitimate claims for citizenship more firmly, it will be all the more important for the principle of difference to be enshrined within a framework of citizens' rights.

Notes

1. The publication in 1988 of Salman Rushdie's *The Satanic Verses* had a significant impact on the politics of race in Britain. In particular, fundamentalist reaction from sections within the Muslim communities fuelled public debates about the issue of cultural differences and the limits of "multi-culturalism".

2. The incorporation into the British nation of colonial immigrants who arrived before 1962 (as well as their family members who arrived later) with full political and civil rights is not unique within Europe. Similarities exist with respect to the position of the Surinamese in the Netherlands and some Algerians in France. Until 1975, the Surinamese were Dutch nationals and citizens, while between 1947 and 1962, the people of Algeria also possessed French nationality and citizenship. As with Commonwealth migrants to Britain, Surinamese and Algerian migrants to the Netherlands and France respectively also enjoyed full and equal rights of political participation. In comparison, most other migrants to western European countries have been non-citizens or "foreigners", possessing few, if any, rights of political participation.

3. This harmonization process was advanced through an agreement reached by EC immigration ministers meeting in London on 30 November 1992 under the auspices of the Ad Hoc Group on Immigration. Like the Schengen and Trevi groups, this group has no official status within the Community and therefore is not subject to scrutiny by the European Parliament. The new policy aims to speed the repatriation of asylum seekers through the development of accelerated procedures to deal with so-called "manifestly unfounded" applications. The new stricter controls mean that asylum seekers will be sent back to the first safe haven or "third best country" passed through on their way into the Community. In effect, this creates a kind of ring fence around the Community. These new rules are similar to the provisions of the recent UK Asylum Act, though the changes signal a considerable tightening up in most other EC states and should lead to a severe reduction in the number of asylum seekers allowed to stay (*Independent* 2 December 1992).

References

Balibar, E. 1991. Racism and politics in Europe today. *New Left Review* **186**, 5–19.
Ball, W. & J. Solomos 1990. Racial equality and local politics. In *Race and local politics*, W.

Ball & J. Solomos (eds). London: Macmillan.

Ben-Tovim, G., J. Gabriel, I. Law, I. & K. Stredder 1986. *The local politics of race.* London: Macmillan.

Billig, M. & P. Golding 1992. Did the race card tip the balance? *New Community* **19**, 161–3.

Bocker, A. 1991. A pyramid of complaints: the handling of complaints about racial discrimination in the Netherlands. *New Community* **17**, 603–16.

Bulpitt 1986. Continuity, autonomy and peripheralisation: the anatomy of the centre's statecraft in England. In *Race, government and politics in Britain*, Z. Layton-Henry & P. Rich (eds). London: Macmillan.

Bunyan, T. 1991. Towards an authoritarian European state. *Race and Class* **32**(3), 19–27.

Butt, J., P. Gorbach, B. Ahmad 1991. *Equally unfair?. A report on social services departments' development, implementation and monitoring of services for the black and ethnic minority community.* London: Race Equality Unit.

Castles, S., T. Booth, T. Wallace 1984. *Here for good: western Europe's new ethnic minorities.* London: Pluto.

Coleman, D. 1991. Multiculturalism or assimilation: still to decide. *Economic Affairs* 17–19.

Cook, J. & J. Clarke 1990. Racism and the right. In *Reactions to the right*, B. Hindness (ed.). London: Routledge.

Esping-Andersen, G. 1991. *The three worlds of welfare capitalism.* Cambridge: Polity.

Forbes, I. & G. Mead 1992. *Measure for measure: comparative analysis of measures to combat racial discrimination in the member countries of the EC.* Sheffield: Department of Employment.

Fryer, P. 1984. *Staying power: the history of black people in Britain.* London: Pluto.

Giddens, A. 1985. *The nation state and violence. A contemporary critique of historical materialism*, vol. II. Cambridge: Polity.

Ginsberg, N. 1989. Racial harassment policy and practice: the denial of citizenship. *Critical Social Policy*, **9**, 66–81.

Ginsberg, N. 1992. Racism and housing: concepts and reality. In *Racism and anti-racism: inequalities, opportunities and policies*, P. Braham, A. Rattanasi, R. Skellington (eds). London: Sage.

Gordon, P. 1989. Citizenship for Some? *Race and government policy 1979–1989*. London: Runnymede Trust.

Goulbourne, H. (ed.) 1990. *Black politics in Britain.* Aldershot: Avebury.

Gregory, J. 1987. *Sex, race and the law: legislating for equality.* London: Sage.

Harrison, M. 1991. Citizenship, consumption and rights: a comment on B. S. Turner's theory of citizenship. *Sociology* **25**, 209–13.

Held, D. 1989. Citizenship and autonomy. In *Social theory of modern societies: Anthony Giddens and his critics*, D. Held & J. Thompson (eds). Cambridge: Cambridge University Press.

Ireland, P. 1991. Facing the true Fortress Europe: immigrant and politics in the EC. *Journal of Common Market Studies* 24, 457–479.

Jenkins, J. 1989. Foreign exchange. *New Statesman and Society* (28 July) 12–13.

Johnson, M. 1991. Health and social services report. *New Community* **17**, 624–32.

Joly, D. & R. Cohen (eds) 1989. *Reluctant hosts: Europe and its refugees.* Aldershot: Avebury.

Labour Research 1990. 1992 and immigration. *Labour Research* (April) 19–21.

Labour Research 1991. Migrants: facing the clampdown. *Labour Research* (February) 17–18.

Layton-Henry, Z. 1990. *The political rights of migrant workers in western Europe.* London: Sage.

Le Lohé, M. 1992. The Asylum Bill: the rôle of the tabloids. *New Community* **18**, 469–74.

Lewis, R. 1988. *Anti-racism: a mania exposed.* London: Charter.

Loescher, G. 1989. The European Community and refugees. *International Affairs* **4**, 617–36.

Lupton, C. & D. Russell 1990. Equal opportunities in a cold climate. In *Public policy under Thatcher*, S. Savage & L. Robins (eds). London: Macmillan.

Mitchell, M. & D. Russell 1989a. Race, the new right and state policy in Britain. *Immigrants and minorities* **8**, 175–90.

Mitchell, M. & D. Russell 1989b. Race and racism. In *Beyond Thatcherism: social policy, politics and society* P. Brown & R. Sparks (eds). Milton Keynes, England: Open University Press.

Ousley, H. 1990. Resisting institutional change. In *Race and local politics*, W. Ball & J. Solomos (eds) London: Macmillan.

Parekh, B. 1991. British citizenship and cultural difference. In *Citizenship*, G. Andrews (ed.). London: Lawrence and Wishart.

Paul, R. 1991. Black and third world people's citizenship and 1992. *Critical Social Policy* **11**, 52–64.

Pearson, G., A. Sampson, H. Blagg, P. Stubbs, P. Smith 1989. Police racism. In *Coming to terms with policing*, R. Morgan & D. Smith (eds). London: Routledge.

Phillips, A. 1991. Citizenship and feminist theory. In *Citizenship*, G. Andrews (ed.). London: Lawrence & Wishart.

Phillips, D. 1987. Searching for a decent home: ethnic minority progress in the post-war housing market. *New Community* **16**, 105–117.

Pierson, C. 1991. *Beyond the welfare state.* Cambridge: Polity.

Rex, J. & D. Mason (eds) 1986. *Theories of race and ethnic relations.* Cambridge: Cambridge University Press.

Salt, J. 1991. South–North migration in Europe today. *Economic Affairs* (June), 15–17.

Sivanandan, A. 1988. The new racism. *New Statesman* (4 November), 8–9.

Smith, S. 1989. *The politics of "race" and residence.* Cambridge: Polity.

Solomos, J. 1989. *Race and racism in contemporary Britain.* London: Macmillan.

Solomos, J. 1990. Changing forms of racial discourse. *Social Studies Review* **6**, 74–78.

Solomos, J. & L. Back 1991. Black political mobilisation and the struggle for equality. *Sociological Review* **39**, 215–37.

Taylor, D. 1991. A big idea for the nineties? The rise of Citizens' Charters. *Critical Social Policy* **11**, 87–94.

Troyna, B. & B. Carrington 1990. *Education, racism and reform.* London: Routledge.

Turner, B. 1990. Outline of a theory of citizenship. *Sociology* **24**, 189–217.

Webber, F. 1991. Refugees: countdown to zero. *Race and Class* 33, 80–85.

Wrench, J. 1991a. Employment and the labour market: report. *New Community* **16**, 275–87.

Wrench, J. 1991b. Employment in the labour market: report. *New Community* **16**, 574–83.

Chapter 7

The making of an underclass: neo-liberalism versus corporatism

Scott Lash

Introduction

My main claim in this chapter is that economic restructuring has forced the structural downward mobility of a large section of the working class into a "new lower class". I want to claim also that a substantial portion of this new lower class is comprised by an "underclass". I want then to argue that the shape of such new lower class formation is dependent on the varying institutional frameworks of regulation that have accompanied restructuring. Specifically, I want to point to the different tendencies developing in Anglo-American neo-liberalism as compared to the corporatism of the German-speaking world.

The underclass

We will begin with William Julius Wilson's (1987) underclass thesis, which has considerable merit. Let us outline its central tenets, attempting to underscore how Wilson's thesis differs from those of neo-conservative underclass analysts.

1. Blacks have not always been members of the underclass. The underclass has been a result of structural change, especially of de-industrialization. Blacks, previously in the working class, have become downwardly mobile into the underclass.

2. Not all members of the underclass are blacks or minorities, and only a portion of blacks are in the underclass.

3. A ghetto culture has developed that in some ways resembles previously described "cultures of poverty". Where neo-conservative analysts have seen

this as endemic to the ghetto, Wilson does not. For Wilson, black culture was largely constituted around work relations, prior to the economic restructuring of the past 20 years. It is only after the jobs have disappeared that these sorts of cultures have developed, in which symbolic resources and meanings have come to be constituted primarily in non-work situations.

Philip Bourgois (1991), in his ethnographic study of Puerto Rican crack dealers in Manhattan, has examined this aspect in a framework similar to that of Paul Willis's *Learning to labour* (1977). On this account, black and Puerto Rican youth were working class kids who in school had learned "to labour" or who were prepared for the world of working class jobs. The problem is that after they had learned to labour, the "working class jobs" had disappeared. And that much of what was left for them was gang-bonding and the culture of the political economy of crack.

4. Wilson's thesis is importantly gendered. The fact that it is focused not generically on "men", but gender-specifically on *males*, has justifiably aroused objections among feminist scholars. Yet the explanatory potential of his focus on the black male has been considerable. First, as in Paul Willis's account, the working class jobs for which these minority working class boys were schooled for were, as was the "schooling", heavily (male) gendered. And the fact that these male jobs have disappeared to be replaced by very much less "male" consumer services jobs or, more likely, by unemployment, is crucial. Upon graduating from such heavily male schooling, black teenage young men must find other outlets for their masculinity, mostly in the sphere not of work but of non-work. Sometimes these can be highly creative, as evidenced by a series of waves of ghetto culture that have swept the whole of western popular culture. But they also can take a less creative and more violent turn.

A major problem in Wilson's work is the attribution of the proliferation of female-headed households to black male joblessness. This seems to deny the powers of agency to black women, who themselves are making conscious choices of living arrangements. Indeed the increase in the labour force participation rate (LFPR) of black American and foreign-born females has established some (very) minimal economic resource bases that make female-headed households possible. Further, a similar proportional increase has been registered among American and European whites, often in situations in which male unemployment is not at particularly high levels (Jencks 1992).

However, structural conditions of the underclass in the United States and elsewhere have also denied very important powers of agency of black males. This has been reflected, for example, in the new black cinema. The unfor-

tunate focus on black male sexual prowess and athletic ability in black popular culture has encouraged a one-sided emphasis on agency, not as "culture",
but as nature. It has encouraged labelling on the part of white employers and
educators. It has set up rôle models for black youth. Consider Roger
Waldinger's (1986/7) theory of ethnically structured labour markets in terms
of hiring queues that agents enter when excluded from other queues. Blacks,
excluded functionally from a number of other labour markets, look to sports
and popular culture or the crack economy as possible alternative routes. The
Jews, excluded elsewhere, joined the queues in the garment industry and the
business side of the entertainment industry. Blacks have had to join other
queues.

Comparable gendered labour force participation rates (LFPR) are of some
significance. In 1986 the LFPR of foreign-born female blacks in America was
about equal to that of native-born black males. In comparison, the rates of
male and female native-born blacks were much closer together than those
of male and female whites. Similarly, in Britain in 1983 the LFPR among all
women was 47.5 per cent; among Afro-Caribbean women it was 68.5 per
cent. In the USA employers have in particular discriminated against black
males in service jobs involving face to face contact with white consumers. In
any event, pecking orders and competition in terms of gendered labour
markets and economic resources are very different in the black community
as compared to the white. This was already the case when black males had
much lower jobless rates and were more likely to have been employed in
industrial jobs. It is more so now. I am not here, it must be noted, defend-
ing the male bias of Wilson's theses. I am however suggesting that their very
gendered (as distinct from gender-blind) orientation raises a whole series of
important explanatory problems.

5. Wilson's theory is pre-eminently spatial. In regard to labour markets,
not only has de-industrialization led to unemployment and downward
mobility for black males (and females), but so has the spatial mobility of the
remaining industrial jobs. These have moved in the USA, on the one hand,
from the northeastern rustbelt to sunbelt. On the other, in the rustbelt they
have moved to far suburbs and "exurbs", hence an inaccessible distance
away from inner city blacks. In addition to industrial jobs, a great number
of retail and consumer service jobs have moved to suburban shopping malls.
Often inner city blacks must do their shopping here as ghetto stores close
down. But only rarely are they *employed* in the suburban malls.

In this context, it is possible to speak of three sorts of American city:
  – De-industrialized cities such as Cleveland, Philadelphia, and Detroit,

which like Newcastle and Liverpool have not made a successful transition from their industrial past
- Restructured cities such as New York and Chicago which, like London and Manchester (after crisis), have made a reasonably successful transition
- Post-industrial cities such as Houston, Denver, Atlanta, and Miami, which were never big manufacturing centres and had their rapid growth spurts in much more recent years; Boston, San Francisco, and Los Angeles are "older" cities that partly fall in this category.

Both work and residential patterns of the underclass bear examination in this context. Wilson's underclass or "ghetto poor" are found almost exclusively in de-industrialized and restructured, and not in post-industrial, cities. The ghetto poor, as defined by Wilson and other urban analysts such as Mark A. Hughes (1990), are those living in census tracts in which over 40 per cent of the population is below the poverty line. In 1970 there were very few of these. In 1980 they multiplied – in de-industrialized cities like Philadelphia and Detroit several fold. However, post-industrial cities have very few of these high poverty districts. They also have relatively few blacks. In fact, the number of such census tracts vastly decreased in Los Angeles from 1970 to 1989, and the absolute number of blacks in Los Angeles' population also decreased. The post-industrial cities were major growth centres in the 1970s. In these agglomerations are found many jobs that require only intermediate levels of education. The education level of American blacks has improved considerably. Nevertheless, the relative absence of blacks in these post-industrial cities means that they are not there to fill the jobs for which their education level qualifies them.

The de-industrialized cities have lost jobs altogether. The restructured cities, in contradistinction – and especially the "global" cities among them – have created awesome numbers of advanced service sector jobs in the city centres. The problem is that these jobs, as John Kasarda (1990) notes, require very high levels of education. And inner city blacks with intermediate levels of qualification cannot fill them. Far suburban and exurban jobs in restructured cities do require such intermediate levels of education. But inner city blacks do not have access to the transportation to travel to them.

The post-industrial cities thrived economically in the 1970s and 1980s in the absence of a substantial black population. Restructured cities (such as, for example, New York) underwent fiscal crises in the mid-1970s, but – with the growth of the advanced service sector – survived. But whereas blacks were previously more central to the economies of such cities, post-organized capitalist growth was achieved without blacks. That is, blacks were excluded and marginalized from the new growth economies, as Fainstein and Fainstein (1989) have noted. The Keynesian coalitions that had governed these cities were based not only on industrial employment and trade union-ism but also on a consensus around welfare state and demand-side politics in respect of blacks and others among the "truly disadvantaged". Post-Keynesian supply-side politics – a consensus of formerly liberal Democrats and Republicans, that Mike Davis graphically describes in *City of quartz* (1990) – have put to one side the welfare state. The newer supply-side poli-tics instead have seen the increasingly economically marginalized blacks, not as a welfare, but as a *policing* problem. Hence the famous "thin blue line" that separates Southcentral Los Angeles from the white districts in the north and west of the city. Hence similar thin blue lines in Britain. In Los Angeles the closing down of the branch plants of auto and other machine-building in-dustries have economically marginalized previously strongly working class and trade-unionized blacks. Opportunity for many of the next post-indus-trial generation seemed to beckon only from the "crack economy", esti-mated from 1985–87 at $3.8 billion.

The spatial and residential processes involved here are complex. First many working and middle class blacks moved out of the deepest ghetto to contiguous areas, so that the former declined in status from 20 per cent to 40 per cent poverty tracts, while many of the latter became 20 per cent tracts (Wilson 1987). A few, but not many, other blacks moved farther out. As in Britain, middle class blacks are more likely to live in poor neighbour-hoods than poor whites, who in the USA mostly live in middle income cen-sus tracts. Thus the American white underclass does not live in "impacted ghettos", i.e. does not live in underclass areas. White areas, despite the ille-gality of restricted covenants, tend to stay lily white, encouraged for example by the "separate incorporation" movements that have sprung up from California to Massachusetts, in which well off white areas can hoard their tax base, so that welfare resources available to inner city blacks decline even further.

Oliver Williamson (1985) has spoken of "markets" and "hierarchies" (i.e. managerial bureaucracies) as two forms of economic "governance". Subse-quent analysts such as Schmitter (1988) have considered additional forms of economic governance such as regulation by the state, by corporatist in-stitutions, through alliances, through networks. A number of these forms of institutional regulation of the economy are at the same time institutions of social and cultural regulation. The point I want to argue here is that the

ghetto has been emptied out of all these economic and socio-cultural institutions – of markets, labour markets, commodity markets and capital markets; of the industrial branch plants of corporate hierarchies, of corporatist
institutions such as trade unions, of welfare state institutions, and of regulation by the family.

Loic Wacquant (1991) has captured this distinction by speaking of the
classic ghetto in organized capitalism as reduplicating each of these institutions found in the dominant society, from church to family to markets, etc.
Disorganized capitalism, in contrast, brings what Wacquant has called the
"hyperghetto", in which all these institutions disappear from the ghetto. The
result, and this is the basis of the constitution of the black underclass, is a
deficit of such institutional regulation. A similar deficit of institutional regulation would seem also to exist in the white ghettos of Newcastle's council
estates and in the east German breeding grounds of gang-bonded neo-Nazi
skinheads, in which the deficit has largely come through the demolition of
the communist state.

Numerical flexibility and migrants

The logical extension of what British analysts have called "numerical flexibility" is inherent in the Japanese and now western development of "lean
production" (Jurgens 1991). The difference is that it is no longer the major
firms that are comprised of privileged "core" workers and part-time and
temporary, numerically flexible peripherals. Instead the peripheral workers
are no longer employed by the large firms at all, as less skilled production
units are spun off and sold on to markets. The revenues realized with such
sales are used to diversify into new areas of quality production. Wages of *all*
workers in these spin-off firms decline, as they enter into subcontracting
relations with major firms. These spin-off, medium-sized, medium-skilled
firms then spin off their own less skilled production units on to subcontractors and so forth. The result is a set of "tiered" or layered subcontractors,
whose very bottom ranks are often "informalized" family firms where females do unpaid, or only partly paid, work *outside* the household. In Japan,
the result is a stratified working class in which two-thirds of manual workers are employed outside primary sector large firms. This sort of phenomenon seems also to be developing in the USA; where analysts have found a
decline in part-time working among women. Instead of core and periphery
workers, there are now core and periphery *firms*. The more expensive

"make" decision is supplanted by the "buy" decision from lower paid sub-contractors. The extent to which such spinning-off has taken place in the British public sector is also noteworthy. Lean production seems to be very much an integral component of diversified (flexible) quality production. And the latter not only assumes reskilling of a considerable proportion of the manufacturing workforce, it also paves the way for substantial amounts of new lower class formation.

Additional recruits to the new lower class have come in neo-liberal societies with relatively open borders such as the USA (but not Britain) in the new immigration. Post-war black migration to US manufacturing cities roughly paralleled similar organized-capitalist immigration patterns into Britain and other European countries that were choked off after the 1973 oil crisis. The new immigration to the USA is mainly a post-organized capitalist phenomenon, opened up especially – after the very low levels of immigration from 1924 to 1965 – in the 1970s 1980s and 1990s, now at a level of 700,000 per year. In terms of mobility, the phenomenon has been one of migrant immobility, blacks staying put, together with white flight from central city areas. And the – mainly Asian and Hispanic – migrants often carry jobs with them. The creation of 25 million jobs in the USA over a period with little if any net job creation in western Europe from 1972 to 1986 is inexplicable without this supply-side contribution of the migrants. Though sometimes the sons and daughters of the migrants are found in the elite universities, the migrants themselves overwhelmingly fill new lower class places. This can be either as entrepreneurs and workers in the very bottom tiered subcontractors of, for example, the garment industry, or in small commercial shops in the ghetto and elsewhere. As in Japan's bottom tier – and this is one reason that "modern" blacks cannot compete here – work is based on a pre-modern family structure, in which women typically do unpaid work in the (informalized) public sphere. A certain amount of the expansion of this sort of work – as Phizacklea (1990) notes – is explicable through the development of specialized consumption, hence the necessity that garments for changeable niche markets must be produced geographically close to demand rather than in the third world. But part of it is explicable only by the supply side. As some of Waldinger's (1986/7) respondents noted, without New York City's new migrants – with native white flight out of the industry – the New York garment industry would have died long ago.

The corporatist alternative?

So far I have discussed only neo-liberal societies. But the implications of corporatist variants of restructuration present a vastly different scenario. Given German potential hegemony in western and eastern Europe, surely corporatism presents an alternative and significant model of accumulation. Corporatist regimes, like the Japanese paradigm, depend on a certain number of "flexible rigidities" in the achievement of economic growth. My argument is that the shift to post-organized capitalist modes of growth does not necessarily lead to significant underclass formation, and variably leads to new lower class formation. Indeed the corporatist route, I shall suggest, tends to lead to much lower levels of development of either. German corporatism – with its solid growth and export levels, its high skill, high value-added production, its continued solid levels of trade union membership and democratic input through workers' councils – seems to many an ideal model for other western European countries. But I shall suggest the existence of a reverse and darker side of Germany's seemingly fortunate flexible rigidities; one that tends to lead to the institutional exclusion of ethnic minorities and women from crucial positions in labour markets and civil society in general.

Much of the previous literature on corporatism has been almost exclusively production oriented. But this second, darker side of the German route to modernization can be understood only when corporatism is understood as a socio-economic complex involving dimensions of both consumption and production. Let us start from the perspective of consumption, with Gosta Esping-Andersen (1990), who describes the – specifically corporatist and Christian – German "welfare state regime". Esping-Andersen distinguishes three welfare state regimes.

First, *"liberal" regime* is based on means-tested public assistance. Liberal regimes also involve low levels of non-means tested, universalist benefits. These are to a greater or lesser degree supplemented by private insurance schemes. This sort of welfare regime has been initially introduced, not by socialist, but by liberal governments. It offers – in correspondence with market principles – neither a welfare net, nor a "family wage". Thus a number of people who might not be labour market participants in other countries are forced on to the labour market in liberal regimes. Female labour force participation rates (LFPR) are not low. But such work is often in poorly paid and downgraded jobs. If liberalism is practised with respect to immigration as well as to the domestic economy, then a large number of immigrant entrepreneurs will open up shop in these welfare state regimes.

The United States comes quite close to the liberal ideal-type. Britain has gone a long way towards becoming liberal on social policy, though not on immigration policy.

Secondly, *social-democratic regimes* of which Sweden is paradigmatic, are based on high levels of universalist, general revenue-financed benefits. They assume the large-scale production of welfare services. Because so much is spent on welfare services, it is not possible to have high levels of transfer payments in social-democratic regimes. However, these are necessary because so many labour force participants receive wages from their activity on the production side of welfare services. The social-democratic model will have quite high female LFPRs. These regimes are typically initiated by social-democratic governments. The British welfare state had a very important social democratic component, which has diminished from the 1980s.

Thirdly, *"corporatist" regimes* are typically introduced by conservatives and/or Christian Democratic governments. They can offer high levels of benefit. They exist to a certain degree in France and Italy. But the corporatist thrust of French and Italian regimes is blunted by the fact that the production side of the economy is largely neo-liberal. It is in Germany (and Austria), where consumption-side matches production-side corporatism, that they assume their full significance. Corporatist regimes are based on the vitiation of the market, not by "modernist" social-democratic social citizenship principles, but by two "traditionalist" principles, based on two traditionalist types of corporate body. The first of these is a set of hierarchically ordered status groups, on which basis a whole set of different social insurance regimes is based.

The second of these traditionalist corporate bodies is the family itself. Corporatist regimes are based on the Catholic principle of "subsidiarity", in which the state is to intervene only once the family's capacity is exhausted. Wage structures in the labour markets are such that the family's capacity is not likely to be exhausted. Men working in highly skilled, high value-added jobs receive effectively a family wage. This is complemented by very high levels of transfer payments to the jobless. The family is thus at the centrepoint of a structure whose implications are to limit new lower class formation. But corporatist regimes must at the same time limit female labour force participation, to the extent that women who would move into consumer service and welfare service jobs in (modern) liberal or social-democratic regimes are kept off the labour market altogether.

There are two broad implications of this.

First, women in the private sphere of the family provide a number of services that are provided in the public sphere in liberal and social-democratic regimes. Consumer service functions provided through markets in liberal regimes are provided by women at home in Germany. There are many fewer women (and men) employed in restaurants, hotels, cafes, and the leisure sector in Germany than in the UK or USA. And very few women (and men) are employed by the welfare state, as in Sweden. Emblematic, and more than emblematic, of this is the lunchtime end to the school day for German pupils, keeping mothers off the labour market. The LFPR in 1991 of German women not in schooling, aged 16 to 64, was 39 per cent. Concomitant with this are especially low rates of births to non-married mothers – less than half the proportion in the UK and about a quarter of that in Denmark.

Secondly, there are very few of the sort of jobs to which women have found access in other western countries. Thus there are few opportunities for women to work in consumer services and welfare services. The German welfare state spends so much on transfer payments, it can afford to spend little on the provision of welfare services. Moreover, there are few opportunities for middle class women to work in the *advanced* services. This is because there are comparatively very few jobs at all in the advanced services. Because of the traditionalism of German life – lower divorce rate, low rates of home ownership, low level of personal finance, etc. – a much lower proportion of the workforce is engaged in the advanced consumer services, for example, law, accounting, estate agents, building societies, architecture, and surveying, etc. Further, studies in Holland and elsewhere have shown that advanced *producer* services have more important output relations with other services than with manufacturing (de Jong et al. 1992). The relative paucity of such firms in Germany means an even lower level of employment in the producer services. In terms of jobs requiring high qualifications, women have often found manual jobs requiring apprenticeships to be more gender segregated than a number of careers requiring higher education. The proportion of the former to the latter is much higher in Germany than in the USA, UK, or the Netherlands. This reinforces female labour force exclusion. Germany is a manufacturing economy – over 40 per cent of its workforce in 1991 was in manufacturing as compared to 20 to 26 per cent in the USA, UK, Japan, and Sweden. It is based on high value-added work, which, given labour market segregation, has encouraged the exclusion of not only women from the labour force, but also of a high proportion of men aged between 55 and 64 (58 per cent in 1985), and of middle class people in their twenties. University degrees are typically taken at the age of 27, delaying labour market entry in comparison with the UK by five to six years.

Corporatist regulation involves economic governance by an extremely dense web of institutions, of bodies that violate the assumptions of neo-classical economics as well as the realities of neo-liberal regulation. These institutions include the state, the family, trade unions, chambers of commerce, education and training institutions, and employers' associations. The anti-modern, "ancient regime" nature of a number of these institutions provides a set of rigidities that allows for flexible economic accumulation on the one hand, but has a set of retrogressive socio-cultural implications on the other. We have discussed these in regard to gender. Let us turn now to ethnicity.

Germany is still very much a *Nationalökonomie*. German industry has very little direct investment in other countries. In contrast, Britain has much higher levels of foreign direct investment (FDI). Germans also have very low levels of portfolio investment abroad. Conversely there are quite low levels of inward FDI and portfolio investment in Germany. In Germany, in relation to Britain, only about a quarter of the proportion of companies of comparable size are publicly quoted on stock markets.

The German state stands in a rather unique position to immigration. It has let in a much greater number of immigrants than Britain. This is true not only of the massive immigration wave of 1988–92, but also is true prior to 1973. It is also very universalist in terms of the almost free movement into Germany of Poles and eastern European Jews. (However, free Polish movement in Germany has served partly as a *quid pro quo* for Poland serving as a buffer state to keep immigrants from the former Soviet Union out of Germany.) Germany finally admitted in 1991, for example, some four times as many asylum seekers as Britain.

The problems arise once the immigrants are inside Germany. First, especially the 1955–73 immigration in particular was anything but liberal, and largely set by agreements of the West German state with, for example, the Turkish government. Once the immigrants are in the country, citizenship, residence, and the ability to open a business are severely restricted. In the light of these kinds of factors it makes sense to speak of a continuum of four levels of socio-political distanciation of immigrants from the host nation:

– *Ex-colonial*, in which important citizenship rights are acquired immediately or soon after entry to host country.
– *Jus soli*, in which for example the sons and daughters of immigrants are automatically granted citizenship rights
– *Voluntarism*, in which even children born to immigrants in the host country – that is, the second generation – must show a commitment to and

knowledge of the political rules of the host country to gain citizenship rights

- *Jus sanguinis*, in which inclusion into citizenship has also an ethnic, or "blood", component.

Almost all advanced countries come under the first two of these categories. Germany, however, comprises a sort of hybrid of voluntarism and jus sanguinis. Voluntarism exists to the extent that German-born sons and daughters (and even grandchildren and great grandchildren) of immigrants must apply for and take examinations for citizenship. German-born sons and daughters of immigrants must even apply for a *residence* permit. The overwhelming majority (less than 10 per cent) of German born ethnic minorities are neither citizens nor residents. By 1981, for example, over 40 per cent of Turkish workers had been in the labour force in Germany for more than eight years and were thus eligible for residence permits. In fact only 0.3 per cent had them and hence lacked *de jure* security of residence. Jus sanguinis applies to the extent that ethnic German, though usually not German speaking, immigrants – who have spent centuries outside Germany – have immediate citizenship and welfare state privileges.

In some of this corporatist "regulation of ethnicity", the state works together with other corporate bodies. During the immigration of the *Gastarbeiter* prior to 1973 the state worked with employers who were recruiting labour. The chambers of commerce have effectively excluded Turks and other sons and daughters of immigrants from getting apprenticeships and hence entry into the skilled trades. When they do manage to achieve entry, it is to the lowest level of such firms. Indeed a study of training in Düsseldorf carried out by Ute Mehrlander and her colleagues (1983) in the early 1980s showed that Turkish families lacked the information networks to place their children in good apprenticeship places. Hence they were dependent on the local employment office. Indeed so few Turks obtained apprenticeships that the sociologists involved in the study had insufficient numbers for a control group to evaluate against German youth. Even when they (the researchers) convinced the Düsseldorf employment office to go out and find the training places for the purposes of their study, the latter were unable to persuade a significant (statistically) number of local employers to take on the Turkish teenagers as apprentice/employees!

In the exclusion of immigrants from gaining access to the labour market as manufacturing entrepreneurs, the state works in tandem with local chambers of commerce. First, the state requires that would-be manufacturers have a residence permit, which few immigrants have. Moreover, they also have to have a special work permit allowing activity as a manufacturing employer. Furthermore, for local chambers of commerce, would-be manufacturers must also pass a *Meisterprüfung* (Master's Exam). This applies also to those who were very highly qualified already in Turkey. Most do not have sufficient written ability in the German language to pass the exam. Finally, few have security of residence, so they do not apply to take the *Meisterprüfung*. The result is the virtual absence of foreign manufacturing entrepreneurs in Germany. In contrast, immigrant Turks in Paris, and Asians and others in the UK and USA, very often enter the garment industry and employ large numbers of ethnic minority female personnel. Hence another component of the new lower class is largely missing in corporatist Germany.

Thus the corporatist variant of economic growth seems to militate against the formation of all of the different fractions of the new lower class. Corporatism tends to inhibit the development of numerical flexibility accompanying lean production as well as the development of consumer services. It tends to inhibit the growth of an underclass in the sense described by Wacquant (1991), partly because of the still tight regulation of ethnic minority residential districts by the very intact family. It tends to limit the entrepreneurial activity of the migrants , who are unable to set up and work in downgraded manufacturing. The cost side of this relative absence of new lower class formation is the persistence of traditional family structures, unacceptable levels of exclusion of women from labour markets, and of minorities from citizenship rights. Whether corporatism, and limits to new lower class formation, can persist with the mass migrations and cataclysmic social change – and its implications of a growing deficit of regulation – that is pouring into western Germany from regions eastwards is yet another question.

Conclusions

We will conclude with a number of observations relating first to the Anglo-American comparison, and second to the effects of re-unification in Germany. The British shift towards neo-liberalism at the end of the 1970s would seem to portend a marked convergence with the American case in terms of new lower class formation. And indeed Britain has undergone class polarization – different from continental countries and similar to the USA – in the creation of a very large, very well paid post-industrial advanced sector upper middle class in business services, high tech, the culture industries, and finance. Further, Britain has created, again only matched in the west by the USA, large numbers of "junk jobs", for a downgraded manufacturing and especially service proletariat. In both countries, many female workers have moved into these mostly private sector junk jobs (in Scandinavia they are primarily in the public sector). And in both the UK and USA – unlike Catholic and corporatist welfare state countries such as France, Italy, and Germany – a large number of these jobs are part-time.

There are also marked parallels between ethnic minorities in the two countries. Afro-Caribbeans, like Afro-Americans, have suffered downward mobility from the working class in a country that is only matched by the USA in the pace and extent of decline of manufacturing industry. In both cases this has been particularly intense for young males, whose occupational positions have declined along with the improvement of the positions of black females. The occupational standing of the present generation of Afro-Britons and black Americans has deteriorated in comparison to their fathers – though black Americans have made marked strides in educational achievement. Here blacks are joined – in new lower class positions without very optimistic upward mobility prospects – by Pakistanis and Bengalis in the UK and Mexican-Americans and Puerto Ricans in the USA. These "brown" ethnic groups in both countries tend, on the one hand, to have lower educational attainment than blacks. On the other hand they are less likely to be unemployed, in that they will be part of traditionalist families and may work in very small, ethnically owned manufacturing or commercial firms. A final parallel is found on the highest rung of the ethnic minority stratification ladder, where the situation of Indians in the UK bears comparison with Orientals (and other Hispanics and Afro-Caribbeans) in the USA. In these cases there is often one generation of new lower class membership and then very fast mobility into the middle classes.

At this point, however, the similarities end. There is nothing even remotely like the level of creation of "junk jobs" in the UK or Europe in the past two decades to parallel the USA phenomenon. The USA has created some 30 million new jobs during this period, while net new job creation in western Europe has been close to zero. This has been accompanied by the above-mentioned mass immigration into the USA from the early 1970s to the present, the migrants often, so to speak, bringing the jobs with them. Britain, to the contrary, has been the advanced country that has above all stood out by the very paucity of the flow of migrants it allows through its frontiers.

The major difference between the two countries of course is the overwhelming social fact of black America. To understand generic social inequality in the USA is first to understand the position of black Americans, whereas in Britain race and gender inequality are still largely subsidiary to the *Vergesellschaftung* of social class. Commentators have even observed that today's open USA immigration policies have been largely aimed at "swamping the blacks" in American inner cities. Andrew Hacker (1992) has also argued that the US is neither "melting pot" nor multi-cultural, but fundamentally a *bi*-cultural society of the blacks and "the rest", in which "the rest "eventually come into line with the cultural assumptions of the WASP mainstream. America's "second culture" and its American underclass are most visibly black. In Britain, to the contrary, the underclass (on Wilson's model) would be overwhelmingly white, concentrated above all in the housing estates of Liverpool, Glasgow, Newcastle, and elsewhere. In the USA such concentrations of white urban poverty just do not exist.

This at the same time brings us to the major shortcomings of Wilson's theory. It is surely the racialization of America's new lower class that gives it the visibility and "impacted ghetto" concentration that gives to it its full significance as *under*class. Whites simply do not face the same obstacles against spatial and social mobility – which consolidate cycles of poverty – that blacks do. And Britain, in comparative perspective, contains neither sufficient numbers of, nor large enough concentrations of, blacks. Thus there is something problematic about the application of the theory to the UK. At the same time difficulties arise in its applicability to the USA, not because Wilson's theory is not sufficiently a theory of social class, but precisely for the opposite reason – it is too much a theory of class to deal with a system of stratification that is fundamentally *racial* in character. Wilson is influenced by social-democratic and (highly) revisionist Marxism. His first highly influential book, *The declining significance of race* (1978) should be taken literally at its title. He argued that black upward and outward mobility meant that class and not race was becoming the most distinctive feature of American society. Wilson's subsequent *The truly disadvantaged* was where he principally developed the underclass thesis, thematizing the downward mobility of a large section of (not race, but) the American working class. And this was inscribed in the logic of economic growth, capital accumulation by another name. What such analyses ignore, however, is for example the continuing geographical segregation of even the black *middle* class, as well as their horizontal occupational segregation in the public sector. It denies that the main social fact involved in US inequality is not class but race.

As for the effects of German unification, one must be even more speculative. Will a combination of re-unification, the opening up of the old

Comecon countries and possible increased integration of the EC lead to neo-liberal convergence in Germany? Since the Second World War Germany has had neo-liberal regulation of product markets. This is why the country can export more than Japan year in and year out, while the *de facto* protectionist Japanese run larger balance of trade surpluses. In contrast, German direct investment and capital markets have been anything but neo-liberal, with very low levels of outward or inward investment. This should change, especially with the opening up of eastern Europe. What will in likelihood develop is a two-way flow (Sassen 1988), with direct investment from German firms especially in (the "buffer countries") Poland, the Czech Republic, Slovakia, and Hungary, while people will flow in the opposite direction either for work or for training.

What is unlikely however is that *labour* markets will come under neo-liberal regulation, at least not labour markets in the country's "primary sector". More likely is considerable growth of a hitherto not terribly significant secondary labour market, which will be neo-liberally regulated. This should grow enormously in view of the level of immigration from the East (and South). This developing social stratification will thus be heavily overdetermined by ethnic and regional stratification. At the top will be western Germans, themselves competing mostly for middle class jobs. From the middle 1980s there has been a deficit in the supply-side of German apprenticeship markets, as West German youth has aspired to middle class occupations. This deficit was at first filled by ethnic minorities, especially Turks. But from the end of the 1980s the desirable large firm apprenticeship places began to be filled by eastern Germans and by *Aussiedler*, i.e. immigrants from Russian and Poland of German ethnic origin (Wilpert 1991).

This growing secondary labour market, not corporatistically regulated by apprenticeships, will be above all comprised of the progeny of 1960s immigrating Turks and 1980s and 1990s immigrating Poles. Here Poles will probably be favoured and the Turks thrust down to the lower reaches of the market to compete with the various groups of 1980s and 1990s *Asylanten*, Romanian Gypsies, Orientals, black Africans, Russians, and Bosnians. The Turks are thus very much cast in the same rôle as America's blacks. And this is because the secondary labour market has vastly changed since the 1960s. Recruited to fill jobs in an expanding manufacturing sector then, they now face a market in which there are many fewer industrial jobs and instead a lot more downgraded service jobs, unemployment, and informal labour market work. Apart from this downward mobility, which the 1980s and 1990s wave of immigrants did not experience, the Turks have like US blacks witnessed the new immigrants – including above all eastern Germans and *Aussiedler* as well as Poles – pass them by in the hiring queues. The Turks have paid into the social insurance funds, while the *Aussiedler* – ethnic Germans who have not paid into these funds – are eligible for full social benefits.

But is this an underclass in the making in today's Germany? The answer to this would seem to be in the affirmative. The underclass, though clearly a post-industrial and post-Fordist phenomenon, seemed to be possible only in neo-liberal social formations such as the USA. Corporatism, with its non-market regulation, high value-added work and developed welfare state, seemed to have the answer. It seemed immune. But the German re-unification, coupled especially with massive waves of immigration, and the recent tendency towards the decline in industrial jobs, has led to a situation in which corporatist (and statist through jus sanguinis citizenship laws) exclusion is even more ruthless than market exclusion into an underclass. This is indeed an explosive mix. And it can only be further exacerbated by the expected Russian migration of the later 1990s and the first decade of the next millennium.

The notion of an underclass best makes sociological sense in terms of its effects in social instability and disorganization. In this context the phenomenon may exist only when downward structural mobility is overdetermined by ethnicity. Though its ethnic minority population is now 5.9 per cent, Britain, with its low levels of immigration and tendencies more towards inclusion into rather than exclusion from *de jure* and *de facto*, social and cultural citizenship, seems unlikely to have a significant underclass. In contrast, Germany, with very strong corporatist and statist exclusion, coupled with high levels of immigration and hence more significant ethnic overdetermination, would seem pre-eminently to fulfil the conditions for underclass formation.

The question of the possible making of a European and specifically German underclass may not even be a matter of whether or not, or even how, but instead a question of where. Will Frankfurt at the dawn of the Third Millennium be Europe s Los Angeles? Is Germany's Rodney King just now growing up in the Turkish *barrios* of Berlin Kreuzberg?

References

Bourgois, P. 1991. In search of respect: the new service economy and the crack alternative in Spanish Harlem. Paper presented at Working Conference on Poverty, Immigration and Urban Marginality, Maison Suger, Paris: France.

Davis, M. 1990. *City of quartz*. London: Verso.

de Jong, M. 1992. Producer services and flexible networks in the Netherlands. In *Regional development and contemporary industrial response*, H. Ernste & V. Meier (eds), 147–62. London: Belhaven.

Esping-Andersen, G. 1990. *The three worlds of welfare capitalism*. Cambridge: Polity.

Fainstein, S. & N. Fainstein 1989. The racial dimension in urban political economy. *Urban Affairs Quarterly* **25**, 187–99.

Hacker, A. 1992. *Two nations. Black and white, separate, hostile, unequal*. New York: Scribners.

Hughes, M. 1990. Formation of the impacted ghetto: evidence from large metropolitan areas 1970–1980. *Urban Geography* **11**, 265–84.

Jencks, C. 1992. *Rethinking social policy. Race, poverty and the underclass*. Cambridge, Mass: Harvard University Press.

Jurgens, U. 1991. The changing contours of work in the car industry. Abteilung Regulierung von Arbeit: Technik-Arbeit-Umwelt, Berlin: Wissenschaftszentrum (WZB).

Kasarda, J. 1990. Structural factors affecting the location and timing of urban underclass growth. *Urban Geography* **11**, 234–64.

Mehrlaender, U. et al. 1983. *Turkische jugendliche – eine berufliche chancen in Deutschland?* Bonn: Verlag Neue Gesellschaft.

Phizacklea, A. 1990. *Unpacking the fashion industry*. London: Routledge.

Sassen, S. 1988. *The mobility of capital and labor*. Cambridge: Cambridge University Press.

Schmitter, P. 1988. Sectors in modern capitalism: modes of governance and variations in performance. Paper presented at Colloquium: Comparing Capitalist Economies, Madison, Wisconsin, USA.

Wacquant, L. 1991. From "black metropolis" to "hyperghetto": race, state and economy in the postfordist era. Paper presented at Working Conference on Poverty, Immigration and Urban Marginality in the Advanced Societies. Paris, France.

Waldinger, R. 1986/7. Changing ladders and musical chairs: ethnicity and opportunity in post-industrial New York. *Politics and Society* **15**, 369–402.

Williamson, O. 1985. *The economic institutions of capitalism*. New York: Free Press.

Willis, P. 1977. *Learning to labour*. Aldershot: Gower.

Wilpert, C. 1991. Migration and ethnicity in a non-immigration country: foreigners in a united Germany. *New Community* **18**, 49–62.

Wilson, W. J. 1978. *The declining significance of race*. Chicago: University of Chicago Press.

Wilson, W. J. 1987. *The truly disadvantaged*. Chicago: University of Chicago Press.

Chapter 8

After the Cold War: the defence industry and the New Europe

John Lovering

Introduction

At the Malta Summit in 1989, Presidents Gorbachev and Bush declared that the "Cold War" was over. It seemed not only that the world might become less dangerous, but that defence spending would fall, releasing resources for more desirable or productive uses, creating a Peace Dividend (Chalmers 1990). However, four years later the only apparent result of changes in defence spending has been severe large-scale job loss.

The perspective presented by the media, consultants, and most academics is that this is merely the transitional cost of change in demand. The few social scientists who have written in this field tend to replicate the optimistic view that we are witnessing the effects of an historic decline in military confrontation. Shaw, for example, suggests that defence cuts signify the beginning of a welcome era of "societal demilitarization" (Shaw 1991). At the policy level, the debate is dominated by the paradigm of "build-down", implying that the changes in the defence industry are equivalent to those experienced in numerous other sectors forced to adjust to new market conditions. There may be some localized difficulties that may demand a localized response, but no change in policy at the national or supra-national level is called for (see for example Financial Times 1 February 1990; Braddon et al. 1991; CEC 1992; Statement on Defence Estimates 1992; Economist 16 January 1993). The Peace Dividend will come in time so long as governments allow market forces to work.

This chapter challenges this interpretation of the changes at work in the European arms industry. It argues that the transition from the Cold War era to a new order entails not just a "build-down" but rather a restructuring. The form of military production that came into being with the Cold War, namely the Military-Industrial-Complex, is collapsing (Kennedy 1988: 159). The business of supplying the military is becoming more closely interwoven into the mainstream of capitalist production. And as a result, the employment it generates is changing in volume and type (Lovering 1993). The transformation has important implications for the European labour market, high-technology industry, and especially for regional development. Of course, it also has major implications for security and defence, and the arms trade.

These outcomes are not pre-ordained. They are dependent on national policies, and the development of supra-national institutions such as the European Community, and the re-invention of organizations such as the CSCE, WEU, and NATO.[1] It is argued here that the political pressures and intellectual biases currently embodied in these institutions are such that they are unable to bring about a significant Peace Dividend. Instead there will be a Peace Penalty, affecting literally millions of Europeans, in several industries and regions.[2] The first section outlines the rôle of arms production in the post-war era. The second identifies two crucial determinants of the current restructuring; the politico-military and industrial dimensions of the integration of Europe. The third discusses the absence of the Peace Dividend, and the inadequacies of the policy debate.

Europe and the arms industry

Europe has not been at war since 1945, but it is one of the world's three leading sites of arms production. The defence spending of EC countries in the late 1980s was just over half that of the USA, roughly the same as that of the USSR, and ten times greater than that of Asia (Renner 1992: 70). Over two-thirds of EC defence spending, and 85 per cent of defence procurement, is accounted for by France, Britain, Germany, and Italy.

German rearmament was prohibited for a decade after the Second World War, and the bulk of defence spending thereafter has been on personnel rather than equipment. Nevertheless, Germany has become an important producer and exporter of military and related equipment, as became clear in the aftermath of the 1991 Gulf War. The defence industries of Britain and France, and to a slightly lesser extent Italy, have been major elements in their national industrial, corporate, and employment structures since the early 1950s. In the 1980s British and French producers vied for third place after the USA and USSR in the ranking of world arms exporters. The Span-

Table 8.1 European defence industry, basic statistics (1990).

	Employment	Major weapons procurement ($)
UK	620,000	7,141
France	400,000	9,100
W. Germany	191,000	5,703
Italy	103,000	3,024
Spain	66,000	904
Belgium	33,000	409
Switzerland	31,000	na
Netherlands	29,000	1,206
Sweden	28,000	na
Austria	16,000	na
Norway	15,000	740
Greece	9,000	663
Finland	5,000	na
Denmark	na	291
Poland	272,000	na
Czechoslovakia	125,000	na
E. Germany	66,000	na
Hungary	10,000	na
Total	2,053,000	

Source: CEC 1992; Renner 1992: 72.   na: not applicable.

ish industry is growing rapidly. Table 8.1 shows employment in European defence industries as the post-Cold War era began. It is generally estimated that the West European defence industry generated over one-and-a-half-million industrial jobs, almost as many as the car industry.

The Military-Industrial-Complex and the post-war regime of accumulation

As Weber emphasized, the state is the monopolist of organized violence, and as such becomes a prime customer for arms, the means of violence. The demand side of the arms market is conditioned by the internal and external relations and military doctrines embodied in the state system (Kaldor 1990). In a capitalist economy, however, the supply side cannot be completely isolated from the dynamics of the search for profits (or the "law of value"). The structure of arms production at any time is therefore contingent upon the way the state system and the economic system inter-relate, the particularities of which have varied through time and space (Mann 1984; Giddens 1985; Lovering 1987).

In the 19th century, the parallel emergence of new nation-states and the spread of capitalist industry resulted in the industrialization of the arms industry. This was markedly international in its orientation; guns were a highly tradeable commodity. In the early 20th century the world armaments market was largely divided up between cartels of giant manufacturers. But the international arms industry collapsed in the mid-1930s as governments rearmed, and in so doing built up comprehensive national arms-producing capacities (Lovering 1993). The "Cold War" arms industry was reconstructed after the Second World War, in the context of the division into US and Soviet spheres of influence. In western Europe it was still overwhelmingly a national business, except to the extent that national industries now formed part of a "bloc-wide" system of production and military force, i.e. those of NATO or the Warsaw Pact (Kaldor 1990). The UK missiles and nuclear weapons industry, and German aerospace, for example, depended on US technology. In eastern Europe, the defence industry was even more closely conditioned by Russian requirements. Some smaller countries, notably Sweden and Switzerland, attempted to be more self-sufficient, in line with their status of "armed neutrality" (Renner 1992: 196).

President Eisenhower's somewhat loose term "Military-Industrial-Complex" (MIC) has been widely adopted to refer to the nexus of capital and state in arms production that emerged with the Cold War (Horowitz 1969). This represents a set of institutions, in both the legal and the sociological sense (Brunton 1992), through which capitalist accumulation was channelled to produce a particular set of use-values. Military customers were able to order the products they desired, while companies were able to achieve a sufficient degree of profit to stay in the game (Melman 1985). Given the intimacy of the supply–customer relationship, the distinction between private and public ownership in the arms industry was relatively unimportant. The leading British arms companies escaped public ownership, for example, although the reverse was true in France and Italy.

From the late 1940s arms spending increased, reaching heights unprecedented in peacetime. In the same period, a new model of economic regulation emerged, and the post-war "long boom" began. The combination of the regulatory apparatus established at Bretton Woods, the adoption of Keynesian national macro-economic management, the importation of American methods and technology into European industry, a national social contract around the welfare state, and not least the economic and social effects of the Cold War, provided the social framework for a New European growth path (Tipton & Aldrich 1987; Gill 1992). The juxtaposition of industrial and military expansion was not coincidental, it was worked for. Leading interests in the USA and its European allies converged around the project of transforming western Europe socially, industrially and militarily (Van der Pijl 1984; Ellwood 1992; Kaldor 1990; Palmer 1987). A cohort of interventionist and Atlanticist academics and advisers helped to move governments towards agreement on the economic and military policy agendas (Ikenberry 1992). From 1948, $13 billion of American aid was pumped into western Europe through the European Recovery Programme (Marshall Aid). A major share of US aid was military, and designed to trigger military spending by recipient countries. The Mutual Weapons Development Programme fostered the development of European defence technologies (resulting for example in the British Harrier aircraft programme). The connection between industrial development and military spending was explicitly stated in the 1951 Organization for European Economic Co-operation (OEEC) European Manifesto: 'by this large increase in production, improvements in living standards and further social progress can be achieved while meeting defense requirements'. In 1953 the European Productivity Agency was set up to crusade for increasing productivity and ensure long-term support for the defence drive (Ellwood 1992: 182).

In the language of the Regulation School, US hegemony made possible the discovery of both a new mode of regulation and a new regime of accumulation. The former rested on a combination of welfarism and anti-communism (Davis 1986; Kaldor 1990; Palmer 1987). The latter consisted of a particular combination of what Hymer has called "horizontal" and "vertical" paths of accumulation. Civilian industry could expand by horizontal accumulation, "making goods available on a broad basis" (Hymer 1972: 119). The democratization of incomes, attributable to the capital labour accord, new industrial relations practices, and the redistribution of wealth imposed in Adenauer's Germany and the new welfare states, underpinned the growth of demand for standardized goods.[3] Meanwhile, military production was driven by highly specialist requirements for ever more sophisticated technologies. The Cold War defence industry was designed to have the capacity to innovate to order, corresponding to Hymer's "vertical accumulation"; "continuous innovation for a small number of people and the introduction of new goods before the old ones were fully spread" (Hymer 1972: 119). If the expansion of civilian industries is characterized as "Fordist", that of the Military-Industrial-Complex must in some respects be characterized as "post-Fordist" (Markusen 1991). State-driven innovation in the military sector generated technologies that would be taken up by market-driven firms on the civilian side. For a time this model of technology transfer worked spectacularly, as manifested, for example, in the air transport or computer industries (Alic 1992).

But this model could function effectively only so long as autarky and corporatism were conducive to a faster rate of technological advance than the more exposed environment of non-defence industries. The very success of the corporate-liberal reconstruction of Europe and Japan meant that this eventually ceased to be the case. In the early 1950s, the defence sector grew much more rapidly than any other, as defence spending outstripped civilian growth, especially in Britain. But thereafter, firms exploiting civilian markets, no longer confined to the national territory, continued to grow rapidly, expanding their division of labour and acquiring the new technological capacities and organizational powers that Adam Smith or Marx would have expected (Markusen 1991; Van der Pijl 1984). The defence sector, meanwhile, became an enclave increasingly suffocated by fiscal crisis, and unable for security reasons to extend the social and technical division of labour at the pace of leading non-defence firms. The MIC lost its monopoly of "vertical accumulation", and with this its relative technological dynamism. Successive weapons projects became enormously expensive, and defence companies were forced to buy in technologies developed in civilian markets (POST 1991; Gummett & Walker 1992; Schofield et al. 1992). About half of current procurement is said to be of "dual use" technologies. In 1988 the British government set up a working group to examine the problem (ACOST 1989).

The 1980s: the Military-Industrial-Complex in decline

As difficulties mounted, governments and defence companies experimented with a variety of reforms. The most politically undemanding strategy was to prop up the MIC by exporting, shedding the costs of supporting the defence industrial base onto military allies. Britain and France in particular promoted exports to the Middle East, and latterly the Far East. Export sales became even more urgent as the long post-war rise in arms spending in advanced capitalist countries came to an end. In the mid-1980s, world arms spending stabilized, then began to decline (in the UK, defence spending fell by a tenth in the second half of the decade, in France the fall was delayed until 1990).

But at the same time the halted growth of oil revenues and increase in third world debt limited the growth potential of export markets (Deger & Sen 1990). By the late 1980s it had become clear to most actors that a more fundamental restructuring would be necessary.

Companies and procurement agencies began a variety of attempts to modernize the arms business. It is said that western Europe was quicker to respond than the USA (*Flight International* 27 May 1992). British and German companies began restructuring in the late 1980s, the Italian and French industries in 1991–92. For governments, this meant more off-the-shelf purchases in the international market. For companies, it meant a series of experiments with acquisitions and divestments, corporate restructuring, joint ventures and collaborative agreements. Leading companies in Britain and Germany are targeting dual use technologies (e.g. British Aerospace, Daimler Benz), while others are hoping to become world players in the arms market by specializing (e.g. GEC, Thomson-CSF). The result is a global web, with regional biases, of formal and informal links between companies. West European defence suppliers (Figure 8.1) now have multiple connections with each other and firms elsewhere, notably in the USA and latterly in Japan and Russia (see Taylor & Hayward 1989; Lovering 1990a 1993; CEC 1992; Dunne & Smith 1992; Gummett & Walker 1992; Walker 1992). Eastern European companies have also sought foreign partners, and Israeli firms have been particularly responsive.

British Aerospace (UK)	ININ (Spain)
Thomson (France)	Thorn emi (UK)
GEC (UK)	Ferranti (UK)[1]
Daimler Benz (Germany)	GIAT (France)
Rolls Royce (UK)	Matra (France)
Aerospatiale (France)	Philips (Netherlands)[2]
DCN (France)	Oerlikon (Switzerland)
Dassault (France)	Nobel (Sweden)
MBB (Germany)	Plessey (UK)[3]
EFIM (Italy)	Siemens (Germany)
FIAT (Italy)	

[1] Since shed most of its defence activity.
[2] Since acquired by GEC.
[3] Since acquired by GEC together with Siemens.

Figure 8.1   Main European arms producers. Source: Anthony et al. 1990; CEC 1992.

The Cold War model of autarkic defence industries serving as supply departments to their national states is being replaced by a model in which commercially oriented companies serve an international market according to more conventional capitalist criteria. Defence-industrial investment is increasingly influenced by the same sort of considerations as non-defence investment. Short-term financial considerations are displacing the former emphasis on long-term national interests. The limited number of customers, massive size of the few suppliers, and sensitivity of the products means that the arms industry still remains unusually subject to monopoly, state interference, and corruption (Fontanel & Smith 1991). But these features are also found in other industries. The production of the means of violence is becoming much more like the production of other commodities, and less a separate, identifiable, and accountable part of state activity.

Restructuring employment

From a labour market perspective the Cold War defence industry was not unlike a massive job creation scheme. Funded by the state with scant regard to cost, most of its output was never used, and much was unusable (Kaldor 1982). But it employed a large, relatively stable, and relatively well paid workforce, approaching two million European jobs even at the end of the Cold War (Table 8.1). In some countries, especially Britain, employment in the defence industry came much nearer to the "Fordist" stereotype than in many civilian sectors (Lovering 1990b). Employment was concentrated in large units and conditioned by corporatist norms, with elaborately formalized internal labour markets. All this is changing as the industry contracts and restructures. The Stockholm International Peace Research Institute (SIPRI) estimated that employment in the arms industry in European NATO countries would fall by up to half between 1985 and 1995, a loss of some 835,000 jobs (Schofield et al. 1992: 2). Since then, future defence spending has fallen, competition in defence markets has intensified, the prospect for saving jobs by diversification into alternative civilian markets has diminished with recession, and many leading defence companies have entered a phase of acute uncertainty. Job losses over the 1990s are likely to be even higher. The US defence industry is expected to lose one million jobs by mid-decade (Roth 1992).

The burden is falling on lower-qualified and routine workers, middle-management and administrative staffs. In Britain, defence industry employment is becoming more segmented as collectively bargained norms are

Table 8.1 Regional dependence on defence industry employment in the EC (NUT II regions).

Ranking	Region
1	Cumbria[2]
2	Essex[2]
3	Bremen[2]
4	Bretagne[1]
5	Aquitaine[1]
6	Lancashire[2]
7	Liguria[2]
8	Provence-Alpes-Côtes d'Azure[2]
9	Centre[2]
10	Limousin
11	Midi/Pyrénées
12	Ile-de-France
13	Friuli-Venezia Giulia
14	Oberbayern
15	Cornwall and Devon
16	Basse Normandie
17	Haute Normandie
18	Avon, Gloucestershire, Wiltshire[2]
19	Hampshire, Isle of Wight

Source: CEC 1992.   [1]"Highly vulnerable"; [2]"Vulnerable".

abandoned, and employers differentiate more systematically between employees with scarce skills and those employed on the basis of labour costs. An assault was launched on the power of the trade unions, especially in the larger companies (although other British and European firms are more hesitant and continue to see unions as allies in labour management and in government lobbying). Remaining employment opportunities tend to be concentrated in higher occupational categories, under new and more individualized terms of employment. The British case is not likely to be unique in kind, although the degree of adjustment may be more severe than in other West European countries.

Employment change is also associated with a change in geographical distribution. The MIC did not obey the same locational rules as civilian industry; established in a relatively small number of regions chosen for industrial and military reasons, it tended to stay there while civilian industries moved on. As a result it became the largest source of stable, high-paid employment, and a key supplier of training in a number of regions that otherwise became disadvantaged. The current restructuring of employment implies a shift of the remaining jobs to new locations. Assembly and production work is being transferred to cheaper labour forces, either by relocating work within companies or via collaboration and subcontracting (Rolls Royce subcontracts part of its military engine work to Spain). In most cases this is not compensating for overall job loss in the industry. Meanwhile, the higher-level research and development activities upon which competitiveness largely depends is being consolidated in labour markets dense with appropriate skills (in the UK this predominantly means the non-metropolitan southeast, in Germany it means Bayern). Geographically, the Cold War defence industry used to sustain islands of modest prosperity (Lovering 1988 1991a). It is now sustaining much smaller citadels of relative privilege.

Figure 8.2 shows the EC regions considered in a recent consultants' report to be most severely affected by job loss in the defence industry. British

Figure 8.2 EC areas most severely affected by job losses in the defence industry.

and French regions head the list. Informally, EC officials have said they expect 80 per cent of the job losses in the defence industry to fall in Britain. This is partly because Britain's was the largest Cold War defence industry, and partly because of the particularly abrupt restructuring strategy of UK companies. Although the bulk of job loss is in relatively advantaged regions, the impact is greatest in non-core regions within the formerly more prosperous countries of the EC: the west coast of England and central Scotland, the north coast of Germany, southeast and southwest France, Wallonia in Belgium, and Liguria in Italy (Lovering 1991a; CEC 1992; Renner 1992). Nearly all these areas lie outside the banana-shaped zone of prosperity running from London to Piedmont. The end of the Cold War arms industry is thinning out employment opportunities outside the EC's central growth zone, heightening the tendency to spatial polarization. If eastern Europe is included, this pattern would be even more pronounced. In the Martin region of Slovakia and parts of Brandenburg, for example, a huge part of employment is threatened by the collapse of the arms industry. (Land Brandenburg 1992; Renner 1992: 206). In Russia, this is said to be responsible for half of all unemployment in 1992 (*Flight International* 18 March 1992).

Constructing the post-Cold War arms industry

The post-Cold War arms industry is being constructed by a small number of large producers, in close if uneasy contact with governments. Governments have faced contradictions in reconciling support for the Single European Market with their desire to retain some national control of arms production, especially in Britain (Schofield et al. 1992). The industry, naturally, exploits governmental contradictions. Defence companies interact closely with the armed services in sustaining the preparedness ethic and in defining the equipment implications of perceived threats (Kaldor 1990). As an institution in the Veblerian sense, a set of relationships and a habituated way of thinking, the MIC is not dead yet (Brunton 1992: 600).

The political power of the European defence lobby, but equally its industrial incoherence, is illustrated by the European Fighter Aircraft (EFA) programme, the major West European weapons project in the 1990s involving virtually all the major contractors directly or indirectly. Governmental approval was won in 1986 after extensive lobbying, especially by British companies and the UK Defence Ministry (Gummett & Walker 1992). Nevertheless, Margaret Thatcher interrogated the Defence Minister (Michael

Heseltine) over what appeared to be a throwback to corporatism (*Independent on Sunday* 5 July 1992). France withdrew to develop its own aircraft, leaving a major division in the putative European defence industry (Smith 1989). In 1992 financial and political pressures in the newly re-united Germany, together with differences with Britain over Europe's defence requirements, led to the announcement that Germany would pull out of production. There were also tensions between German and British companies. Deutsche Aerospace (DASA) proposed setting up a joint European company to make the aircraft, but British Aerospace resisted, apparently in order to keep its US options open (*Financial Times* 2 September 1992). There was allegedly a feeling that the British had got the lion's share of EFA radar contracts. The differences were patched up, after much lobbying and wrangling over legal commitments, and the Eurofighter project was reborn (*Financial Times* 11 December 1992). But future work sharing arrangements have yet to be settled, the production timetable is unclear, potentially competing products are under development in France, the USA and elsewhere, and the political support for continued spending is not assured.

Co-operation between the leading European defence companies is likely to increase, and a cross-national European defence industry is almost bound to emerge by the end of the decade, but many obstacles have to be overcome (Smith 1989; *Flight International* 5 June 1991). The construction of the Cold War European defence industry was planned, the transition to its successor is not. Europe lacks both the political and the economic institutions that would be required to replace the anarchy of the restructuring of the arms industry with order.

The indeterminate character of Europe as a military entity

In the first place, the political and military identity of Europe is a matter of dispute. A major question in the 1990s is how far and in what form the European Community will observe Weber's dictum that a state is defined by its "monopoly of the legitimate use of physical force". Section 223 of the Treaty of Rome allowed member states to block EC action in the defence field, but it was widely expected, especially after the Maastricht agreement, that this clause would become obsolete. The EC bureaucracy and some prominent Euro-politicians intend the EC to form not only a new political bloc but also a military one. But while some (especially Britain) advocate this to sustain the US alliance, others (especially France) believe that Europe should form an independent military apparatus. Nevertheless, the Franco-German brigade was established in 1992 as an embryonic European Army. The Gulf War and crisis in the former Yugoslavia precipitated further efforts to pull together an EC security policy. Europe's security and military apparatus in Europe now looks likely to be built from some combination of a "neo-Atlanticist" framework based on NATO, and a "West-Europeanist" structure in which the WEU would be subordinate to the EC (Hyde-Price 1992). Nevertheless, the shape of the future European military identity, and especially its implications for the defence industry, remain hazy. Historically, most federal states began by unification on defence policy; in the EC this is coming last.

This is largely because the job is already being done by the USA, or "Globo-cop" as *Time Magazine* put it on 1 April 1990. US defence spending may be under pressure in the Clinton administration, especially the half devoted to NATO. But it seems highly unlikely that the American military apparatus in and around Europe will rapidly be replaced by an equivalent European one. No EC country has yet urged complete US withdrawal from Europe. The armed European super state is still in the realm of fiction. Europe seems unlikely to develop a structure capable of organizing and funding autonomous military power rapidly enough to change the course of the restructuring of the defence industry.

The absence of a transformative European industrial strategy

Not only is Europe's politico-military character not yet settled, its future economic development is also a matter of some debate. The development of EC industrial policy has been hesitant and contradictory (Cutler et al. 1989; Grahl & Teague 1990). The Commission itself favours a more interventionist approach, but the prevailing policies limit support for "industrial champions", whether defence companies or otherwise. The defence sector managed to secure some benefits from EC technology policy in the 1980s such as the ESPRIT and EUREKA programmes (the latter was presented by its French sponsors as a European response to the US Strategic Defence Initiative). The Independent European Programme Group (IEPG), now renamed the Western European Armaments Group (WEAG), attempted to take the lead in unifying the European armaments market, launching the European Cooperative Long-Term Initiative in Defence (EUCLID) in 1990. But the tensions between this attempt to preserve capacity through the "juste retoure" principle and the free market policy enshrined in the Single European Act have grown (Gummett & Walker 1992). The *Financial Times* commented on 23 February 1990 that the IEPG's interventions looked like "a grudging response to preempt EC effort to apply liberalisation measures in arms".

The industry is nevertheless lobbying vigorously. Companies object to the lack of planning in defence procurement, and in some countries, notably Britain, want policy changes to help diversification (SBAC 1992). Trade unions and an increasing number of local authorities across western Europe are also calling for a strategy for the defence sector, especially measures to assist badly hit regions (IMPS et al. 1991; ACC et al. 1992). In Britain these campaigns forced the Labour party to propose a Defence Diversification Agency in the run-up to the 1992 general election. In Germany the union IG Metall, in collaboration with defence companies (notably in shipbuilding) and states in north and east Germany, has called for special support for marketing and investment leading to conversion (Land Brandenburg 1992). A number of Italian local authorities advocate interventionist public conversion policies, and trade unions have developed model bargaining agreements to put conversion on the industrial agenda (Renner 1992).

Since 1990 the Socialist Group in the European Parliament has demanded that the EC adopt an explicit policy for the defence industry. In 1991 and 1992 the EC included defence dependent regions in those eligible for the 40m ecu PERIFA scheme, which funds small, innovative industrial and training projects. In March 1992, EC ministers met for the first time to discuss the crisis in the defence industry, but failed to agree. In January 1993, pressure from MEPs resulted in Parliament approval for KONVER, a five-year programme with an initial annual budget of 140m ecus to assist diversification in areas hit by defence cuts, via the existing structural fund system. This represented a major step, but the scale of response is still modest (140m ecus is less than 0.005 per cent of EC spending on major weapons procurement alone). The President of the European Community, Jacques Delors, has said that the defence industry should be a priority area for "industrial mutation", along with motor vehicles and electronics, to be targeted by the reformed EC structural funds. But so long as EC industrial and economic strategy in general remains a matter of intellectual and political contention, the impact of such proposals remains uncertain (Ramsay 1992). In the meantime, the effective response is limited to a series of efforts directed at "mopping up" the consequences of job loss.

For all its state-like trappings, the EC has so far evaded the implications of militarization (Lodge 1990: 66). The relationship between its military rôle and industrial development is even farther down the agenda. European capitalism as a whole is in a sense leaderless, lacking a unified direction (Glyn & Sutcliffe 1992). In this vacuum, the restructuring of the European defence industry is being determined by diverse individual responses to a combination of inconsistent policies and volatile market forces. Capital in the defence sector is breaking beyond its hitherto national "containers", yet endeavouring to retain as much domestic support as possible. New competitors are entering, notably Japan, Korea, and Israel, and former members of the Warsaw Pact (Lovering 1991b). The west European arms industry is devolving into a small set of large companies drawing on an international group of supplies, exploiting a variety of markets at the national, regional, and world levels as best they can. The arms export scandals uncovered since the Gulf War reveal something of the complexity and intractability of the forces at work (Cowley 1992).

The absence of a Peace Dividend and the "democratic deficit" in Europe

The end of the Cold War signified not "demilitarization" (Shaw 1991) but "remilitarization". In keeping with postmodern tendencies, the production of the means of violence is becoming less politically and industrially *visible*. On the demand side, the nation-state is very much alive and well, contrary to many predictions (Picciotto 1991). While its ability to sustain the welfare project is in question, the state's efficacy as an instrument of social control through the monopoly of organized violence remains unrivalled (Hirst & Thompson 1992; Townsend 1992). This translates into the demand for arms. Although world defence spending is expected to fall by a third to 1995, this will reduce it only to the average level of the Cold War period (Roth 1992). And some expect it to start growing again in the late 1990s (*Flight International* 27 May 1992). The demand is met by a business that is increasingly penetrated by the revolutionary dynamics of capitalist production. The demise of the Military-Industrial-Complex is giving rise to a more complex production system, crossing national boundaries and sectoral and labour market categories.

The Peace Dividend is not being generated within the defence industry. Five years of restructuring have not resulted in any major examples of "arms conversion" in west European defence firms (CEC 1992; Renner 1992; Schofield et al. 1992). Many in the trade unions and peace movement have argued that defence companies could and should "convert" to produce needed civilian technologies: for example, waste reduction, environmental control systems, energy saving, undersea exploitation, and civilian transportation (Southwood 1990). But the market, as interpreted by investors and managers, believes otherwise. Diversification predominantly means rationalization and acquisition, rather than a shift of resources in production. The precise form of restructuring varies somewhat between countries. The rhetoric of plant-level conversion is more acceptable in German and French companies than in British ones, because the former pay more regard to the views of the trade unions. In British companies, some conversion proposals have been opposed precisely because they imply workforce influence in company decisions (Lovering 1991b). But despite these national differences, the general trend is for retrenchment into defence and large-scale job loss (CEC 1992).

In principle, a Peace Dividend could still arise despite the inflexibility of the companies, if governments used savings on the defence budget to reduce taxation or increase spending on other activities. But the predominant approach to public finance in the current environment is such that the latter is unacceptable. The prevailing model of economic management stresses competitive deflation (Lipietz 1992). German re-unification has added to the deflationary impulse in Europe (Glyn & Sutcliffe 1992). Defence cuts are being absorbed into generic public spending economies. In effect, the Peace Dividend in Europe is being used to help finance the management of recession.

The limitations of the current policy debate

The policy debate on the defence industry in Europe is currently dominated by a tussle between advocates of free markets and nationalistic defenders of industrial interests. On the right the dominant consensus is that public spending to promote conversion, especially at plant level, would be wasteful, another case of government intervention that is inevitably likely to do more harm than good (Statement on Defence Estimates 1992; *Economist* 16 January 1993). Companies should learn to respond to market forces, although this may require some cultural adjustment. If they then choose to remain in the arms market, it can be assumed that this is the right course. The Peace Dividend will come from the lower burden of public spending. A conservative minority favour a more interventionist policy to sustain the defence industry as a strategic national or alliance asset (Smith 1989).

The left is also split between those who advocate a policy of benign neglect and interventionists. Some welcome market forces in the defence sector on the grounds that they will purge the economy of an economic liability (Dunne & Smith 1992). A policy intervention is likely to be captured by the companies, resuscitating the defence lobby and leading to inefficiency (Fontanel & Smith 1992). Others take the view that a policy of abstinence means standing by while jobs are lost and national and regional capacities disappear (IMPS et al. 1991). In the peace movement the emphasis is on the moral unacceptability of high defence spending, and especially the arms trade, backed up by claims that it is also economically damaging (Southwood 1990). Arms conversion is urged on moral and practical grounds. There is perhaps a general consensus that the prospects for changing "swords into ploughshares" within defence companies are very limited except without a change in their environment. For this, some kind of macroeconomic and/or industrial policy is required. A report to the Parliamentary Office on Science and Technology recently concluded that the real issue is "how to turn around a country's manufacturing industry and its technological base . . . to meet the present need for a successful high-technology civil industry" (Schofield et al. 1992: 85). Some interventionists advocate borrowing from models in France or Germany.

Conclusion: the arms industry and the European growth path

The emphasis is on the need to adapt to market forces, the parties differing over the kind of policy that is believed to promote this, and the emphasis they give to the company, regional, and national levels. The problem is beginning to generate research and innovations. But this approach leaves aside the question, what sort of market is it that firms should be adapting to? The question would not be worth asking at the local level, but in the context of the unification of Europe it becomes important. The debate over the arms industry, especially in Britain, lacks a European dimension.

The creation of a European state apparatus has been legitimized on the grounds that it implies the possibility of greater social control over the economy (Palmer 1987). The larger the state, the greater its power to create and contain markets through public spending on areas of unexpressed demand, support for long-term investment deemed insufficiently profitable in the short term, the prohibition of undesirable trades, and regulation of the terms of employment. European unification came just as the "project" of western capitalism had reached a crisis point, raising the possibility of the creation of a new development path (Lipietz 1992: xi).

But Europe's present institutions and discourses allow little space for real debate at this level. The EC itself is constitutionally unable to take a lead. For policy makers to "pick a dynamic development path" they would need not only the full powers of a state, but also an agreed view of what sort of economic and social structure they wanted to achieve (Begg & Moore 1992: 83). The hegemony of neo-liberalism in Europe disallows any such vision, reducing the goal to one of process, the agenda of "enabling" market processes to work effectively. There is little recognition that the state system – formal and informal – necessarily plays a crucial rôle in structuring the configuration of these market forces. The discourse of post-Fordism seems paradoxically to have induced a corresponding myopia on the left. Talk of intervention is dismissively associated with subsidies and protectionism, rather than public choice over patterns of supply and demand, the purposes and instruments of regulation, or the direction of accumulation.

But all markets are "political", and the state cannot but exert an influence (Hirst & Thompson 1992). This point, the political nature of choices, is being raised in American campaigns to divert defence spending into infrastructure (Markusen & Yudken 1991). But it is still inaudible in Europe. What is missing is a sense of history. The crisis in the defence industry is the result of the dismantling of the Cold War model. This was created as part of a continent-wide package of innovations on both the supply and demand side. The Marshall Plan, NATO rearmament, and the development of the welfare state (and their correlates in the East) triggered a redirection of demand, the construction of a new industrial apparatus, and the establishment of a new growth path. Europe in the 1990s is being rebuilt in the absence of a debate over what sort of growth path it should adopt. The question of what sort of economy and society Europeans want is simply not being posed. The question of what sort of arms industry it needs is lost in this silence.

Meanwhile, the post-Cold War arms industry is rapidly taking shape according to its own privatized imperatives. These do not in general happen to coincide with the improvement of the rest of European industry, civilian needs, or the reduction of world military tensions. It seems absurd that a potentially beneficial reduction in arms spending is being translated into a chronic jobs crisis. But such is the logic of neo-liberal capitalist Europe. The disappearance of the Peace Dividend ultimately reflects the enormity of the so-called "democratic deficit".

REFERENCES

Notes

1. The WEU (West European Union) was founded in 1954 as the result of an attempt to establish a European military identity. The CSCE (Conference on Security and Co-operation in Europe) was founded in the 1950s at Soviet initiative as a pan-European security conference. It expanded to over 50 members after 1989.
2. This chapter does not discuss the effects of reductions in armed services personnel, which pose further problems.
3. The Fordism literature draws out the relationship between horizontal accumulation (mass-production of standardized commodities) and the reproduction of standardized lifestyles and consumption patterns (Castells 1989; Lipietz 1992; Kennett in this volume).

References

ACC, ADC, AMA 1992. *The impact of reduced military expenditure on local economic activity: a case for European Commission assistance.* Joint submission by the Association of County Councils, the Association of District Councils, and the Association of Metropolitan Authorities.

ACOST 1989. *The defence R & D base.* Advisory Council on Science and Technology. London: HMSO.

Alic, J. A. 1992. *Beyond spin-off: military and commercial technologies in a changing world.* Boston: Harvard Business School Press.

Antony, I., C. Allebeck, H. Wulf 1990. *West European arms production.* Stockholm: SIPRI.

Begg, I. & B. Moore 1992. Industrial regeneration and economic redistribution. In *A more perfect union? Britain and the New Europe*, D. Miliband (ed.), 83. London: Institute of Public Policy Research.

Braddon, D., A. Kendry, P. Dowdall, P. Cullen 1991. *The impact of reduced military expenditure on the economy of South West England.* Bristol: Bristol Polytechnic Research Unit in Defence Economics.

Brunton, B. G. 1992. Institutional origins of the military-industrial complex. *Journal of Economic Issues* **22**, 599–622.

Castells, M. 1989. *The informational city: information technology, economic restructuring and the urban-regional process.* Oxford: Basil Blackwell.

CEC 1992. *The economic and social impact of reductions in defence spending and military forces on the regions of the Community.* Brussels: Commission of the European Communities.

Chalmers, M. 1990. The peace dividend: a European perspective. In *European security: the new agenda*, 87–102. Bristol: Safer World Foundation.

Cowley, C. 1992. *Guns, lies and spies.* London: Hamish Hamilton.

Cutler, T., C. Haslam, J. Williams, K. Williams, 1989. *1992 – The struggle for Europe.* Oxford: Berg.

Davis, M. 1986. *Prisoners of the American dream.* London: Verso.

Deger, S. & S. Sen 1990. *Military expenditure: the political economy of international security.* SIPRI Security Strategic Issue Papers. Oxford: Oxford University Press.

Dunne, J. P. & R. Smith 1992. Thatcherism and the UK defence industry. In *1979–1992: The economic legacy*, J. Michie (ed.), 91–111. London: Academic Press.

Ellwood, D. W. 1992. *Rebuilding Europe: western Europe, America and postwar reconstruction.* Harlow, England: Longman.

Fontanel, J. & R. Smith 1991. A European defence union? *Economic Policy* **13**, 393–424.

Giddens, A. 1985. *The nation-state and violence: Volume two of a contemporary critique of historical materialism.* Cambridge: Polity.

Gill, S. 1992. The emerging world order and European change. *Socialist Register*, 157–96.

Glyn, A. & R. Sutcliffe 1992. Global but leaderless: the new capitalist order. *Socialist Review*, 76–95.

Grahl, J. & P. Teague 1990. *1992 – The big market.* London: Lawrence & Wishart.

Gummett, P. & W. Walker 1992. Changes in defence procurement and the European technology base. In R. Coopey, G. Spinardy & M. Uttley (eds) *Defence science and technology: adjusting to change.* Hurwood.

Hirst, P. & G. Thompson 1992. The problem of globalization: international economic relations, national economic management and the formation of trading blocs. *Economy and Society* **21**, 357–96.

Horowitz, D. (ed.) 1969. *Corporations and the Cold War.* New York: Monthly Review Press/ Bertrand Russell Peace Foundation.

Hyde-Price, A. 1992. Alternative security systems for Europe. In *European security – towards 2000*, M. C. Pugh (ed.), 124–39. Manchester: Manchester University Press.

Hymer, S. 1972. The multinational corporation and the law of uneven development. In *Economics and the world order from the 1970s to the 1990s*, J. Bhagwate (ed.), 113–40. New York: Collier-Macmillan.

IMPS, MSF, TGWU 1991. *The new industrial challenge – the need for defence diversification.* Institution of Professionals, Managers and Specialists, London: Manufacturing Science, Finance, Transport and General Workers' Union.

Ikenberry, J. 1992. A world economy restored: expert consensus and the Anglo-American postwar settlement. *International Organizations* **46**, 289–321.

Kaldor, M. 1982. *The baroque arsenal.* London: Deutsch.

Kaldor, M. 1990. *The imaginary war: understanding the East–West conflict.* Oxford: Basil Blackwell.

Kennedy, P. 1988. *The rise and fall of the great powers.* London: Unwin Hyman.

Land Brandenburg 1992. *Ratgeber konversion.* Potsdam: Land Brandenburg.

Lipietz, A. 1992. *Towards a new economic order: post-Fordism, ecology and democracy.* Cambridge: Polity.

Lodge, J. 1990. European Community security policy: rhetoric or reality? In *European security – towards 2000*, M. C. Pugh (ed.), 227–51. Manchester: Manchester University Press.

Lovering, J. 1987. Capitalism, militarism and the nation-state: towards a realist analysis. *Environment and Planning D: Society and Space* **5**, 283–302.

Lovering, J. 1988. Islands of prosperity. In *Defence expenditure and regional development*, M. Breheny (ed.), 29–48. London: Mansell.

Lovering, J. 1990a. Defence spending and the restructuring of capitalism: the military industry in Britain. *Cambridge Journal of Economics* **14**, 453–67.

Lovering, J. 1990b. A perfunctory sort of post-Fordism. *Work, Employment and Society*, Special Issue, May, 227–51.

Lovering, J. 1991a. The changing geography of the military industry in Britain. *Regional Studies 25*, 239–79.

Lovering, J. 1991b. *The defence industry after the Cold War*. London: Campaign for Nuclear Disarmament.

Lovering, J. 1993. Restructuring the British defence industrial base after the Cold War: geographical and institutional perspectives. *Defence Economics* (forthcoming).

Mann, M. 1984. Capitalism and militarism. In *War, state and society*, M. Shaw (ed.), 25–46. London: Macmillan.

Markusen, A. 1991. The military-industrial divide. *Environment and Planning D: Society and Space* **9**, 391–416.

Markusen, A. & J. Yudken 1991. *Dismantling the Cold War economy*. New York: Basic Books.

Melman, S. 1985. *The permanent war economy*. New York: Touchstone Books/Simon & Schuster.

Palmer, J. 1987. *Europe without America?* Oxford: Oxford University Press.

Picciotto, S. 1991. The internationalisation of the state. *Capital and Class* **43**, 43–64.

POST (Parliamentary Office on Science and Technology) 1991. *Relationships between defence and civil science and technology*. London: HMSO.

Ramsay, H. E. 1992. Whose champions? Multinationals, labour and industry policy in the European Community after 1992. *Capital and Class* **48**, 17–39.

Renner, M. 1992. *Economic adjustments after the Cold War: strategies for conversion*. Dartmouth: United Nations Institute for Disarmament Research.

Roth, R. T. 1992. The impact of decreased defense spending on employment in the United States. *Armed Forces and Society* **18**, 383–405.

SBAC 1992. *Briefing papers*. London: Society of British Aerospace Companies.

Schofield, S., M. Dando, M. Ridge 1992. Conversion of the British defence industries. Peace Research Report 30. School of Peace Studies, University of Bradford.

Shaw, M. 1991. *Post-military society*. Cambridge: Polity.

Smith, R. 1989. *The changing face of industrial Europe: the defence industries*. Paper presented at Royal Institute of International Affairs, 4 October.

Southwood, P. 1990. *The peace dividend in the 1990s*. London: Campaign for Nuclear Disarmament.

Statement on Defence Estimates 1992. London: HMSO.

Taylor, T. & K. Hayward 1989. *The UK defence industrial base*. London & New York: Brassey's Defence Publishers.

Tipton, F. B. & R. Aldrich 1987. *An economic and social history of Europe from 1939 to the present*. London: Macmillan.

Townsend, P. 1992. *Hard times: the prospects for European social policy*. Eleanor Rathbone Memorial Lecture. Liverpool: Liverpool University Press.

Van der Pijl, K. 1984. *The making of an Atlantic ruling class*. London: Verso.

Walker, W. 1992. Defence. In *Technology and the future of Europe*, C. Freeman, M. Sharp, W. Walker (eds), 365–82. London: Pinter/Science Policy Research Unit.

Chapter 9

The collapse of Soviet socialism: legitimation, regulation, and the new class

Larry Ray

This chapter offers a preliminary exploration of the background to current struggles over economic ownership and control (and hence new dynamics of exclusion) in post-communist systems. It argues that these struggles originate in the systemic dynamic and crisis-logic of the former system. Reform communism, illustrated here largely through the Gorbachev period and its aftermath, represented attempts among the intellectual and political elite to initiate systemic adaptation to long-range structural problems, without undermining the existing mode of appropriation. Beginning in the 1960s, but emerging more clearly in the 1980s, reforms were intended first, to improve motivational inputs into the system (for example through work discipline and incentives); secondly, to shift steering capacity towards latent means of co-ordination (especially through the second, or informal, economy); and thirdly, to sustain outputs of allocative resources, thus forestalling systemic collapse. Although these initiatives failed on one level, in relation to the political system, at a deeper level they perhaps enabled the existing mode of domination to reproduce itself within post-communist society more effectively than under the old regime. This possibility is illustrated with reference to how the former elite stratum, the nomenklatura, are transforming bureaucratic power into economic capital. Finally, it is suggested that analysis of this process might offer ways of examining the relationship between societal breakdown and the emergence of new forms of social integration.

Mode of domination and legitimation

The "social nature" of Soviet-type societies (STS) has been the subject of a long-running debate, which this is not really the place to recapitulate. Nonetheless, in order to develop a model of systemic regulation in STS, and to identify the emergence of new types of ownership in the present transition, it is necessary briefly to define the key features of this social system, and the following definition is offered. State-socialist societies were often described as forms of status group domination, where the power of the privileged stratum, the nomenklatura, arose from bureaucratic position rather than class location. A central feature of the Soviet system was bureaucratic control of the means of production, and a fusion between economic, political, and cultural imperatives. The principle of profitability was subordinated (or suppressed) by other considerations, which were determined by a network of impersonal relations of dependence such that the bureaucracy decided what to produce and how to deploy the gross product.

However, an alternative definition is provided by the well-known theory of "state capitalism", according to which integration within the global economy obliged STS to submit to the capitalist laws of value. In consequence, they were subject to the same kind of crisis-tendencies as western capitalist societies. This view further entails a kind of convergence thesis that claims that monopolization and state regulation in capitalist economies finds a parallel in STS, where the bureaucracy performs the rôle of the collective capitalist, or the "personification of capital" (Callinicos 1991: 39). The absence of extensive markets or private productive property, then, does not preclude the description of STS as capitalist, or "militarized state capitalism" (Callinicos 1991: 19). Beneath this analysis (if not always acknowledged) lies the extensive literature pointing to the independent power of administration in both capitalist and socialist societies and the expanding rôle of the state in a period of monopoly capitalism, and the early Frankfurt School's account of authoritarian state capitalism.[1]

"State capitalism", however, is a problematic notion. Of course, one can call a system by whatever name one chooses, but this description does not reveal much about the structure or development of STS. A fairly unexceptional definition of "capitalism", I would have thought, would refer to a system where, despite state regulation, substantial means of production are privately owned; investment decisions are led by anticipated profit; economic rationality is divorced from socio-institutional limitations, so dominating social development, including the pattern of state intervention, which in turn operates within parameters of capital accumulation (e.g. Rakovski [Kis] 1978). Further, money in capitalism is the social form of value, which begets more value within a division of labour where the capitalist proprietor has command over labour. However, this command is circumscribed by the conditions of the wage contract within a legal framework.

However, *none* of these conditions obtained to any significant degree in STS. On the contrary, there was an absence of large-scale private production; dissolution of boundaries between state and economy resulted in profit being subordinated to state allocation and the appropriation of use-values. Money was not the real medium of exchange, since the majority of capital goods circulated through interdepartmental requisition (Mandel 1977: 567), and consumption goods (especially housing, domestic fuel, transport, and food) were heavily subsidized. This in turn resulted in production that could not satisfy solvent demand, thus STS were prone to crises of under- and not over-production. There was no proper wage contract, since the apparatus that controlled the means of production (such as Gosplan in the USSR) also commanded labour and set rates of pay and consumption subsidies. It is true that an un-consumed surplus product was accumulated by the bureaucracy, and that wage labour was generalized throughout the system, but neither of these in themselves render STS "capitalist", since both can be found in complex pre-capitalist societies. Similarly, STS could not be described as "capitalist" simply by virtue of their linkage with the global economy, any more than could, say, the Ottoman Empire.

A number of theorists, such as Djilas (1957), Rakovski [Kis] (1978) or Konrad & Szelényi (1979), while accepting many of the above points, argued that the bureaucratic elite in STS constituted a "new class". Planners and intellectuals, defined by their possession of technical expertise and bureaucratic power rather than private property, disposed of resources and a social surplus that had been produced by workers with no control over the ends to which it was put. Voslensky (1984) and Zemtsov (1976, 1985) argue similarly, but both use the term "class" rather loosely, pointing to the ability of the bureaucratic elite to consolidate their position via the intergenerational transmission of cultural capital. This took place through access to elite schools and universities, foreign trips, dachas, privileged occupations, as well as the opportunity to amass private fortunes through *blat*, or corruption (Zemtsov 1976: 23). However, as Ferenc Fehér, György Márkus, and Agnes Heller (1984) argue, the term "class" might not be appropriate, since the corporate rulers were defined neither by property nor market relations. Indeed, Voslensky himself argued that the new class was by the 1980s coming to feel anxious that its rule was "terminable without notice", since it lacked an independent base of ownership in civil society (1984: 240).

There might be good grounds, then, for regarding STS as bureaucratic caste rather than class societies. Ernst Mandel (1977, & 1991) has written of the parasitic bureaucracy, which unlike a real ruling class was unable to base its material privileges on the coherent functioning of the economic system. The privileges of the ruling group were dependent upon their position in hierarchy, where the bureaucracy tended to form groupings of mutual support, from which they could control fiefdoms (e.g. Khrushchev's buddies from the Ukraine; Brezhnev's mafia of Dnipropetrovske; or Gorbachev's friends from Stavropol). As a bureaucratic stratum, the nomenklatura were defined by access to privileges secured by their position and by rights to dispose of productive resources, both of which followed from status rather than ownership. Since this involved regarding particular spheres of control as personal "fiefdoms", state socialism was sometimes described as a kind of "socialist feudalism" (Voslensky 1984: 70). Further, the mechanism of elite recruitment through the nomenklatura appointments created a mode of domination and social regulation specific to state-socialist societies.[2] This was a bureaucratic system of control established in the 1920s when the Party list, drawn up by the Organburo and ratified by the Central Committee, controlled appointments to all significant positions, including nominally "elective" ones (Hough 1969: 153; Rigby 1988). The exceptional comprehensiveness of the system converted its occupants into a distinct social category defined by common behavioural, attitudinal, and organizational features (Hill 1988).[3]

What mechanisms, though, were available for the transmission of elite culture and privileges? That is, how secure was the nomenklatura; how did it reproduce itself and maintain group boundaries? Being embedded in clientelistic structures meant that the inter-generational transmission of cultural and material capital was uncertain, since membership was dependent upon the continued approval of superiors and local party organs, rather than an independent base in civil society. During the Stalin period, officials were denied personal assets and their dependence on Stalin's personal patronage was reinforced in various ways.[4] Further, in the Great Purges of the 1930s Stalin turned the NKVD[5] on the nomenklatura in an ultimately unsuccessful attempt to undermine the power of local organs (Getty 1985). Even so, Yezhov's terror had left the party apparatus vulnerable to purges, and it was only under Khrushchev and Brezhnev's generation of leaders that these "revolutions from above" ended (Fehér & Arato 1989).[6] After Stalin, the nomenklatura consolidated into cadre-patrons, or what Jowitt (1983) calls "political principals", overseeing a system founded upon an administrative hierarchy in which the primary agent is the fiscal corporation, rather than the entrepreneur. Moreover, after Stalin the nomenklatura enjoyed high security of tenure (Hirszowicz 1986: 129), which offered opportunities for widespread corruption integral to the system of rewards. However, these were still not formally embedded in social norms and rules, nor were they inheritable rights in the form of alienable capital.

Legitimacy and regulation

How, then, did the institutional structures of the Party reproduce themselves, and to what extent were they embedded in cultural values and social practices? Fehér et al. pointed out that,

> If a social order survives for sixty years, it is appropriate to raise the question of its legitimacy... According to one formulation of Max Weber, a social order is legitimated if at least one part of the population acknowledges it as exemplary and binding and the other part does not confront the existing social order with the image of an alternative one as equally exemplary... Consequentially the Soviet social order can be conceived as a legitimate one, even though only the Party... acknowledge[s] the order as exemplary and binding
> (Fehér et al. 1984: 138).[7]

However, more detailed analysis of legitimation in STS is complex for at least three reasons. First if, as Heller (1982) has argued, eastern European regimes (by contrast with the Soviet Union) were undergoing "protracted legitimation crises", then legitimation *per se* is not a satisfactory account of their survival for 40 years or so. Secondly, legitimation is a complex process linked, as Habermas has suggested, to motivational inputs (from the cultural system); the generation of solidarity, or social integration (the social system); and fulfilling required administrative outcomes (the administrative system).[8] Thirdly, in capitalist societies, the concept of legitimacy derives from the dissolution of traditional structures, so that world views that once generated an undisputed order dissolve into disputable and competing interpretations. Administrative power then confronts the potential challenge of justifying itself and having to secure agreement from citizens to norms of government. However, in the absence of both the market as a regulator of autonomous groups, and a public sphere where legitimacy questions could arise, it might be more appropriate to speak of the relationship between state

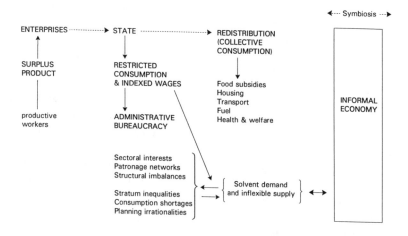

Figure 9.1 The redistributive economy.

and society in terms of ideological mobilization, social contract, and acquiescence than of "legitimacy".

Indeed, David Lane (1979) has argued that in order to compensate for lack of procedures for generating consensus, the Soviet state closely linked social integration to the system of resource allocation, thereby rendering subjects dependent on and acquiescent to state agencies for their material well-being. This notion of functional legitimacy, based on dependence rather than consent, is also developed by Maria Markus (1982) and Jadwiga Staniszkis (1992: 101–2), who point to the importance of substantive legitimation through social security, income maintenance, housing subsidies, health, and welfare, allocated on the basis of what Weber called substantive rationality.[9] This notion is elaborated again in what Szelényi, Hegedus, Tosics and others have called the "redistributive economy" (Figure 9.1) as a mechanism of resource allocation and regulation. This concept, derived from Polanyi's distinction between transactive (market) and dispositive economic relationships,[10] refers to a system of state-regulated collective consumption, where "the state redistributes a surplus . . . which was never accumulated in personal incomes . . . but which was directly centralized in the state budget and reallocated according to centrally defined goals and values" (Szelényi 1979). Further, Szelényi argues that the redistributive economies differentially benefited the higher nomenklatura and intellectual strata, that is they operated in part as exclusionary mechanisms. In the absence of generalized market systems of allocation, the redistributive economies generated complex bureaucratic rules of allocation that gave rise to social inequalities based on privileged access to resources through occupation, patronage, and sectoral influence within the planning bureaucracies. In housing allocation, for example, the nomenklatura and intelligentsia were over-represented in better-quality state dwellings, while manual workers were highly represented in the private, self-build sector (Szelényi 1983: Dangschat 1987; Musil 1987; Tosics 1987) At the same time though, the redistributive system obliged subjects to sell their labour to the state, which instituted dependence on corporatist structures.

Nonetheless, the generation of acquiescence through bureaucratic corporatism involves rule through visible structures of political intervention, and carries a higher de-legitimation risk than rule through the invisible mechanisms of the market. The later is a de-politicized form of regulation (in so far as market mechanisms take on the appearance of being autonomous and inevitable) whereas administrative-political resource allocation involves identifiable decision-making structures. As Wesolowski (1972: 183) put it,

> [i]n socialist societies the unequal distribution of goods in high demand is made through the mechanism of government decisions . . . the government assumes the rôle of direct regulator. This explains [why] . . . people with insufficient incomes tend to blame the government. . . rather than the more favoured groups.

Thus economic disputes (such as strikes) could very easily turn political and call the rule of the Party into question. Confronted with a serious crisis then, a political elite in these circumstances might attempt to better secure its rule through shifting towards the more de-politicized regulation of the market.

This is arguably what began to occur as problems of regulation through central planning grew more complex. Since coercion, though an evident feature of the system, was insufficient to guarantee the rule of the Party, socialist states were confronted with problems of management and regulation. These in part were concerned with operating the redistributive economy that during the 1960s and 1970s increased in complexity as it began to shift away from the Stalinist concentration on autarkic development through capital goods production, towards increased personal consumption and a more flexible planning system. They were further concerned with managing systemic irregularities that arose from the planning mechanisms themselves. For example, enterprises hoarded capital equipment against the possibility of future shortages; local party secretaries colluded with factory managers to procure materials or falsify data; enterprises relied on "storming" at the end of the planning cycle to fulfil monthly quotas.[11]

Not only this, but by the 1960s long-range problems in the Soviet economy were apparent. Much national product growth resulted from oil and gas production, which involved high capital investment and transportation costs. Since 1945 each 1 per cent increase in growth had required a 1.4 per cent increase in investment and a 1.2 per cent increase in raw materials supply (Guber 1985). Moreover, as the geographical integration of the USSR weakened with population dispersal, so logistical problems accumulated. For example, coal from Siberia increased in cost two times with every 1500 km transport (that was why nuclear reactors were situated in the more populous western USSR) (Walker 1988: 70). Between the 1950s and 1980s the annual growth rate fell from 11.4 per cent to 3.6 per cent, and although by 1980 the USSR produced twice as much steel as the USA, its output of finished products was smaller (White 1992: 106). Moreover, imported technology and the increasing pressure of competing with Western military systems highlighted the poor differential productivity of the USSR (which ran at about

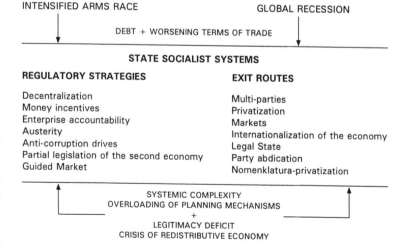

Figure 9.2 Regulatory strategies and exit routes.

70 per cent of US industry, with much higher energy consumption). Increasing proportions of foreign currency earnings from oil and gas exports were being used to pay for grain imports (which in turn were used as cattle feed to support meat consumption) and for imports of Western technology. This resulted in accumulating indebtedness, such that by 1985–86 the USSR's foreign debt stood at $24 billion (Carlo 1989), and by 1990 had risen to around $100 billion. This was combined with inflationary pressure from a budget deficit in 1989 of 120 billion roubles, representing 11–12 per cent of GNP (compared with a US deficit of 4 per cent) and public expenditure that exceeded revenue by 7.3 per cent (White 1992: 132).

By the 1980s, then, STS confronted two loci of crises, arising from global and internal environments (see Figure 9.2). From the global environment, an accelerating arms race that was increasingly technologically-driven, along with growing foreign indebtedness, exacerbated the systemic dysfunctions of the Soviet planning mechanisms. From the internal environment, the redistributive economy became difficult to sustain, as it was over-burdened by increasing complexity and steering problems. Exit routes from these crises increasingly involved delinking the rule of the nomenklatura from the redistributive economy.

Second society and informal economy

To understand how STS remained integrated for as long as they did, one needs to appreciate the importance of the increasingly tolerated parallel or "second" society alongside the "official" economy. Exclusion from the redistributive effects of the state sector generated informal dynamics of inclusion. Shortages resulting from the redistributive mechanisms were (partially) filled through informal networks, and by symbiotic exchanges between the informal sector and the state, based on patrimonial protection through mutual security and political corruption (Fehér 1983; Jowitt 1983). In response to scarcities of distributive goods, officials developed coping mechanisms in the form of clientelist networks and horizontally integrated relationships that spanned all levels, from local councils to the Politburo (Baker 1982: 44). Moreover, informal bureaucratic exchanges were replicated by more extensive social networks of the second society, which offset shortages and planning deficiencies through mutual assistance, reciprocal labour exchanges, barter of scarce commodities and, eventually, petty commodity production.[12] The boundary between tolerated and illegal economic activity was indistinct and fluid, permitting a vast network of transactions that contributed to consumer satisfaction, and provided an outlet for antisystemic sentiments and activities. Sampson (1985–6) describes the informal sector as a "de-bureaucratized" social space, characterized by relationships of mutual obligation and patronage, which not only survived well within "the interstices of bureaucratic organization" but also to some extent assisted the latter to function. Thus when, for example, the local mayor mobilized relatives to help out with the voluntary work brigade to fulfil a production quota, he or she was solidifying non-formalized relations of personal obligation that had only the appearance of commitment to the motivational requirements of the regime. Moreover, planners relied on the ability of people to provision themselves via informal channels. Davies (1988) describes how increased prices, combined with scarcity of welfare resources were absorbed by local communities through the "self-management of austerity", which was dependent on the deployment of women as unpaid carers and low-wage workers.[13] Thus the division of labour between the "command economy" and "second economy" was

> much more than functional, it [was] an ingenious, not fully conscious, not fully accidental arrangement that sustains and reflects the invidious distinction . . . between the privileged exclusivity of the cadre stratum, . . . on the one hand, and the dependent, privatized situation of the politically excluded on the other.
>
> (Jowitt 1983)

However, the second society had dysfunctional as well as functional consequences for the state sector. On the one hand, it drained state resources both directly (through theft, moonlighting, etc.) and indirectly, by siphoning off motivational inputs, as attitudes towards the official economy became increasingly cynical and apathetic. The latter contrasted with relations of trust, reciprocity, and self-interest in the second economy (Bugajski & Pollack 1989: 187).[14] On the other hand, these defensive reactions, rational enough in a chronic shortage economy (Kornai 1986) themselves exacerbated the kinds of shortages and dysfunctions referred to above (hoarding, falsifying data, storming, etc.). Further, Hankiss points out that the terms "official" and "second" societies do not refer to two groups of people, but to two dimensions of social existence governed by different organizational principles (1991: 310). Conflict between the two, therefore, indicated a fundamental contradiction in the social system.

Reform and crisis

Under the impact of multiple crisis tendencies, Party planning bureaucracies developed successive attempts at technocratic adjustment that eventually led towards an abandonment of the redistributive economy altogether. The trajectory of the various reform programmes from the 1960s through to *perestroika* and *glasnost* was to protect the identity of the system in two ways: first, to consolidate its functional legitimacy by improving motivational inputs through a combination of improved work discipline and financial incentives; secondly, to offset administrative crises partly by deploying techniques latently stored in the learning capacity of the second society (especially expanding the scope for market allocation) and partly by deploying more sophisticated managerial and productive technologies. Indeed, the Party was a vehicle within which (generally, but not always internal) debate took place on technocratic solutions to systemic inefficiencies.

The reform proposals that emerged in the post-Brezhnev period (after 1982) were part of a long-term process of attempted systemic adaptation to systemic problems. In 1965, Abel Aganbegyan (Institute of Economy of Siberia, Novosibirsk and later architect of *perestroika*) identified the major problems of the Soviet economy in terms of slow growth, over-extended commitments to defence, and extreme centralism, and concluded that the planning model of the 1930s was no longer workable (Hosking 1985: 363–4). This analysis was the basis for the hesitant Kosygin and Aganbegyan/Liberman reforms in the 1960s. Although these reforms ran aground after 1968, other experiments in self-management and financial accountability within specific enterprises continued through 1970s (as they did in East Germany and Hungary). Further, alongside experiments in enterprise autonomy a debate continued among economists and sociologists through the 1970s, for example in *Dengi i Kredit* (Money and Credit).[15] These developed strategies for reducing the inflexibility of Gosplan, but also challenged many assumptions of the redistributive economy. In December 1980 these debates spilled into the public domain with a piece in *Pravda* by Gavril Popov (economist at Moscow University and again later a member of Gorbachev's team) that advocated wages cuts, work incentives, and planned unemployment.

In 1984 Andropov commissioned the Novosibirsk Institute of Economics and Organization of Industrial Production to produce a critical analysis of the entire system of economic management. In the resulting analysis, the sociologist Tanya Zaslavskaya attacked the rigidity of the planning system, corruption, inflexible work practices, and the "inhibition of market forces". She identified middle-ranking bureaucrats, planners, and enterprise managers as the most likely opponents of reform, since they would defend their privileges. Indeed, she identified a division between "qualified, energetic, and active managers" who realize the system is not working, and the "apathetic, elderly, less qualified groups . . . who bear witness to the famous principles of 'I need no more than anybody else'" (Zaslavskaya 1984). Her report signalled a turn away from even the pretence of upholding egalitarian values. Rather, it argued that,

> [t]he social mechanism of economic development at present operating in the USSR does not ensure satisfactory results. The social type of worker formed by it fails to correspond not only to the strategic aims of developed socialist society, but also to the technological requirements of contemporary production.[16]

Before long, Gorbachev and Yeltsin were repeatedly to attack managers of the Brezhnev period as an "inert stratum of careerists with a party card". Systemic problems were identified in part in terms of technology-deficit, in part with reference to out-moded values that failed to stimulate innovation, but also in terms of the nomenklatura system itself. *Perestroika* was to involve an attempt at restructuring motivational inputs to the system, in the course of which a transition from status to class-based power became possible.

Gorbachev, representing a new generation of post-Stalinist communists (with close KGB connections) intent on improving the functioning of the system, launched the programme of restructuring at the 27th Party Congress. This set out a programme that had its origins in debates of the past two decades and concentrated on economic modernization. It called for price flexibility (linked to demand); an end to the tutelage of ministries over enterprises; farms would be free to dispose of surpluses on the open market; workers' incomes would correspond to the quality and quantity or work done; and enterprises would be responsible for losses. Further, military and civilian industries would be integrated to facilitate technology transfer and the deployment of advanced productive skills.

Such major changes, however, required the construction of new constituencies favouring reform (Hauslohner 1989), which in turn involved a gradual de-linking of the Party from the structures of economic power as well as a collapse in central systems of regulation. However, the enterprise-based nomenklatura had already become highly interpenetrated with the informal economy and the culture of illegality, and one consequence of *perestroika*, by giving greater latitude to local decision-making and market allocation, was to make more manifest the latent practices and networks of the second economy. Moreover, the larger the sphere of economy and society outside the control of the planning bureaucracy, the greater were the difficulties of legitimacy-generation, not least because the resources at their disposal diminished (Batt 1991: 13; Murphy et al. 1992). Thus the unintended consequence of the reforms was to undermine further the functional legitimacy upon which the bureaucratic privileges of the nomenklatura was based. One exit from this impasse was to seek a new settlement based on a separation of the social reproduction of the nomenklatura from the bureaucracy and political system. Perhaps acknowledging this, by the mid-1980s, younger members of the nomenklatura-intelligentsia tended to favour an extensive enlargement of the scope of democratic pluralism and market forces.[17] It is important to stress that these policy innovations came initially not so much from a challenge to the Party from without, so much as from within the Party and planning bureaucracy itself (though it was later taken up by others).[18]

In response to motivational crises the bureaucratic elite attempted to reactivate motivational inputs in various ways. These included improving labour discipline (e.g. the anti-alcohol campaigns and increased surveillance over time-keeping); offering wage incentives; widening participation in enterprises, with more local autonomy and employee self-management; but, above all, shifting resource allocation in the direction of the market. Incentive schemes and work-discipline were linked to an effort to substitute the ethics of social security and equality (*garantirvanost*) with market rationality. Experiments in workers' democracy, such as the 1987 Law on Enterprises (enterprise managements were to be elected by the collective) gave way to consolidating the powers of managers, who were increasingly in a position to become owners of productive property (the 1990 Law on Enterprises re-established managers' control).[19] Later, the Central Committee Plenum in 1987 went further than the 27th Party Congress, and called for nothing less than the "radical reform" of management leading to extensive marketization. However, increasing the scope for initiative and market forces did not arrest economic decline. Prices continued to rise, shortages increased, labour discipline worsened, with 30 per cent more days off in 1989 than 1988 (White 1992: 133). In May 1990 the Prime Minister of the Russian Federation, Ryzhkov, proposed a "regulated market", followed by Shatalin's "500 Days Programme" for a transition to the market and a "hard rouble". In August 1990, Gorbachev himself identified free enterprise as the "motor" of economic growth, and private property as the *only* guarantor of democracy and human rights (*Pravda* 19 August 1990).

New class formation?

Naturally enough, many commentaries of the Gorbachev period tended to focus on its immediate objective, namely to preserve the political system through opening up new channels of inclusion. For example, Fehér et al. argued that Gorbachev's reform programme aimed to make technocratic adjustments such as changes in the leadership, local democracy, or limited legalization of private enterprise and co-operatives. It is then claimed that these failed because they were too limited, whereas radical reform would have called into question the power and privilege of the corporate ruling group (Heller & Fehér 1990: 25). However, in 1989 unfolding events were already more complex than this. The 27th Congress of the Party, after all, had launched an assault on the very privileges of the nomenklatura upon which the identity of the system was supposedly based. Yet at a deeper level, the underlying identity of the system actually reproduced itself within a class system of new property relations. The crisis of the political system and the crisis of social integration were actually to facilitate the transformation of the bureaucratic nomenklatura into the nucleus of an accumulating class.

The reform strategy had been to increase the scope of the latent capacities of the second economy to generate motivational inputs and co-ordinate allocative mechanisms. Once the redistributive economy had become inviable, though, the Party, and indeed the structure of the Soviet Union itself, could no longer guarantee the social reproduction of the nomenklatura.[20] Ivo Mozny (1991) argues that by the 1980s the nomenklatura's power, derived from bureaucratic position rather than ownership, was uncertain since property could not be transferred through inheritance. Thus to facilitate intergenerational reproduction they permitted the political guarantees of public ownership to disintegrate along with the political system that had served them previously. Similarly, Hankiss has suggested that the large-scale appropriation of state property by the former nomenklatura was facilitated by a "grand coalition" between intellectuals and the state-bourgeoisie, in which both collaborated to transform state assets into private capital, an arrangement from which both benefited (Hankiss 1990: 250). This claim does imply a level of collusion that might be difficult to document, although there is evidence for the more general claim that former nomenklatura are emerging as new property owners. This section presents some examples of this, while raising questions about the type of new class that might be forming.

The transformation of the nomenklatura-stratum into nomenklatura-capitalists needs to be understood in the context of economic problems of post-communism. Post-communist economies face problems of developing a strategy for privatization; and of regulating the new mode of private accumulation. Problems of the transition from a monopolized economy to a market have been exacerbated by declining production and accelerating inflation. Meanwhile, the rapid growth of the market sector in which prices are still highly distorted has led to the concentration of economic activity in speculative operations rather than restructuring and investment (Glaziev 1991). In relation to the latter, Filatotchev et al. (1992a, 1992b) identify problems of obsolete plant and old technologies, artificial prices, histories of planned unprofitability, a dearth of bidders, no local capital market, and enterprises that own cultural centres, housing, polyclinics, sports facilities, kindergartens, etc. that potential purchasers would not want. Finally, even if all the savings of the ex-USSR in 1990 (700bn roubles) were available for investment, this would amount only to about 25 per cent of the base-value and current assets (2700bn roubles) (Fischer et al. 1992).[21]

Against this background, two types of buy-outs are taking shape. (Since this is an account of indigenous class formation, foreign purchase is excluded from the discussion.) In the first type, managers lease assets from the state. By 1991 there were 2400 leased manufacturing enterprises in the USSR, producing 5.2 per cent of total output. In the service sector, employees leased about 2000 retail organizations, 33,000 shops and over 2000 workshops (Filatotchev et al. 1992), and against a rapid decline in production during 1990–91 of 13 per cent, leased activities increased output by 3.5 per cent (*Birzheviye Vedomosti* 1 January 1992). In the second type of privatization, the liquidation of enterprise and plant assets is followed by a management buy-out (MBO) using bank credit and plough-back funds from the old enterprise. This (often called) "spontaneous privatization" enables former managers to become owners of productive resources in a situation where economic restructuring is subject to little regulation. (Levitas & Strzalkowski 1990; Hausner 1991; Kowalik 1991; Mandel 1991). These might be called nomenklatura buy-outs (NBOs).

The latter is not a uniform process and itself takes at least two forms. First, there is the legal purchase of state enterprises by former managers (whose investment capital might well have been accumulated through *blat*); and secondly, there is the acquisition of state property by virtue of the new owner's current position and privileges. The latter involves the extensive transformation of state assets into private property through illegal conversion, where the practices and networks established in the second economy come into their own.

For example, in Leningrad, 250,000 foreign currency roubles were moved from the Soviet executive committee's account into Lentok (a private firm) as joint-enterprise capital. On instructions from the mayor, the account was then moved to the Russian Ballet fund, in Switzerland. Among the small entrepreneurs backing Lentok, one-fifth were powerful founders – administrative bodies, who supplied them with buildings and state funds for capitalization. Members of Soviet executives were frequently setting up small firms, funded by the city. (*Izvestia* 10 October 1990).

Moscow markets are completely monopolized by the "mafia" structure of a single market that makes thousands of roubles a day. The "mafia" is a growing fusion of the bureaucracy, economic administrators, and "affairists" of the private sector, who create shortages through monopoly structures, and illicitly transfer state resources and funds into private hands (*Komsomolskaya Pravda* 12 December 1990).

There have further been suggestions of arbitrary pricing and deals between enterprises and customers.[22] The economist, Sergei Kugushev, reports that there are three groups of major property owners. First, there is the administrative-management segment of the Party, who are creating banks. Secondly, there are top ministry officials, such as the erstwhile USSR Ministry of Gas, which has become Gazprom Co; or the Ministry of Construction in the northwest, which is now Severo-Zapad (NW) Construction Co. Public funds are converted into share capital, and the directors become shareholders. Thirdly, there are the Soviets, such as the Moscow River Borough Soviet Executive Committee, which turned over its best stock to the Energia Interbank Association, and became its executives. Laws will regulate this process, Kugushev suggested, only when it has been completed (*Komsomolskaya Pravda* 6 February 1991).

Kugushev continues to the effect that there is a "larcenous bourgeois class rapidly taking shape", a theme developed by David Mandel (1991), who argues that the conversion of state assets into private capital involves collusion between administrators and the shadow (*tenevaya*) economy, consequent on the weakening of central control (*Rashidovshchina*). Joint ventures are set up for sale abroad, or to the private sector, a process that the Law on Co-operatives has facilitated. Whereas exchanges within the state sector are non-monetary, sub-contracting work to co-operatives turns non-cash credits into cash. "Joint venture construction" companies, or agricultural co-operatives, can make profits of 4000 per cent by importing and selling computers – not building or producing food at all. David Mandel (1991) concludes that "transition to the market" involves the formation of monopolies, through which public wealth is illicitly transferred into private capital. Further, this process is not restricted to the former USSR. In relation to Poland, Jerzy Hausner refers to the "self enfranchisement of the nomenklatura", as factory directors serving commissions preparing for privatization were first appointed as liquidators, and subsequently took top positions in enterprises taking over the assets of state firms (Hausner 1991: 18).

Nomenklatura-privatization has implications for new patterns of inclusion and exclusion from the economic and political process, and has in consequence become highly controversial. The Russian Politika Independent Research Centre report on the administrative apparatus claimed to have identified a "nomenklatura underground" in the "Military-Industrial-Complex" and the shadow economy. Moreover, it is claimed that this underground controls the entire "non-communist press"; the General Management Office of President's staff; Rutskoi's extreme right-wing populist campaign against "profiteering middlemen and speculators"; and the Democratic Reform Movement (largely responsible for ousting Gaidar as Assistant Prime Minister in favour of Viktor Chernomyrdin in December 1992). Whether true or not,[23] these allegations illustrate how the regrouping of the nomenklatura has become a centre of political controversy, manifest for example in the conflict between Yeltsin and the "conservative" Congress of Peoples Deputies.[24] The issue to some extent underlay both the stormy meeting of the Congress in December 1992, and Yeltsin's ongoing dispute with Ruslan Khasbulatov (Speaker of the Russian Parliament).

Yeltsin, Yegor Gaidar, and Gennady Burbulis (First Deputy Head of the Russian government) had attempted to block nomenklatura-privatization through a combination of controls on asset conversion, and the development of an alternative scheme of voucher privatization. The latter involves plans to issue privatization vouchers, of which 25 per cent of enterprise assets go to employees as non-voting preference stock; 10 per cent to employees as voting stock available for purchase; the rest to be auctioned to the public, who will be able to "buy" shares with vouchers. Other controls include a ban on state employees being stock holders, and obliging company executives to declare sources of income (*Rossiiskaya Gazeta* 17 January 1992). However, whether these will prevent spontaneous privatization is far from certain.[25] The Piyasheva-Selunin Group[26] have claimed that since the bulk of the population have no savings, the real buyers of state enterprises will still be commercial organizations set up by the former nomenklatura,[27] a process they describe as "a special, socialist form of corruption, one that . . . surpasses all Sicilian models" (*Smena* 28 April 1992). Instead, the Piyasheva-

Selunin Group have advocated that nomenklatura-appropriated property should be returned to the people free of charge, the bulk of which should go to labour co-operatives, which would become joint-stock companies with individuated ownership.[28]

On the other hand, some commentators such as Hankiss (1990) or Boris Rumer (1991) claim approvingly that nomenklatura-privatization represents the formation of an accumulating capitalist class. Rumer argues that "ministers, party bosses, university figures, leaders of government agencies, and industrial executives . . . are laying the foundations for a viable market economy. It would be a mistake to underestimate the business acumen of the nomenklatura". From this point of view, NBOs might have a significant contribution to the process of privatization in that they harness managerial talent developed over years of informal negotiation required to meet planning targets, along with knowledge of networks and rules of barter. Speculation is good in itself, the argument goes, irrespective of who the new owners are, so long as they are entrepreneurial. Arguing against broad-based employee ownership schemes, Anatoly Chubais insists that "entrepreneurs are a specific socio-psychological type who will not be found by distributing capital collectively" (*Izvestia* 26 February 1992).

However, it is not yet clear that the ex-nomenklatura *are* emerging as a capitalist class in the sense that Hankiss or Rumer imagine. Levitas & Strzalkowski (1990) argue that state assets are being appropriated mainly for consumption. Why, they ask,

> should one make the long-term investment in domestic skilled labour and technology, if through a combination of a little industrial collusion and some personal connections one can re-write tax legislation, export credits and bank policies? Or. . . why not simply sell off your newly-acquired state factory . . . and live off the interest one can earn in a Swiss bank?

Indeed, it has been suggested that uncontrolled exports of capital from Russia has resulted in $20 billion (more than Russia's annual state budget) being deposited abroad in 1991 (*Nezavismaya Gazeta* 6 March 1992). As a bureaucratic stratum, the nomenklatura were essentially consumers of a social surplus rather than an accumulating bourgeoisie, and the transition to capitalist economy would require, in addition to a restructuring of ownership relations, a cultural value shift towards ethics of accumulation. This in turn presupposes the grounding of markets and new forms of ownership in appropriate non-market relations, that is, supportive (though constraining) social, organizational, institutional, and normative frameworks. The culture of the shadow economy, though, is hardly likely to offer a sufficiently complex regulating institutional framework for capital accumulation and organizational co-ordination.

Conclusions

This chapter explores ways of making sense of certain tendencies in the dynamics of exclusion in the post-communist world, with reference to transitions from status to class power. Most illustrative material has been drawn from Russia, partly to avoid over-burdening the account with the complexity of being in several countries at once, although many of the general tendencies identified here, especially nomenklatura-privatization, can be identified elsewhere in the post-communist world. It is too soon to say what implications this might have for the subsequent development of the region, its external relations, or for the stability of the transition itself. However, some lines of analysis can be suggested.

The collapse of state socialism was a crisis of a mode of regulation, which opened up the potential for a new system of domination, within which the former nomenklatura could convert bureaucratic power into capital. However, it has been seen that this is still a contested process, the outcome of which remains undecided. It is possible that an absence of sufficient alternative buyers for state industries will open the way for nomenklatura-privatization to become the dominant pattern of asset conversion. However, even if there is more to nomenklatura-privatization than short-term asset-striping, that is, if there is the nucleus here of an accumulating capitalist class, it might have difficulty anchoring itself in institutional norms.

The discussion has suggested that systems will have self-reproductive capacities only so long as they are embodied within wider socio-cultural processes. It is far from clear whether this can occur here. Really, the critical issue for the future of the post-communist countries, especially for the stability of plural democracies, is whether the process of privatization can be brought within the framework of legality and regulated by an institutional public sphere. Yet, nomenklatura-privatization might be inimical to pluralization and democratization. The disintegration of the redistributive mechanism and its familiar consequences – the collapse of social infrastructures, hyper-inflation and unemployment (or its imminent threat) – have created acute social disorganization and the potential for mass social protest (which thus far has actually been rather muted). Still, the issue of social protection, of how to manage the transition without disastrous consequences, will be critical for the stabilization of post-communist societies. However, it is the political group-ings with (allegedly) the closest connections to the former nomenklatura (such as Rutskoi's Free Russia party) that attempt to mobilize resentments caused by marketization, often under an authoritarian and antisemetic programme, such as the (now banned) National Salvation Front, or Zhirinovsky's Liberal Democrats.

This alliance between the former nomenklatura and anti-democratic forces is not really surprising. Given that nomenklatura-privatization is illicit and largely risk-free asset conversion, a kind of frontier capitalism, it trades upon a culture of illegality (which previously subverted the official systems of allocation from within). The formation of institutional structures, and the regulation of new markets within non-market relations by contrast, would bring this illicit process within a legal regulatory framework. However, former Moscow mayor Gavriil Popov perhaps speaks for a wider social trend when he justifies his appropriation of state assets, claiming that "a revolu-tion is now occurring, and in a revolution laws no longer have any mean-ing, so I am not going to abide by any set of laws, either union or republi-can ones" (Medvedev 1991). In summary, to paraphrase the well-worn epigram, the old structure of social integration is dying but the new cannot yet be born. In the interregnum a great variety of morbid symptoms are likely to appear.

Note added in proof

The above discussion addresses the situation as it developed during 1992, at the end of which year the Yeltsin–Gaidar vision of mass popular privati-zation combined with economic shock therapy was effectively terminated with Gaidar's removal. During 1993 the dominant trend of asset conversion remained nomenklatura-privatization whereas the creation of a new insti-tutional framework (property law, land redistribution, bankruptcy procedure, the reorganization of monopoly enterprises, regulation of foreign trade) was eclipsed by the struggle between Presidential and Parliamentary factions within the political system. The denouement of this struggle, the battle for the White House in October 1993, has, for better or worse, broken the dead-lock, but it remains unclear what the implications Yeltsin's victory for the structural transformation of the Russian economy might be. That the pre-viously centrist Scientific-Industrial Alliance (representing enterprise managers) supported Khasbulatov and Rutskoi is a measure of its loss of confidence in President Yeltsin. Moreover, during 1993 employers' and managers' organizations began to distance themselves from particular political factions, constructing instead more independent, pressure-group netweorks. Developing a new Government economic strategy will therefore require negotiation with managers, enterprise collectives (along with trade unions, although these are presently rather fragmented) towards devising a workable legislative regulatory framework. The upshot of this will very probably be to formalize the de facto property relations that have emerged spontaneously during the immediate post-communist transition.

Notes

1. See for example Postone & Brick (1982). Weber's general observations on bureaucratization were relevant of course, along with Bruno Rizzi's *Bureaucratization of the world* (1939), whose notion of "bureaucratic collectivism" influenced Trotskii, and appeared in the latter's *The USSR in war* (1939).

2. There is no space here to describe the system in detail, but see Hough (1969) or Voslensky (1984). According to Voslensky, recruitment was particularistic and clientelistic, operating through "recommendation" of individuals from higher to lower committees, although Hough detected evidence of appointment according to merit too (1969: 175). By the early 1980s the Soviet nomenklatura consisted of about 250,000 people (about 0.1 per cent of the population) (Voslensky 1984: 95).

3. A similar pattern developed in other communist regimes. In Hungary, for example, by 1949 over 90 per cent of newly appointed high-level bureaucrats were from the party list (Hankiss 1990: 45), and in Poland by 1953 only 2.2 per cent of managerial positions were filed by non-Party members, compared with 17 per cent in 1949 (Majkowski 1985: 100).

4. Such as the packets of money, often of insubstantial amounts, that were delivered from Stalin to high-ranking officials (Voslensky 1984: 214).

5. Narodny Kommissariat Vnutrennikh Del (People's Commissariat for Internal Affairs, later of course the KGB).

6. Indeed, Khrushchev's decline 1958–64 was the result of his behaving in an increasingly arbitrary manner and ignoring his patronage commitments with the Central Committee (Hill 1988).

7. They claim that legitimation in the Soviet Union shifted from a "charismatic totalitarian" (Stalinist) to a "traditional" (post-Stalinist) mode. Depiction of the Soviet Union as "traditionalistic" is problematic though, and is discussed in Ray (1993: Chapter 6).

8. This is, of course, a highly summarized form of arguments developed at length in a number of works, such as *Legitimation crisis* or *The theory of communicative action*. I discuss the usefulness of Habermasian critical theory for analysing STS in Ray (1993).

9. An argument that is also pursued in Konrad & Szelényi (1979). Weber described

substantive rationality as "the provisioning of given groups of persons with goods
... under some criterion of ultimate values, which are often geared to social justice"
(Weber 1978: 85).

10. Both types of society can have trade and money, but in the dispositive type prices
    are not regulated by the market, but fixed by a sovereign authority. In the
    transactive type, traders exchanges goods at market prices (Polanyi 1957).

11. Storming refers to accelerated production to meet planning targets. For example,
    "We never use a screwdriver in the last week" said a worker at a Lithuanian televi-
    sion factory, "We hammer the screws in. We slam solder the connections, cannibal-
    ize parts from other TVs . . . and the management is pressing us to work faster"
    (Walker 1988: 42).

12. Since a great deal of these exchanges were non-monetary, it is difficult to estimate
    the size of the informal sector, even if reliable data were available. A report to the
    Central Committee of the Communist Party in 1987 estimated that 1.5 billion rou-
    bles a year were tied up in the second economy (White 1992: 118) (i.e. 0.2 per cent
    of GNP), but this was probably an under-estimation.

13. Elson (1988) points out that the "success" of informal economies, small-holder pro-
    duction, or reciprocal labour exchanges in state socialism was always dependent on
    women's labour, in a context of patriarchal relations, generally combined with first-
    economy employment.

14. However, Sampson (1985–6) warns against romanticizing social relations in the in-
    formal sector, which could be as conflictual and exploitative as those in bureaucratic
    apparatuses.

15. The transliteration of Russian newspaper and journal titles follows that in the *Cur-
    rent digest of the post-Soviet press.*

16. Zemtsov (1985: 166) points out that it is inconceivable that such an attack could
    have been launched publicly without the approval of Andropov himself, who he
    suggests had linked up with the sociologists "over the heads of the Party apparatus".

17. This observation is based in part on interviews I conducted with members of the
    Research Bureau of the Hungarian Socialist Workers' party in October 1985, and
    in the Research Bureau of the Marxism-Leninism Institute in Sofia, September
    1988.

18. Social movements arising in the last few years of communist rule in the USSR or-
    ganized predominantly around civil rights, trade union, ecological, and national-
    ist issues, and often held anti-capitalist views. For a review of social movements in
    this period, see Hosking et al. (1992).

19. In the process, however, other forces with an independent trajectory were released
    (notably an openly authoritarian nationalism), but this would be the subject of
    another paper.

20. Kagarlitsky (1990: 61–2) for example claims that once the flow of redistributive
    resources from Moscow began to subside, local nomenklatura in the republics
    speedily threw in their lot with nationalist Popular Fronts.

21. In an economy that is not extensively marketized, estimates of asset values such as
    these, and others given below, are rather notional.

22. For example, the Moscow Ventilator Factory was leased and bought out at an arbitrary price of 6.5m roubles in 1990, the major corporate customer, Svetlana, providing an interest-free loan in return for future supplies at a reduced price.

23. Nomenklatura conspiracy theories should be treated with some scepticism, since they have been convenient explanations for policy failures (Yeltsin for example explained that measures for social protection were making little headway because of "sabotage and inactivity on the part of authorities at the local level") (*Rossiiskaya Gazeta* 17 January 1992).

24. Forcing post-communist politics into familiar categories of "conservative" and "radical" can be misleading, as can the characterization of "radicals" as pro-market and "conservatives" as statist. The political terrain is shaped by new patterns of inter-elite competition that have less to do with *whether* than *how* to privatize. The anti-Gaidar faction at the Congress tended to oppose price de-regulation and favour social protection, but support nomenklatura-privatization.

25. Indeed, some critics have accused Yeltsin of tolerating or encouraging nomenklatura-privatization. Burbulis claims that Yeltsin's desire to "conserve experienced personnel" is a continuation of the old policy (*Nezavisimaya gazeta* 24 January 1992), and that privatization through the State Property Committee is "only good for people with "shady" money" (*Nezavismaya Gazeta* 18 March 1992). Stanislav Shatalin (President of the Reform Foundation) describes Yeltsin's decree combating corruption as a "fig leaf", creating only the illusion of struggle (*Izvestia* 28 April 1992).

26. L. Piyasheva (Deputy General Director, Moscow Mayor's Office); Members of Moscow Economic Council: A. Isayev (Dir. Institute of Economics Planning and Management of the Aircraft Industry) V. Selyunin (economist and public affairs writer) G. Lisichkin (economist) S. Khokhlov (adviser to Research Centre on Private Law) S. Alekseyev (member of Russian Academy) B. Pinsker (Surgeon).

27. Gorbachev has also argued for turning property over to producers free of charge (*Komsomolskaya Pravda* 29 May 1992). His critique of Yeltsin's privatization programme drew the accusation from Yeltsin of "aggravating political tension – in essence, . . . constituting a destabilization of the social and political situation in the country" (*Izvestia* 3 June 1992). In October 1992 Gorbachev was to have his freedom of movement briefly curtailed.

28. A proposal denounced by Anatoly Chubais (architect of the Government programme) as "the latest resurgence of the Bolshevik mentality" (*Izvestia* 26/ February 1992).

References

The following newspaper sources were used (volume and numbers refer to issues of the Current Digest of the (post) Soviet Press): *Pravda* 19.8.90 (vol. 42, no. 37); *Izvestia* 10.10.90 (vol. 42, no. 41), 26.2.92 (vol. 45, no. 9), 28.4.92 and 3.6.92 (vol. 45, no. 21); *Komsomolskaya Pravda* 12.12.90 (vol. 42, no. 50), 6.2.91 (vol. 43, no. 7), and 29.5.92 (vol. 45, no. 20); *Birzheviye Vedomosti* 1.1.92 and *Rossiiskaya Gazeta* 17.1.92 (vol. 45, no. 2);

Nezavisimaya Gazeta 24.1.92 (vol. 45, no. 3), 6.3.92 and 18.3.92 (vol. 45, no. 11); *Smenal* 28.4.92 (vol. 45, no. 17).

Baker, R. 1982. Clientelism in the post-revolutionary state: the Soviet Union. In *Private patronage and public power*, C. Clapham (ed.), 36–52. London: Pinter.

Batt, J. 1991. *East Central Europe from reform to transition*. London: Pinter.

Bugajski J. & M. Pollack 1989. *East European fault lines, dissent, opposition and social activism*. London: Westview.

Callinicos, A. 1991. *The revenge of history – Marxism and the East European revolutions*. Cambridge: Polity.

Carlo, A. 1989. Contradictions of *Perestroika*. *Telos* **79**, 29–48.

Dangschat, J. 1987. Social disparities in a 'socialist city' – Warsaw. *International Journal for Urban and Regional Research* **11**, 37–60.

Davies, T. 1988. A framework for relating social welfare policy to economic change: evidence from Hungarcity. In *Social welfare and the market*, F. Millart (ed.), 36–80. London: LSE.

Djilas, M. 1957. *The new class*. London: Hudson.

Elson, D. 1988. Market socialism or socialization of the market? *New Left Review* **172**, 3–44.

Fehér, F. 1993. *Dictatorship over needs*. Oxford: Basil Blackwell.

Fehér, F., A. Heller, G. Márkus 1984. *Dictatorship over needs – an analysis of Soviet Societies*. Oxford: Basil Blackwell.

Fehér, F. & A. Arato (eds) 1989. *Gorbachev: the debate*. New York: Humanities Press.

Filatotchev, I., T. Buck, M. Wright 1992a. Privatization and buy-outs in the USSR. *Soviet Studies* **44**, 265–82.

Filatotchev, I., T. Buck, M. Wright 1992b. Privatization and entrepreneurship in the break-up of the USSR. *World Economy* **15**, 505–24.

Fischer, S., L. Summers, W. Nordhaus 1992. Stabilization and economic reform in Russia. *Brookings Papers on Economic Activity* **1**, 77–126.

Getty, J. A. 1985. *Origins of the Great Purges – the Soviet Communist Party reconsidered 1933–38*. Cambridge: Cambridge University Press.

Glaziev, S. 1991. Transformation of the soviet economy: economic reforms and structural crisis. *National Economic Review* **138**, 97–108.

Guber, A. 1985. *Intensified economy and programmes in science and technology*. Moscow: Novosti Press.

Hankiss, E. 1990. *East European alternatives – are there any?* Oxford: Clarendon.

Hankiss, E. 1991. The "second society": is there an alternative social model emerging in contemporary Hungary? In *Crisis and reform in eastern Europe*, F. Fehér & A. Arato (eds), 303–34. New Brunswick: Transaction Books.

Hauslohner, P. 1989. Gorbachev's social contract. In *Gorbachev – the debate*, F. Fehér & A. Arato (eds), 88–123. New York: Humanities Press.

Hausner, J. (ed.) 1991. *System of interest representation in Poland*. Crakow: Crakow Academy of Economics.

Heller, A. 1982. Phases of legitimation in Soviet-type societies. In *Political Legitimation in communist regimes*, T. H. Rigby & F. Fehér (eds), 45–63. London: Macmillan.

Heller, A. & F. Fehér 1990. From Yalta to glasnost: the dismantling of Stalin's empire.

Oxford: Basil Blackwell.

Hill, R. J. 1988. The *Apparatiki* and Soviet political development. In *The Soviet Union – party and society*, P. Potichnyj (ed.), 3–25. Cambridge: Cambridge University Press.

Hirszowicz, M. 1986. *Coercion and control in communist society – the visible hand of bureaucracy*. Brighton: Harvester.

Hosking, A. 1985. *A history of the Soviet Union*. London: Fontana.

Hosking, G., J. Aves, P. Duncan 1992. *The road to post-communism – independent political movements in the Soviet Union 1985–91*. London: Pinter.

Hough, J. F. 1969. *The Soviet prefects: the local party organs in industrial decision-making*. Cambridge, Mass: Harvard University Press.

Jowitt, K. 1983. Soviet neotraditionalism: the political corruption of a Leninist regime. *Soviet Studies* **35**, 275–97.

Kagarlitsky, B. 1990. *Farewell perestroika – a Soviet chronicle*. London: Verso.

Konrad G. & I. Szelényi 1979. *Intellectuals on the road to class power*. Brighton: Harvester.

Kornai, J. 1986. The Hungarian reform process - visions, hopes, and reality. *Journal of Economic Literature* **24**, 1687–2037.

Kowalik, T. 1991. Marketization and privatization: the polish case. *Socialist Register* 259–77.

Lane, D. 1979. Soviet industrial workers: the lack of a legitimation crisis? In *Legitimation of Regimes*, B. Denitch (ed.), 177–94. London: Sage.

Levitas, A. & P. Strzalkowski 1990. What does "Vwlaszczenie Nomenklatury" [propertization of the nomenklatura] really mean? *Communist Studies* **2**, 413–16.

Majkowski, W. 1985. *People's Poland – patterns of social inequality and conflict*. London: Greenwood Press.

Mandel, D. 1991. The struggle for power in the Soviet economy. *Socialist Register* 95–127.

Mandel, E. 1977. *Marxist economic theory*. London: Merlin Press.

Mandel, E. 1991. *Beyond perestroika*. London: Verso.

Markus, M. 1982. Overt and covert modes of legitimation. In *Political legitimation in communist regimes*, T. H. Rigby & F. Feher (eds), 82–93. London: Macmillan.

Medvedev, R. 1991. Politics after the coup. *New Left Review* **189**, 91–110.

Mozný I. 1991. Proc tak snadno? (Why so easy?) *Sociologický Casopis*, Prague: SLOM

Murphy, M., A. Shleifer, W. Vishny 1992. The transition to a market economy: pitfalls of a partial reform. *Quarterly Journal of Economics* **107**, 889–906.

Musil, J. 1987. Housing policy and the sociospacial structure of cities in a socialist country. *International Journal of Urban and Regional Research* **11**, 27–36.

Polanyi, K. (ed.) 1957. *Trade and market in early empires*. Glencoe, Illinois: Free Press.

Postone, M. & Brick 1982. Critical pessimism and the limits of traditional Marxism. *Theory & Society* **11**, 617–58.

Rakovski, M. [Janos Kis] 1978. *Towards an east European Marxism*. London: Allison & Busby.

Ray, L. J. 1993. *Rethinking critical theory – emancipation in the age of global social movements*. London: Sage.

Rigby, T. H. 1988. Staffing the USSR incorporated – the origins of the nomenklatura system. *Soviet Studies* **40**, 523–37.

REFERENCES

Rumer, B. 1991. New capitalists in the USSR. *Challenge* **34**(3), 19–22.

Sampson, S. 1985–6. The informal sector in eastern Europe. *Telos* **66**, 44–66.

Staniszkis, J. 1992. *The ontology of Socialism*. Oxford: Clarendon Press.

Szelényi, I. 1979. Social inequalities in state-socialist redistributive economies. *International Journal of Comparative Sociology* **19**, 63–87.

Szelényi, I. 1983. *Urban inequalities under state socialism*. Oxford: Oxford University Press.

Tosics, I. 1988. Inequalities in east European cities: can redistribution ever be equalising . . . ? *International Journal for Urban and Regional Research* **12**, 133–6.

Voslensky, M. 1984. *Nomenklatura – Anatomy of the Soviet ruling class*. London: Bodley Head.

Walker, M. 1988. *The waking giant – the Soviet Union under Gorbachev*. London: Sphere.

Weber, M. 1978. *Economy and society* (2 vols). Berkeley: California University Press.

Wesolowski, W. 1972. The notions of strata and class in socialist society. In *Social inequality*, A. Beteille (ed.), 122–48. London: Penguin.

White, S. 1992. *Gorbachev and After*. Cambridge University Press.

Zaslavskaya, T. 1984. The Novosibirsk paper. *Survey* **28**, 88–108.

Zemtsov, I. 1976. *Partiji ili mafia? Razvorannaya respublika* Paris: Les Editeurs Reunis.

Zemtsov, I. 1985. *Policy dilemmas and the struggle for power in the Kremlin – the Andropov period*. Fairfax, Virginia: Hero Books.

Chapter 10

Privatization, class and interest formation in eastern Europe[1]

Terry Cox

After the momentous political events of 1989 and 1990 in eastern Europe, when seemingly unmovable political structures were dismantled and replaced in a matter of weeks, there was a widespread assumption in the media and among politicians that social and economic changes could occur almost as rapidly. In particular, it was often assumed that a programme of market reforms and privatization could provide the remedy that would revive ailing economies of eastern Europe and establish a firm basis for democratic development. Among the main components of such reforms were price deregulation, liberalizing foreign economic links, the transfer of state-owned enterprises into non-state and private ownership, support for the establishment of new private businesses, and various supporting legislation, for example, laws governing bankruptcy, the provision of credit, and taxation.

Of particular importance in the reform strategies have been the policies aimed at the expansion of a private sector through encouraging new small businesses and by means of privatization of state assets. Discussion of such issues has often been based on a particular set of sociological assumptions concerning the necessity to create a new commercial middle class as a social basis for the stable operation of both a market economy and a pluralistic political system. Usually absent from such discussions, however, has been any suggestion that privatization is likely to lead to social and economic exclusion on a large scale, involving not only bankruptcies and redundancies, but also the loss of access to various goods and services formerly available through the state and the workplace. Moreover, since 1990, far from achieving its general social aims, it has become clear that the implementation of privatization reforms is proving to be a slower and much more painful process than many had originally assumed.

The extent of private-sector growth

The extent to which reforms have been implemented varies considerably between different countries.[2] At one extreme, reforms in Albania and most parts of the former Yugoslavia have scarcely begun. Meanwhile, in Romania, Bulgaria, and some former Soviet republics such as Ukraine and the Baltic republics, privatization legislation has been adopted or is in advanced stages of preparation, but very little of the programme has been implemented so far. Romania has a slight lead over the other countries in this category, but even there only one state enterprise was fully transferred to private ownership in 1992. In all these countries the main sphere of private sector activity is in small-scale farming and services. In Romania, after initial confusion, around 70 per cent of collective farmland has now been transferred to private farmers, but there are still doubts about the ownership of some farmhouses.

In Russia, although there is much discussion of privatization and a very ambitious programme has been put into operation, the general situation suggests at best that a very problematic economic transformation is taking place. While the number of small-scale and family-based businesses has increased, the crucial process of privatizing large state enterprises has met with many setbacks and is only now beginning in earnest. Building on some of the limited reforms in Soviet legislation of the last few years, a growing amount of economic activity is now organized outside direct state control. By the end of 1991 around 21.3 per cent of the workforce worked outside the public sector, of which 3.8 per cent were clearly employed in private enterprises, mostly on a very small scale. For the rest, however, the situation was more complex, since they worked in enterprises involving elements of both private and public ownership combined in a variety of ways.[3]

Some privatization of larger and medium-sized enterprises has taken place, but the evidence is difficult to interpret. According to one source, there were 45 legal privatizations of state-owned enterprises by September 1991, involving 7000 employees.[4] There have also been privatizations of enterprises in trading, catering, and repair services, along with nearly 500 small industrial concerns (employing less than 200 people). By 1 April 1992, the percentage of small enterprises in Russia that had been privatized was 0.7 per cent each in the retail trade and public catering, and 0.5 per cent in services. By 1 March 1992, although 26500 new private farms had been registered, they still owned only 2 per cent of the land in Russia (Yavlinsky 1992: 7). There have also been illegal transfers of state-owned assets into joint stock company property, by means of which state managers sought to turn themselves into private owners. One source has estimated there were more than 3000 such illegal or semi-legal transformations.[5]

The situation probably varies considerably between different parts of the country, depending partly on the degree of enthusiasm of local officials for privatization. Nizhni-Novgorod, Moscow and St Petersburg are probably the leading cities in the proportion of municipal assets that have been privatized. In St Petersburg, in the 12 months ending 31 October 1992, out of a total of around 2500 small businesses (shops, restaurants, and factories) owned by the local authority, 1500 had been sold (*Guardian* 31 October 1992). During 1992, in an attempt to boost privatization at a national level, the Russian government borrowed from the Czechoslovak experience (see below) and issued vouchers to the adult population to be exchanged during the following year for shares in privatized enterprises.

Considerably more privatization has already taken place in Hungary, Czechoslovakia,[6] and Poland, although by quite different mechanisms in each case (Fischer 1992). In Czechoslovakia by the end of 1991 there had been a fourteenfold increase in the number of small entrepreneurs since 1989, and 10,000 small shops and catering establishments were privatized during 1991. Since then, during 1992 a scheme of mass privatization was implemented, involving first, the sale of vouchers to the public at discount rates, and then the auctioning of state enterprises allowing voucher holders to exchange their vouchers for shares in enterprises. In practice nearly three-quarters of all voucher holders opted not to handle the transactions themselves but to sign up with one or other of over 400 hundred independently formed investment fund organizations. By November 1992, 80 per cent of the shares of 1490 former state enterprises had been purchased in this way.

In Poland, various political conflicts and scandals led to a postponement of a large-scale privatization programme, similar to the Czechoslovak model, aimed at the 400 leading state enterprises. The programme envisaged the establishment of several state-owned investment funds, to be managed by Western experts. Shares in these funds would then be distributed free to every Polish adult citizen. However, despite the failure of the legislature to approve the mass privatization scheme, there has been a rapid growth in the Polish private sector, resulting both from private purchases of over 500 small and middle-sized state firms that had gone into liquidation, and from the setting up of new private firms. Over 80 per cent of the country's retail trade is now in private hands, mostly of small family businesses, along with a growing share of some sectors of wholesale trade. According to official estimates, which may be underestimates, at the end of 1992 the private sector accounted for around half of the Polish GDP and over half of all employment.

Yet another different pattern of change has been experienced in Hungary. In some ways Hungary has had a head start on the others. "Market reform" within the state-managed system had gone farther under the communist regime there than in other east European countries, and during 1991 and 1992 Hungary also attracted more than half the foreign investment in eastern Europe. By the end of 1991, 8000 joint ventures were in operation, and it is estimated that around 80 per cent of the privatization that took place during 1992 was financed by foreign capital. By contrast, private ownership by Hungarians is concentrated in the small business sector. According to some unofficial reports the private sector overall produced 50 per cent of GDP in 1991 (Slay 1992: 100).

The focus on privatization through sales to foreign companies developed after 1989 as a reaction against charges that state managers were turning themselves into private owners through "spontaneous" privatizations. However, following a further public reaction against the growing concentration of foreign ownership of Hungarian business, new schemes were introduced during 1992 to stimulate domestic privatization. This include help for smaller state enterprises to organize their own privatization with the help of an outside consultant, measures to help break up state enterprises into smaller parts so that it would be easier to attract local buyers, and the transfer of some state property to non-state owners such as universities. Such moves reflect a realization among Hungarian policy-makers that, with most of the attractive Hungarian companies already sold to foreign concerns, the pace of private-sector growth could slow considerably in future years. Indeed, there is some concern among Hungarian policy-makers that the present growth rate of the private sector will remain insufficient to offset the declines registered in the state-owned sector (Okolicsanyi 1992: 32).

Thus, the general situation in eastern Europe suggests at best that a very difficult economic transformation is taking place. While the number of small-scale and family-based businesses has increased in most countries, the crucial process of privatizing large state enterprises has met with many setbacks. On the basis of a comparative review of the progress of privatization measures in most of eastern Europe up to mid-1991, Jackson concluded that:
- "All aspects of the process are more complicated than initially perceived"
- "It will take much longer to complete than had initially been envisaged"
- "There will necessarily be more political conflict in the process" (1991: 45).

Developments since then have produced little to change such conclusions.

The politics of privatization

As Jackson suggests, political conflicts have been among the major causes of impediments to privatization throughout eastern Europe. The issues over which disagreements have arisen include the extent of foreign investment and control of former state enterprises; the extent and form of the restitution of the rights of former owners of property that had been nationalized by the communist regimes; the transfer of private ownership of enterprises to former managers, communist politicians, and government officials (so-called "nomenklatura-privatization"); the transfer of ownership to the workforce of an enterprise as a whole; and schemes for "mass privatization" in which state property is distributed to the population in general. While debate on these issues has proceeded among policy-makers and politicians, at the same time political changes have brought privatization into the new realm of parliamentary politics, occasioning wide-ranging debates between parties in the parliaments and in the press of many east European countries.[7]

The relative significance of each issue and the character of the "solutions" sought have varied between different east European societies, depending on the relative strength of various social interests and on the character of the economic structure in each society before the change of regime. For example, Hungary's experience of privatization has been influenced by its unique experience in eastern Europe of a long period of economic reform, beginning in 1968, which devolved a significant amount of decision-making to enterprise managements and helped create a more market-oriented management culture than in its neighbours. Partly as a result of this, it has been easier to interest Western companies in investment and joint venture arrangements than in other parts of eastern Europe. Furthermore, it has been suggested that the same reforms also contributed to a general depoliticization and the growth of a more privatized outlook among the Hungarian working class than in some neighbouring countries (Szelényi 1988).

In Czechoslovakia, a different combination of factors contributed to the politics of privatization taking on a different character. As in Hungary, but for different reasons, the working class, along with many other sections of society, became depoliticized and turned inward to focus on more privatized concerns. While the defeat of the reform movement of 1968 had contributed to a general disillusionment with politics, government policies to improve living standards helped forestall the developments of any strong oppositional political culture. In the new conditions after the end of communist rule, and under the influence of the campaign of Vaclav Klaus and his associates, there was no clear source of opposition to privatization. Consequently the government was able to risk a highly political form of privatization, highlighting the economic interests of each individual member of society through the voucher scheme of mass privatization.

By contrast, in Poland a history of very active and organized working class opposition to the communist regime, along with strong popular support for economic independence from either Russian or German influences, has contributed to yet another different framework within which privatization goals are pursued. Unlike Hungary, there has been greater resistance to foreign ownership of Polish industry, and greater support for the ownership rights of the enterprise workforce. In addition, the fragmented nature of Polish parliamentary politics and the frequent changes of government in recent years delayed agreement on a wider programme of privatization on either the Hungarian or Czechoslovak models. In the absence both of clear government policies and of sources of investment from within the country, the predominant form of privatization has been the so-called "liquidation privatization", in which enterprises have been broken up and the more profitable parts have been sold, or more often leased, to private businesses often owned by former managers and officials in state enterprises.[8]

In other societies where privatization reforms are now under way, further variations on the forms of the politics of privatization are beginning to emerge. While none are likely to be able or willing to follow Hungary's strong foreign orientation, many others have been attracted by Czechoslovakia's approach to mass privatization. This is seen as offering two advantages. First, in the absence of strong foreign investment rates, it solves the problem of there being no native investors with sufficient capital, apart from local organized crime and some former state managers, both of whom attract popular opposition as potential owners. Secondly, it offers a means of legitimating privatization and market reforms more widely by seeming to give everyone an equal stake in the ownership of capital. Voucher-based mass privatization schemes have now been introduced in Russia and Romania, and are on the policy agenda elsewhere.

Meanwhile, the rôle of the old "nomenklatura" continues to be a significant issue throughout eastern Europe. In some countries, where the nomenklatura have managed to retain some power or influence, they have tended to resist or delay calls for privatization, such as in Serbia and Romania, and to a lesser extent in Bulgaria and the Ukraine. In other countries, to varying degrees, they have sought to transform themselves into new private owners, notably in Croatia, but also in Poland, Russia, and elsewhere (see Ray in this volume).[9]

A sharp debate has developed around the question of the nomenklatura. On the one hand, it is argued that officials and functionaries of the old ruling parties, as well as leading bureaucrats in the old state institutions and managers of state-owned enterprises, are the only people in the population with the necessary or technical skills to run newly privatized companies. On the other hand, there have been various objections. On political grounds, some new governments have a history of opposition to the Communist party and its client state officials, and therefore tend not to approve of collaborating with their former opponents. There are ethical objections too, they argue, in that such privatizations are no more than attempts to steal public property.

Privatization strategies involved governments in conflicts, not only with enterprise managements, but also with workers. While the rôle of workers' organizations and trade unions was strongest in Poland, it was also important elsewhere, including in Russia and Romania. In order partly to placate workers' unease, the Russian government built into their scheme of mass privatization complex arrangements to allow workforces to choose between three different patterns of privatization of their workplaces, each involving a different proportion of shares to be allocated to the workers (*Financial Times* 2 October 1992). A major problem of privatization for the working class throughout eastern Europe has been that, although they were excluded in many ways both from material rewards and from effective decision-making in the old system, private ownership and the market economy threaten new and potentially harsher forms of exclusion. Not only are job definitions, wage rates, negotiating procedures, and fringe benefits likely to be redefined by new private owners, but many workers face much larger problems in the form of redundancies and the abolition of the provision of housing, health care, and various social services by enterprises.

Conceptualizing social transformation

In view of the wide range of differences in interest and policy over the issues of privatization and marketization, how should we evaluate the changes that are taking place? The most common approach in media discussions, and in the burgeoning economic and public policy literature on privatization, is to see the problems that have arisen as temporary setbacks to a necessary change that will take place. Explanations of the causes of the problems are often couched in terms of specific factors such as a loss of entrepreneurial spirit in eastern Europe as a result of communist rule, a lack of capital among the local population, and excessive caution on the part of Western governments and businesses. Such analyses are often accompanied by a policy outlook that David Stark has described as "capitalism by design", an approach that assumes economic transition is "a problem to be solved by the rationalist design of economic institutions" (1992: 17).

A better way of approaching the issue of transformation, Stark argues, is to ask more basic questions about the nature of social relations in those societies undergoing transformation, and investigating not only changes but also elements of continuity. This approach has the advantage of highlighting ways in which different eastern European societies are, to some extent, undergoing different transitions, and it does not assume that all are proceeding to the same outcomes. The precise character of both the transitions and the outcomes depends partly on the interactions, decisions, and choices made by members of a society, and partly on characteristics of that society preceding its transformation. In other words, there are social structural features, based on the old-established patterns of relations between social groups, that will in some cases provide barriers to change or, in other cases, openings allowing change while channelling it in certain directions. In order to understand such structural constraints in a more systematic way, it is necessary to decide what were the key characteristics of the old social structure that are likely to have such a continuing influence. In order to do this, it may be useful to go back to theoretical writing on the social structure of Soviet-type societies before their transformation.

During the years that the Soviet Union and the Soviet-type societies of eastern Europe existed, a wide range of theories were put forward with the aim of distinguishing their main defining social characteristics. These ranged from the official state view in such societies that they were "socialist" to views that they were exploitative class societies of some type or other. Perhaps the most illuminating theory in terms of its ability both to explain the gradual changes taking place within those societies, and to connect to empirical research evidence, was the theory of State Redistributive Society, originally developed within eastern Europe by Hungarian sociologists Georg Konrad and Ivan Szelényi (1979). In their view, the expropriation of the working class in Soviet-type societies was enabled by control over the institutions and mechanisms of redistribution in society. The basic division in Soviet-type societies was between the direct producers and those whose work involved the redistribution of the surplus or who had a vested interest in this process.

To begin with, the rôle of redistributor was monopolized by the elite of the ruling Communist parties, but in time, Szelényi argued, it would be extended to the intelligentsia, seen as all those with the intellectual capital enabling them to claim expertise in managing the complex issues of social organization. The conditions for the rise to power of a redistributor class had been created by the abolition of private property in the means of production, and the consequent control of property by state officials as part of their jobs. In such conditions there was greater scope for the holders of knowledge to exert an influence.

In the 1980s, the theory was adapted by Szelényi to take account of new trends that had become clear by then. According to his revised version, the political bureaucracy did not give up their state power to the intelligentsia in the way he had earlier predicted, although they did increasingly share power at least with the technical intelligentsia. However, the biggest change, happening most clearly in Hungary, was in the position of the working class and peasant workers.

> Through a silent revolution from below, workers and peasant-workers gradually carved out greater freedoms for themselves, not through collective political action but through everyday economic practices. This silent revolution dissolved class conflict at the point of production and eased class antagonism between redistributors and direct producers. The Hungarian workers, unlike their Polish counterparts, lost interest in trade unions. Even the level of their wages declined in importance for them . . . For them life began after they left the gates of the enterprise.   (Szelényi 1989: 222)

For Szelényi, the key development was not a political one, but the "silent revolution" itself. He argued that in Hungary under Kádár initial attempts from above to reform the state economy were unsuccessful and so the bureaucracy coped with the situation by quietly withdrawing its restrictions over private activity. The main tendency in the Hungarian class structure, therefore, was "socialist embourgeoisement", in which former workers and peasant workers became part-time entrepreneurs in a "second economy" existing alongside the state economy without overthrowing it.[10]

As a result of these trends, developing strongly in Hungary, but in more muted forms elsewhere as well, the societies of eastern Europe could no longer be seen as organized according to one single economic logic. They now contained two different organizing principles, one based on bureaucratic management of the economy and redistribution of the surplus, and the other based on market exchange and small-scale private ownership. This in turn gave rise to two distinct but overlapping hierarchies of stratification based on either the first or the second economies, as shown in Figure 10.1.

In illustrating his approach, Szelényi used examples from Hungarian society, and he has been criticized for over-generalizing from the particular experience of Hungary (e.g. Feher et al. 1983). Certainly, it must be recognized that the emergence of a second economy was not as pronounced in other east European societies as it was in Hungary. However, even for the Soviet Union, where legal restrictions on independent commercial activity remained much tighter than in many other east European countries, by the 1980s economists were recognizing the importance of a second economy (e.g. Grossman 1990), and furthermore, sociologists were discussing a general "privatization" of social attitudes and lifestyles (e.g. Shlapentokh 1989). In principle, therefore, Szelényi's approach can be seen as applicable to east European societies generally. This was recognized, for example, by Kolankiewicz & Lewis in their adaptation of his dual stratification scheme for Polish society (1988: 63–5).

Although Szelényi's approach did not resolve all the conceptual problems that have dogged the study of east European societies, its main strength lay in its ability to connect better with empirical material than the other theories discussed above. Of particular interest was the focus on the two coexisting economic structures that made up the structure of east European so-

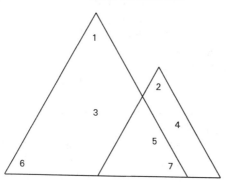

The emergent dual system of social stratification
Bureaucratic-redistributive order

Positions:

1 Cadre elite; 2 new entrepreneurs; 3 bureaucratic middle class; 4 full-time self-employed; 5 part-time self-employed; 6 workers in distributive sector; 7 workers in private sector.

Figure 10.1 The dual class structure of east European societies (Szelényi 1986/7: 126).

cieties. This offered more than the descriptive models of stratification shown above. Referring to the work of E. O. Wright on western societies, Szelényi likened his own approach to the idea of different class positions existing within different "modes of production" or structures in the same society. Also, it should be noted, his approach, and that of Wright, has a long pedigree dating back at least to the writings of Lenin (1921) and Kritsman (1928) on Soviet society of the early 1920s. Although Lenin and Kritsman would not have recognized the idea of co-existing *modes* of production within the same society, and preferred to talk about co-existing socio-economic structures, they too saw different class positions arising from each such structure and went on to discuss the complex patterns of inter-relations between classes that might emerge.[11]

The main purpose in such theorising, Szelényi suggested, was that it "offers insights about the alternative strategies of class alliances" (1986/7: 130). On this basis, he went on to outline and speculate about different scenarios of such class alliances, trying to trace emerging patterns of alliances and conflicts between classes on the basis of their positions within either the redistributive sector, the market sector, or a contradictory location within both (Szelényi 1986/7: 132–41; 1989: 228–32). This reveals an important strength in Szelényi's approach in its concern with processes, in this case of emerging class alliances, rather than simply with structural determination of interests and life chances.

Furthermore, unlike most other theories of east European social structures, it did not ignore the question of human agency in its examination of the larger-scale processes of social change. Especially in his detailed study of the second economy, Szelényi shows how the emergence of the "second economy" structure can be traced to the individual options people took in entering a particular "class trajectory" that moved them from a social position as a worker or peasant to one of cadre elite or "socialist entrepreneur" (1988: 61–75).

Unlike other available theories, Szelényi's approach is thus well equipped to deal with the question of social transformation. Although he developed it to understand the underlying transition of the re-emergence of rural entrepreneurs within Soviet-type society, it also offers insights into the current transitions. Its strength is that people can be seen as "bearers" or "agents" of particular cultural positions from which they derive significant interests and attitudes. In dealing with the problems and issues confronting them in social life, they will opt for certain choices on the basis of their existing interests and attitudes and thereby enter new class trajectories that provide them with new interests and attitudes. For a time they may therefore occupy positions in different co-existing structures and display complex or even contradictory sets of interests and attitudes.

The approach outlined above offers ways of understanding a period of change in which there is a contradictory situation between forms of economic behaviour conforming to different logics or organizing principles. In this context the idea of co-existing "structures", each with their own patterns of stratification, seems a useful way of identifying the elements that in reality are inter-relating and inter-penetrating in a complex fashion. While Kritsman identified as many as six such structures in the Soviet Union of the 1920s, Szelényi proposed two for Hungary of the 1980s.

Now, since the change of regimes in eastern Europe, it seems plausible to suggest three. Alongside the "state redistributive" and "second economy" structures proposed by Szelényi, there is, at least in embryo, a third "capitalist" structure. While it shares a focus on the large-scale organization of production with the state redistributive structure, and an orientation to the market and private ownership with the second economy structure, its combination of these, and the specific logic of its operation, call for treating it conceptually as a third distinct structure.

Of course, Figure 10.2 represents a "snap-shot", frozen in time. In reality the current period is marked by a great deal of social mobility, not simply up or down scales of stratification, but across from one to another as well. Many people probably occupy positions within different structures concurrently as they wait to see which way the economy will turn, and in the meantime maximize their opportunities to earn a living by combining different jobs or economic activities. Meanwhile, and for the foreseeable future, the result will be a very fluid class structure reflecting, and arising out of, the sum total of all the personal manoeuvres people make as they try to secure, improve, or defend their sources of income and life chances.

From the existing evidence, a number of transitions and combinations at an individual level can be suggested. Some possible examples are listed in Table 10.1. Various finer distinctions should also be introduced in the categories in Table 10.1 to give a clearer picture of the different interests that people may take on. For example, there may be differences in outlook, interests and life chances between entrepreneurs a) in the second economy, operating in a subordinate relationship to state enterprises, under contract to them, dependent on them for supplies, power, or marketing; b) running larger independent firms in the new capitalist economy, making contracts with suppliers, customers, and employees as independent actors in a fully

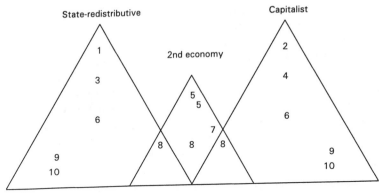

1 Old state elite; 2 New state elite; 3 Directors of state enterprises; 4 Nomenklatura owners;
5 Entrepreneurs; 6 Managers and professionals; 7 Petit bourgeois/full-time self-employed;
8 Part-time self-employed; 9 Skilled workers; 10 Unskilled workers.

Figure 10.2 The emergent three-way system of social stratification.

Table 10.1 Transition since the change of regimes in eastern Europe.

Previous position	Now replaced by, or combined with
Old state elite	New state elite, nomenklatura owner, professional/managerial, worker, unemployed
State enterprise director	Nomenklatura owner, professional/managerial, entrepreneur, worker, unemployed
Professional/managerial	New state elite, entrepreneur, petit bourgeois, part-time self-employed
Second economy entrepreneur	Capitalist entrepreneur, worker, unemployed
Skilled worker	Entrepreneur, petit bourgeois, unemployed

marketized context; c) operating in the new capitalist economy but under restrictions imposed by contracts with larger foreign firms. Differences within other categories are also likely, for example, between managers or workers in state, second economy, or capitalist enterprises.

Privatization and changing social interests

It is in the context of such a shifting class/group structure that market reform and specific policies such as privatization have been introduced. It can be suggested that each of the above-mentioned groups or classes will respond to the new situation, including the proposed new economic policies, on the basis of its own interests. It can also be suggested that these interests derive partly from the position of that group in the complex of social relations that made up the old institutions and the old social structure, as well as partly from the new emerging interests that groups or parts of old groups are now developing. Seen in this light, a policy issue such as privatization ceases to be simply a reform that encounters problems from unreconstructed aspects of the old society, and becomes part of the contested terrain of politics where each group attempts to define it in its own way, and seeks to adapt it according to its own interests.

It was noted above that privatization policies include a variety of different measures, and that there has been a debate over which combination of measures should be adopted with different permutations chosen in each of the countries of eastern Europe. Now it is possible to see the privatization debate as a contest between different social groups, and each type of policy measure as representing the chosen option of a different group. Political struggle is taking place, not only over the issue of privatization in general, but also by each group for its own "privatization" and against the versions of competing groups.

A variety of types of privatization can be identified and defined in terms of the social group to whose interests it conforms:

- "Nomenklatura" or "spontaneous" privatization, promoted by the old economic elite, especially directors of state enterprises and economic officials in Party and government bureaucracies
- Various state-regulated forms of privatization, promoted by the new governing elite that has emerged from the competitive elections following the fall of the old regime
- Purchase by foreign capital, serving the interests of international capitalist interests as well as an emerging domestic "client" business interest
- Formulation of new native businesses, either newly formed or growing on the basis of former second economy concerns, serving the interests of the new entrepreneurs
- Reprivatization of businesses and land, i.e. restitution of property to former owners or their heirs
- Worker share-ownership schemes to provide workers with a stake in newly privatized companies for which they work
- The general distribution or sale at a low price of shares in former state enterprises to the general public; in some cases this may be seen as in the

general public interest by large sections of society, while it may also be in the specific interest of elite groups who see it as a means of legitimising privatization, from which they will draw greater benefits than the rest of the population.

Each of the above "models" of privatization represents more than policy options. They can be understood sociologically on three further dimensions. First, each can be seen as the "project" of one or more social groups and, if implemented, it would form the basis of a potentially distinct "element" or "socio-economic structure" of a new transitional society. Secondly, each can be understood as the subject of a contest between different groups on the basis of their interests. As a result the precise characteristics of the programme could change according to which interests predominate. Thirdly, each could be changed or undermined as a result of a contradiction in the aims of a particular social group between interests and attitudes derived from their position in the old social structure and interests as they are now developing.

Hopefully, the use of this approach can reveal in greater complexity the nature of the social factors affecting privatization and market reform. Instead of only seeing constraints arising from groups whose interests are opposed to change, it should be possible to understand the way change is also influenced both by the way in which different groups pursue different definitions of privatization with the result of counteracting each other, and by the way their own aspirations are internally contradictory.

Constraints arising from conflicts between groups

As noted above, two of the main competing privatization programmes are "spontaneous" or "nomenklatura"-privatization, and state-regulated privatization. There is clearly a contest going on between sections of the old elite and state enterprise managers on the one hand, and the new political elite on the other. At different times and in different countries it may vary between degrees of conflict and compromise, but underlying the situation a general conflict of interests is likely to remain, whether it is acted upon or not.

The project of "nomenklatura"-privatization adopted by elements of the old elite and managers has been partially successful. However, it has also been partially blocked by a political campaign against its "theft" of public property, and by the introduction of legislation promoting state-regulated privatization. This represents the counter-project of the new political elite. However, the contest does not end there. First, because the legislation for state-regulated ownership changes must then go through a period of media and parliamentary debate, there is scope for counter-measures from supporters of nomenklatura legislation. Secondly, because in many countries the passage of legislation and its implementation tend to be long-drawn-out processes, the resulting confused situation will continue to provide opportunities for covert nomenklatura privatizations.

The situation is then complicated further by the problems of lack of capital and markets faced by both of the main powerful groups. To some extent both groups have sought to overcome such problems by attracting the interest of foreign partners or buyers, especially from multinational companies. Both nomenklatura and state-backed new owners have sought joint venture deals with foreign companies, and many of the state-regulated privatizations may go to foreign buyers. This, however, poses the problem of what some have called the "Latin Americanization" of eastern Europe, involving the division of the societies into a modern Westernized and foreign-controlled enclave developing some aspects of the economy but also syphoning off profits to the advanced capitalist countries, and a less developed national sector starved of investments and modern technology and remaining under the control of the political elite. To the extent that such a trend develops, locally based privatization and the extensive marketization of the economy will be impeded by the vested interests of international capital and a new local "comprador" bourgeoisie.

In the "Latin Americanization" scenario, local, small, private enterprises are more likely to retain the characteristics they developed as subordinated and only partly market-oriented concerns, starved of investment and based on low levels of skills and technology. Whether this will happen, however, may depend on a fourth privatization programme: that of the small second economy entrepreneurs developing into a more commercialized small business sector. There may be some opportunities for this group, especially in light industry and in the provision of consumer goods and services, both to new private companies and to their employees and beneficiaries. However, such growth is dependent on the success of large-scale privatization in turn. Furthermore, small business is in a weak political position to pursue its programme in most countries of eastern Europe. Even in Hungary small businesses face high levels of taxation and a lack of investment support and technical services from government. Furthermore, interest group organizations supporting them are mostly excluded from policy discussions.

The final major actor in the contest over privatization, the working class, has had only a minor rôle so far. In parliamentary politics, a distinct workers' voice is generally weak.[12] In the case of Poland too, despite the former strength of Solidarity, the representation of distinct working class interest has declined. In most countries, with the coming of contested electoral politics there has been a drastic decline in the numbers of working class MPs.

However, in extra-parliamentary politics, industrial workers form a potentially strong pressure group in many countries. In Russia, according to Mandel (1990), the workers, especially the miners, have been effective in industrial action, and in the 1989 strike they showed they were capable both of developing a clear consciousness of their interests, and of establishing their own very effective organization. In reviewing the period after the miners' strike, and especially a movement within the working class in favour of workers' self-management, Mandel (1991) expressed hope that they will be able to build a democratic movement to pursue their own interests in the face of attempts from supporters of both of the main privatization programmes to recruit them to their cause. In Poland during 1992, workers showed growing hostility to marketization, privatization, and the increasing levels of unemployment and inflation they were giving rise to. In response to strikes and threats of further industrial action, the government responded by offering a "pact on enterprises" allowing unions some say in how enterprises were to be privatized. Growing working class opposition to existing programmes could lead to increased support for the idea that the workers should become the sole owners of their own enterprises through worker self-management schemes – an approach advocated by some activists in both Russia and Poland. Alternatively, if rises in prices and job losses continue, and more state enterprises go into liquidation, workers may react to their growing social and economic exclusion through more outright opposition to privatization and marketization in general.

Constraints arising from contradictions within groups

It should be noted that, although different programmes for privatization can be connected with the interests and reform "projects" of particular social groups or classes, contradictions may equally arise between interests and attitudes shaped by each group's past social position and the programme it currently adopts. As a result, although a group may formally adopt and pursue a particular version of privatization, it may also tend to defend interests or preserve attitudes that would undermine truly market-oriented behaviour. It may, therefore, successfully pursue its programme of privatization only to deprive it of real content. The available literature suggests tendencies of this kind within the new political elites, nomenklatura owners, and the small-scale second economy proprietors.

The most striking feature of the new political elites in most east European countries is that large numbers of them have a background in the old system. Although some former academics and intellectuals have risen to power, such as Havel in Czechoslovakia, Antall in Hungary, or Sobchak and Popov in Russia, many others are more like Yeltsin in having a background in running the old system. In Hungary, by 1991, "only 100 out of the top 700 old nomenklatura positions changed hands since the Antall government took office" (Tokes 1991: 259). Therefore, the state-directed privatization programme is likely to be in the hands of people whose previous experience in economic decision-making has been described as follows:

> Because the entire decision-making system was but an aggregate of constantly changing and inherently unstable bargaining relationships, none of the participants had a clear sense as to their precise decision-making competency at any given time. What followed from this was rôle ambiguity and the tendency for making excessively cautious use of one's nominal administrative powers.
>
> (Tokes 1991: 246)

A similar case about the survival of old attitudes and practices can also be made for the new nomenklatura owners. There have been many accusations against them that they have used former political connections rather than business skills to gain control of their former state enterprises. It can also be argued that this group is still profoundly affected by links with the old system. David Stark, for example, has suggested that in Hungary the key question is how far the "networks of affiliation" of such groups impede or enable marketization to take place. The problem, he argues, is that the social networks of groups interested in privatization have already been shaped by their modes of operation in the old state-managed economy, and the kind of links that enabled success in that context may impede members dealing with each other in market relationships.

In the case of the enterprise directors, Stark suggests, the networks will be too "clanlike". By this, I interpret him to mean that under the old system success depended on developing relations of trust and mutual dependence between enterprise managers and other state officials in order to deal with delays and bottlenecks in the supply of factors of production, or to ensure the enterprise was given realistic plan targets. Such "networks of trust . . . will be used to defend perceptions of 'interests' shaped by long-standing habits and routines inimical to marketisation." (1990: 390).

On the other hand, according to Stark, small-scale producers in the second economy will not have sufficiently cohesive networks to operate under true market conditions. In their case, their marginal position in relation to the state-managed economy did not allow them to build up networks of mutual support to any significant extent. Their links were either based more on the nuclear family, or were closely subordinated to large public enterprises (1990: 390–1). Partial support for this view is given by Kuczi & Vajda (1990: 341–3), who distinguished two different kinds of "small entrepreneur". The first group, comprising mainly artisans and retailers, are described as traditional. They wish to maintain a strong family basis to their activities, which they see as a source of subsistence rather than profit.[13]

Conclusion

The discussion above offers a framework for thinking about the processes of economic reform and privatization in eastern Europe and the social factors that are likely to affect them. A great amount of new research is currently being carried out, and the data it will produce should help reach firmer conclusions in the future. However, the impression so far is that the processes of privatization and marketization face formidable and complex social barriers. While a small-scale private sector is growing in most of eastern Europe, it is not clear that it has yet shed its subordinate and subsistence character to provide any substantial basis for the growth of commercial businesses. Meanwhile the privatization of state enterprises is taking place very slowly. It has already encountered complex patterns of opposition from different social groups. Much will depend on the extent to which key groups are able to benefit from the transformation, or how far they are excluded from various sources of income, influence and services. It is not yet clear that privatization will be able to meet such demands.

Notes

1. The ideas in this paper have been shaped in the course of discussions with colleagues in eastern Europe, especially in Hungary and Russia. In particular I would like to thank Attilla Agh, Gabriella Honszki, Grigorii Pershin, Rozalina Ryvkina, Agnes Vajda, and Laszlo Vass. Of course, they may not agree with what I have written here, and any errors of fact or judgement are my own.
2. In addition to the sources cited specifically below, this section draws mainly on the *Financial Times, Special Supplement on Privatization in eastern Europe*, 3 July 1992, the special issue on privatization of *RFE/RL Research Report*, Vol.1, No.17, 1992, and B. Slay 1993. In attempting to measure the extent of increase in the private sector, a number of problems are encountered. First, accurate figures are not available for

all types of ownership change; secondly, different categories are used in different countries to classify the ownership changes that have occurred; and thirdly, it is often assumed that measures to remove enterprises from direct state management should be counted as a form of privatization. However, bearing these problems in mind, the following general description is offered.

3. The figures provided here were calculated from *Ekonomika i Zhizn*, No.2 1992.

4. "The Russian Economy in 1991", published by the Russian Academy of the National Economy, Moscow 1992, and quoted in Bush 1992: 43. It is not clear from the source, but this report may be referring only to the privatization of state *industrial* enterprises.

5. Bush 1992.

6. At the time of writing, Czechoslovakia was still one country. No attempt is made here to speculate on how far Slovakia and the Czech Republic may diverge in their experience of economic transformation after 1992.

7. E.g. for a reconstruction of some of the issues that were raised in the Hungarian debates, see Stark 1990.

8. For further discussions of the politics of privatization in Hungary, Czechoslovakia, and Poland, see Fischer 1992.

9. In Russia, for example, a study of Moscow's new large-scale private business owners estimated that of the 2500 people who owned or personally controlled private enterprises with assets of more than one million roubles 12 per cent came from former nomenklatura positions. Most had previously held posts in the Communist party or central government ministries (Kryshtanovskaya 1991). Studies of Poland and Hungary reveal similar trends but point out that because of the now dubious legal position of such privatizations, accurate figures are difficult to find (Jackson 1991; Milanovic 1991). Milanovic offers the following examples of the means by which such privatizations were carried out: "Almost the entire capital of an enterprise would be leased out on favourable terms to a private firm owned by . . . a former manager who would then re-employ enterprise workers and continue production . . . Alternatively, a state enterprise would agree to sell output at official prices to a private company that would later resell the state goods at higher free market prices . . . In some instances, enterprises were bought at low prices by former managers, or anybody else who had sufficient influence and interest to do so." (1991: 15)

10. He developed this idea in detail in his book, *Socialist entrepreneurs* (1988).

11. For further discussion, see Cox (1986).

12. Although there have been attempts to form a strong Labour party in Russia, so far party politics is not well developed and most deputies were not elected on clear party platforms. In Hungary, according to Tokes (1991: 254), there was a tacit agreement between all parties involved in the national Round Table talks that laid down the basis for the democratic transition, that there would be no party to represent working class interests.

13. However, the same study also revealed a second group made up of more mobile and better-educated entrepreneurs who were committed to expanding their business and making profits.

References

Bush, K. 1992. Russian privatization program accelerated. *RFE/RL Research Report* **1**(30).

Cox, T. 1986. *Peasants, class, and capitalism*. Oxford.

Feher, F., A. Heller, G. Markus 1983. *Dictatorship over needs*. Oxford: Basil Blackwell.

Fischer, B. 1992. Large privatization in Poland, Hungary and Czechoslovakia. *RFE/RL Research Report* **1** (44).

Grossman, G. 1990. The second economy of the USSR and eastern Europe. *Berkeley-Duke Occasional Papers on the USSR*, 21.

Jackson, M. 1991. The progress of privatization. *Report on eastern Europe* **2**(31).

Kolankiewicz, G. & P. Lewis 1988. *Poland: politics, economics and society*. London: Pinter.

Konrad, G. & I. Szelényi 1979. *The intellectuals on the road to class power*. New York: Harcourt.

Kritsman, L. N. 1928. Klassovye gruppirovki krest'yanskikh khozyaistv. *Na Agrarnom Fronte* **4**.

Kryshtanovskaya, O. 1991. Soviet millionaires. *Moscow News* 29.

Kuczi, T. & A. Vajda 1990. The social composition of small entrepreneurs. *Acta Oeconomica* **42**(3/4).

Lenin, V. I. 1921. *The tax in kind*. Reprinted in Collected Works 32. Moscow: Progress Publishers.

Mandel, D. 1990. Rebirth of the Soviet labour movement. *Politics and Society* **18**(3).

Mandel, D. 1991. The struggle for power in the Soviet economy. *Socialist Register 1991*.

Milanovic, B. 1991. Privatization in post-communist societies. *Communist Economies and Economic Transformation* **3**(1).

Okolicsanyi, K. 1992. Hungary: modest growth of private companies. *RFE/RL Research Report* **1**(2).

Shlapentokh, V. 1989. *Public and private life of the Soviet people*. Oxford: Oxford University Press.

Slay, B. 1992. Economic reformers face high hurdles. *RFE/RL Research Report* **1**(1).

Slay, B. 1993. The east European economies. *RFE/RL Research Report* **2**(1).

Stark, D. 1990. Privatization in Hungary: from plan to market or from plan to clan? *East European Politics and Societies* **4**(3).

Stark, D. 1992. Path dependency and privatization strategies in East Central Europe. *East European Politics and Societies* **6**(1).

Szelényi, I. 1986/7. The prospects and limits of the east european new class project. *Politics and Society* **15**.

Szelényi, I. 1988. *Socialist entrepreneurs*. Cambridge: Polity.

Szelényi, I. 1989. Eastern Europe in an epoch of transition. In *Remaking the economic institutions of socialism*, V. Nee & D. Stark (eds). Palo, California: Stanford University Press.

Tokes, R. 1991. Hungary's new political elites. In *Democracy and political transformation*, G. Szoboszai (ed.). Budapest: HPSA.

Yavlinsky, G. 1992. Spring '92: reforms in Russia. *Moscow News* **21**.

Index